the Fine Delight

the Fine Delight

Centenary Essays on Gerard Manley Hopkins

edited by
Francis L. Fennell

A Campion Book

Loyola University Press
Chicago, Illinois

Loyola University Press
3441 North Ashland Avenue
Chicago, Illinois 60657

Library of Congress Cataloging-in-Publication Data
The Fine delight: centenary essays on Gerard Manley Hopkins/edited by
    Francis L. Fennell
       p.   cm.
    Essays were delivered at a Hopkins Centenary Conference sponsored by Loyola
University of Chicago, April 7–8, 1989.
       ISBN 0-8294-0627-1
       1. Hopkins, Gerard Manley, 1844–1889—Criticism and interpretation—
Congresses. 2. Christian poetry, English—History and criticism—Congresses.
I. Fennell, Francis L. II. Loyola University of Chicago. III. Hopkins Centenary
Conference (1989: Loyola University of Chicago)
PR4803.H44Z6265 1989
821'.8—dc20   89-13476
                                                                         CIP

To R. B.

The fine delight that fathers thought; the strong
Spur, live and lancing like the blowpipe flame,
Breathes once and, quenchèd faster than it came,
Leaves yet the mind a mother of immortal song.

Nine months she then, nay years, nine years she long
Within her wears, bears, cares and combs the same:
The widow of an insight lost she lives, with aim
Now known and hand at work now never wrong.

Sweet fire the sire of muse, my soul needs this;
I want the one rapture of an inspiration.
O then if in my lagging lines you miss

The roll, the rise, the carol, the creation,
My winter world, that scarcely breathes that bliss
Now, yields you, with some sighs, our explanation.

Hopkins

Contents

Preface

Six of the eight essays in this volume were delivered first as papers at a Hopkins Centenary Conference sponsored by Loyola University of Chicago, April 7–8, 1989. A seventh, by Peter Milward, S.J., would have been given at the conference had distance not been prohibitive. An eighth essay, by the editor, addresses some of the larger questions which a centenary conference like this one has to consider, whether directly or indirectly. The lively exchange at the round-table discussion that followed the presentation of the essays has been recorded in an appendix.

The contributors were told that they could preserve the distinction between oral and written discourse—in other words, that the printed version of their paper could develop arguments or offer illustrations that were impossible or undesirable in a public address to a mixed audience which did not have texts available. Some have taken the opportunity to expand their papers considerably. At the same time they have heeded the original request to direct their argument not just to the Hopkins scholar but also to the general reader and lover of poetry.

The planners of the conference had several criteria for choosing those who would give papers. First, they wanted people who had lived with the poetry a long time, people who could bring to the general topic of "Hopkins After One Hundred Years" a mature reflection and a settled judgment. Second, they wanted contributors who had established strong reputations as publishing scholars. Most often this reputation derives from publications on Hopkins, but the planners also wanted to allow for scholars who have loved and taught Hopkins for many years but whose publications are in other areas. Finally, the planning committee wanted diversity: they wanted men and women; they wanted Catholics and non-Catholics;

they wanted those whose graduate training was British and those whose education was American. They also wanted to include scholars who represented the fields (or movements) and the institutions important to Hopkins himself: examples of the former are classical literature, the Pre-Raphaelites, philosophy, and theology; of the latter, Oxford University and the Society of Jesus. Such diversity has a twofold purpose. First, it permits a more balanced assessment of Hopkins' achievement as a poet. Second, it illustrates many of the critical approaches which have characterized Hopkins scholarship. Thus the volume includes an example of: the study of self-textualization in poetry (Downes), a feminist reading (Sulloway), cultural history (van Beeck), a thematic analysis (Walhout), textual exegesis (Donohue), language study (Bender), an examination of sources (Milward), and an evaluative criticism (Fennell). The essays of course encompass much more than these brief phrases suggest.

The planning committee is grateful to the Illinois Humanities Council for external funding for the conference, and also to Drs. Alice Hayes, James Wiser, and Robert Harvanek, S.J., of Loyola University of Chicago for securing various types of internal funding. The university's Office of Research Services arranged to have the manuscript typed by the very able Ms. Joan Allman. The editor was helped by a semester's leave of absence that, among other things, allowed for the timely appearance of this book during the centenary year.

But perhaps the final word of thanks should be reserved for the poet whose works we honor. The "fine delight" of the title refers both to Hopkins's poetry and (in its original context) to the poet's source of inspiration. The reader will, it is hoped, see also how much the poetry has in turn fathered (and mothered) grateful and appreciative responses in these contributors. Yet as T. S. Eliot said of another poet on a similar occasion, "His grave needs neither rose nor rue nor laurel; there is no imaginary justice to be done; we may think about him, if there be need for thinking, for our own benefit, not his."

F. L. F.

Religious Consciousness in Hopkins

David Anthony Downes

In celebrating the centenary of the death of Gerard Manley Hopkins, we ask ourselves why his life and career have become for many readers significant aids for reflection on some of the deepest awarenesses in our own lives. The first answer I was given to this question was provided in an exchange with Theodore Roethke who, contrary to all his antipathy for things academic, volunteered to become a member of my doctoral committee to oversee a dissertation on Hopkins. He asked me "why Hopkins," and I sputtered something about religious consciousness. Since I knew his impatience with academic bureaucracy, and in the hope that he might withdraw from the committee, I asked him "why Roethke." He spent an hour or so telling me why, the crux of which was Hopkins is a modern poet and hence his contemporary. What Roethke meant is the general subject of this essay: modernity as "I-ness" and the sacred.

The dominant creative spirit that has shaped modern literature has been the intention to make its subject *selfness*. Moreover, the creative impulse towards autobiography has its roots in the culture of nineteenth-century Romanticism, as much contemporary scholarship has shown.[1] It was in the last century as well that literary self-representation, along with its self-reflexive character, took on efforts to express the dynamics of the epistemology of selfness.[2] The literary forms that have resulted from such poetic intentions by the author, as we know, have been, and continue to be, uniquely responsive to the expressive understanding of himself as his subject.

1

This critical focus has not yet been applied fully to Gerard Manley Hopkins, whose works, curiously, have had two temporal lives: Hopkins lived and composed his poems entirely within the historical frame of the Victorian Age, yet his work was not published until the twentieth century. However, his placement as an early modern poet is not based on any mere accident of literary history. We read Hopkins as our contemporary because his poetry is as expressive of the modern consciousness as is the poetry of T. S. Eliot, William Butler Yeats, or Wallace Stevens. Indeed, we are this year commemorating the centenary of Hopkins' death to honor a poetic genius who speaks directly through his work to our hearts and heads as if a hundred years were but yesterday.

What makes Hopkins' work a really fascinating modern literary case wherein to experience the meaning of selfness in poetic form is that, perhaps in greater detail than any other modern poet, Hopkins provides us with a prose outline of his own philosophical and theological notions that explain his understanding of the positing of the self, the structure of the self, the dynamic energies by which the self makes representations of others and the self, and a vision of the destiny of selfness. Unlike reading the canons of other modern poets, where we have to resort to much critical supposition on these matters, in Hopkins there is a definitiveness about the order of existence on which all his poetry rests. In the richness of the intellectual fundament which underlays his poetry, Hopkins' canon stands as an imposing corrective to the current critical effort to deconstruct the self, both psychological and literary, and thus to effect a destruction of the integrity of Being, Knowing, and Saying.

To begin with, let us clarify what is meant by the phrase "textualization of the self." To Hopkins, all Being is energy; he held that the only, but monumental, difference between God and everything else was that God is infinite Being. This energy he called "stress" or "instress." Hopkins also held that acute observation of anything especially reveals its individuality: thus everything exists as a distinct self. This must mean, he inferred, that the energy that is *common Being* forms into unique shapes, what he called "scapes" or "inscapes." Existence, then, is a vast array of inscapes of instress, shapes of energy, and each of these is unique and, as important, each possesses within its conjunction of Being and form the tendency to realize its nature fully. As Hopkins put it, everything utters itself. Self-declaration is always, of course, according to the scale of each thing's nature. The scale on which human nature functions is at a radically different level of existence from that of common nature, for the human self has the power to be reflectively self-expressive; that is, every human has a unique energy shape, a consciousness, which has distinct powers of awareness that are retrospective, introspective, or prospective. According to Hopkins, every human self enacts itself through self-awareness, and every enactment, which he called stressing and instressing, results in self-reflection, or in Hopkins' terms, self-scaping and inscaping.

The human person, then, acts out selfness, each act being a partial reflection of the unique *I* that each person is. Our awareness of our self-awareness, then, gives us special powers for *uttering* ourselves in all our words, acts, and thoughts, for each of us plays a vital role in inscaping the energy of our selfness. I call this "self-textualization" both in a figurative and literal sense. Utterance can take many modes, but each can be reduced to a linguistic base, which is to say, every authentic self-utterance is a symbol reflective of the consciousness of self. Of all of the symbols that each of us utters, those which are the most deep in the structure of the self are word-symbols, for the reflective consciousness carries on its narrative of selfness essentially in linguistic forms. As Hopkins put it so tersely: "To be and to know or Being and thought are the same. The truth in thought is Being, stress, and each work is one way of acknowledging Being and each sentence by its copula *is* (or its equivalent) the utterance and assertion of it."[3] Human life can be seen in the broadest sense , then, as self-texts to be read and interpreted according to their extant state. We all read and reread these self-texts in order to carry on the task of positing our selfness.

Writers, of course, leave us formalized self-utterances in their literary works. The poetic character of language and its importance for the positing of selfness was summed up by

Jacques Lacan: "For in its symbolizing function the Word is moving towards nothing less than a transformation of the subject to whom it is addressed by means of the link which it establishes with the one who emits it. . . ."[4] Hopkins called this link, "the stem of stress between us and things to bear us out and carry the mind over."[5] It is poesis or creation in and through which mankind dwells as selfness in the world. Paul Ricoeur wrote, in commenting on a line of poetry in Holderlin, "poetically Man . . . dwells on this earth: to the extent to which the poetic act is not a pure extravagance but the beginning of the end of a wandering by means of an act of creation, poetry makes it possible for man to dwell on earth. This occurs when my normal relationship to language is reversed, when language speaks. Thus man responds to language by listening to what it says to him." Ricoeur goes on: "The poem suggests that man dwells on earth insofar as a tension is maintained between his concern for the heavens, for the divine, and for the rootedness of his own existence in the earth."[6]

In the perspective of these thinkers, poetry, in the fullest sense of the word, is the way a human person posits selfness, dwells as "that amphibious piece," (as Thomas Browne called the human being[7]) who locates identity within the domain of words wherein each lives the progression of life as self-texts. Let us now look at some of Hopkins' poetry from the vantage point of this poetic phenomenology of selfness.

The first and perhaps most powerful self-text in Hopkins is his poetic canon itself. No poet has ever expressed the energy of self-being more completely than Hopkins did. Art is a special contemplative energy of the mind, according to Hopkins; thus "poetry is speech framed for contemplation. . . . Poetry is in fact speech only employed to carry the inscape of speech for the inscape's sake, . . . inscape of spoken sound. . . ."[8] These definitions emphasize words as sounds, as language energy in forms of rhythm, internal rhyme, consonantal chiming, alliteration, "vowelling"; all of these patterns of purposed language energy coalesce to achieve the utmost distinctiveness of utterance of an inscape in the most inscaped self-utterance, what Hopkins called "brilliancy, starriness, quain, margareting."[9] These poetic techniques produce a poetic language that can be called in texture *muscular*, a poetic pumping iron, if you will. Here is a sample that is literally "muscular" as well, for it is Hopkins' inscaping about the muscle of "Harry Ploughman":

Hard as hurdle arms, with a broth of goldish flue
Breathed round; the rack of ribs; the scooped flank; lank
Rope-over thigh; knee-nave; and barrelled shank—
    Head and foot, shoulder and shank—
By a grey eye's heed steered well, one crew, fall to;
Stand at stress.[10]

What stands forth here is not only Harry's sinewy, burly self; as a figural self-text, Hopkins stands forth as potently powerful in his poetic "sinew service," standing in the stress of his mightily expressive selfness. All of Hopkins' poems exhibit this energy of words conquering their energies in representing the reflections of selfness. Every poem in his canon echoes and re-echoes his famous declaration: "Nothing else in nature comes near this unspeakable stress of pitch, distinctiveness, and selving, this self-being of my own."[11] "Stand at stress" is the key symbolic self-text for selfness in general, Hopkins' selfness, and his poetry in particular.

Such unmatchable selfness, Hopkins argued, could only come from a super energy of Selfness—God. In positing one's own selfness, God's Selfness is perceived as the great archetypal representation of selfness in the consciousness. This being so, it follows that the texture of the reflective acts of consciousness which produces authentic selfness is a religious experience insofar as individual selfness is empowered by Being-energy in common with God. Every human representation of the "I- ness" of the self involves divine energy and thus has divine meaning as well. Hopkins called it the divine "play" in human selfness. The symbolized reflections, then, by which the human self posits its "I-ness" are implicitly religious.

All symbolization of God, of course, works by negative analogy; thus the analog usually helps us to understand more than anything else the analogist. Yet in the evidence provided by his many attempts, Hopkins' poetic symbolization of God places his work in the first rank of religious poetry. There is no room here to list all of his self-texts of the Selfness of God. Borello's *Concordance* has fifty-eight listings under the word "God";[12] reading the poetic passages to which these numerous listings refer reveal the creative effort with which Hopkins expounded on the Selfness of God in his consciousness, His presence in nature, and His role in human experience, all touchstones of the greatest religious poetry. No passage in Hopkins' poetry is more reflective of the positing of God in his consciousness than the thirty-second stanza of his great religious poem "The Wreck of the *Deutschland*:"

> I admire thee, master of the tides,
>   Of the Yore-flood, of the year's fall;
> The recurb and the recovery of the gulf's sides,
>   The girth of it and the wharf of it and the wall;
> Staunching, quenching ocean of a motionable mind;
> Ground of being, and granite of it: pást áll
>   Grásp Gód, thróned behínd
> Death with a sovereignty that heeds but hides, bodes but abides.
> (118)

Hopkins often used water in all of its physical attributes to symbolize the imponderable immensity of the energy of the Selfness of God. Here God is imaged as supercontroller of natural energy, the outer limits of all spiritual and intellectual energy. Yet God— the superconductor of light, fire, motion, and transformation, Hopkins' main metaphors for God's grace— restrains His powerful energies, allows all the inscapes of energy that He has set in action to express, each in its own way, the ultimate scape of their being. Perhaps Hopkins' key symbols for God are the words *master* and *mastery* which suggest ultimate finesse.

Unfortunately, the human consciousness, in carrying on the task of expressing in its reflections the "I" of the self, experiences what Hopkins called "distress." To "instress" in selving meant to Hopkins to turn on the soul's spiritual energy at its highest level in circuit with God's creative current, grace. The soul's stress-energies are of two kinds—the mind and the will. To spiritualize a sensory image, turning a simple apprehension into a judgment, is the instress of mind energy; to posit one's self in an act of choice is an instress of the energy of the will. "Distress," then, is a destructive conduction of these spiritual energies with the result that they lose their connections with the creative energies the Creator has put in force. Hopkins wrote of the Creator's energies: "All the world is full of inscape, and chance left free to act falls to an order as well as purpose."[13] But beneficent chance can be disordered by the distressing energy of the will. This is what happened in the rebellion of Lucifer and the disobedience of Adam and Eve, which are the sacral archetypes for Hopkins' symbolization of evil in the world and in the self —the distress of selfness that breaks the circuit of human and divine coenergies.

Evil takes two forms in experience. Both manifestations are powerfully expressed in Hopkins' religious poetic texts. The first is natural evil. The poetic symbols Hopkins used might be categorized under "spoiling and wrecking." There are sweet sadness passages in the early poems: for example, those in "A Vision of Mermaids," in which he depicts the spoiling of the simple apprehension of the senses; or the "little sickness in the air" that he found in spring; or the wrecking in his epitaph for Jane Green, "Her prime of life—cut down too soon / By death." In the mature poetry, spoiling is everywhere, nowhere better summed up than in the lines from "God's Grandeur":

> Generations have trod, have trod, have trod;
>   And all is seared with trade; bleared, smeared with toil;
>   And wears man's smudge and shares man's smell: the soil
> Is bare now, nor can foot feel, being shod. (128)

For me the sonnet "Felix Randal" is a particularly powerful expression of spoiling. In this poem Hopkins gives us a picture of Felix, who once was a "mould of man, big-boned and hardy-handsome" but who now is dying, wasting away, "pining" his "Fatal four disorders" until "sickness [breaks] him."

"Wrecking" is another form of evil pervasive in Hopkins'

poetry. Wrecking might be viewed as a dramatic version of spoiling. The most famous "wrecking" poem, of course, is Hopkins' ode about a real shipwreck, that of the German ship the *Deutschland*. Hopkins' understanding of that tragic event and his efforts to inscape his reflections in poetic texts opened up a central thematic symbol of evil in his poetry; in his own words from the ode, it is "not out of his [Christ's] bliss"

> Springs the stress felt
> Nor first from heaven (and few know this)
> Swings the stroke dealt—
> Stroke and a stress that stars and storms deliver. . . .(111)

"Swings the stroke dealt" suggests sudden and final destruction about which Hopkins often pondered as a particularly virile form of natural evil. The blinding snow and freezing cold on the *Deutschland* comes to mind, and the lasting squall in the foundering of the *Eurydice*, about which Hopkins wrote in another shipwreck poem:

> Some asleep unawakened, all un-
> Warned, eleven fathoms fallen
>
> Where she foundered! One stroke
> Felled and furled them . . . . (135)

These forms of external evil are the dismal consequences of some aboriginal calamity in Creation. In Hopkins' fifty-six uses of the word *world,* most are expressions of a warped existence. In his poetry Hopkins gave powerful credence to evil powers anterior to any human involvement, echoing the great archetypes of evil found in pre-Christian and non-Christian mythology. Hopkins' direct symbolization of evil rampant in the world is in a Christian context; namely, evil expressed in the form of the serpent. He stressed the dragon symbol; he wrote, "if the Devil is symbolized as a snake he must be an archsnake and a dragon." He went on to depict the dragon as a reptilian form of life which attempts to incorporate in its anatomy and

behavior the entire gamut of natural life, a biological indul-
gence that Hopkins saw as endemic to its evil nature: "I
suppose the dragon as a type of the Devil to express the
universality of his powers, both the gifts he has by nature and
the attributes and sway he grasps, and the horror which the
whole inspires." If God is prime stress, then, the Devil is prime
distress. As Hopkins put it: "God gave things forward and
perpetual motion; the Devil, that is/thrower of things off the
track, upsetter, mischief-maker, clashing one with another
brought law of decay and consumption in inanimate nature,
death in the vegetable and animal world, moral death and
original sin in the world of man."[14]

Out of this dark vision, then, Hopkins wrote many poetic
texts which speak of wrecks, ruins, storms, strokes, floods, and
destructive fires. His poetic consciousness was so shaped by
this sense of external evil pervading the world that he wrote
whole poems reflecting his awareness, none more powerful
than his sonnet "Spelt from Sibyl's Leaves," with its threaten-
ing tone of oncoming "Disremembering, dismembering | all
now." A lesser known poem, but no less powerful in its
expressions of the fright of evil, is an untitled poem which
opens:

> The times are nightfall, look, their light grows less;
> The times are winter, watch, a world undone:
> They waste, they wither worse; they as they run
> Or bring more or more blazon man's distress. (161)

Lucifer's hell is the distress of his darkness (death) which
makes him a detester and dissembler of light (life):

> The dark-out Lucifer detesting this
> Self-trellises the touch-tree in live green twines
> And loops the fruity boughs with beauty-bines (129)

This fragment, which appeared with the draft of "As kingfishers catch fire," brings us to that other great symbolism of
human consciousness—sin. Hopkins' symbolization of sin, of

course, came primarily from scripture. With profound reflections he responded to the opaque images in the sacred texts regarding evil as sin. It is accurate to say that this symbol received major attention in his prose canon as well. In these writings, he traced out his own understanding of the nature of human personality, the character of human volitional energy, and the structural faults that bedevil human choice. These considerations were central to Hopkins' response to the *kerygma* of sacred scripture, for he held that the deepest understanding of sin lay in perceiving the true conditions of human volitional powers. Moreover, to Hopkins the most telling utterance of selfness is expressed in choice. Choice is the primary self-textualizing power. In our choices we determine the "I am" of our "I-ness." His poetry, then, is filled with such words as accepting, bidding, choosing, electing, giving, buying, purchasing, begging, releasing, and offering.

There are two notions in Hopkins' epistemology of self that need to be emphasized. The first is that individual selves are energies that come from God and therefore operate in, and through, His divine aegis. Hopkins expressed this understanding in the poem "Thee, God, I come from, to thee go":

> Thee, God, I come from, to thee go,
> All dáy long I like a fountain flow
> From thy hand out, swayed about
> Mote-like in thy mighty glow. (169)

This being so, then selfness means locating "I-ness" as part of, and responsive to, infinite energy, the stress of God. In the same poem, he wrote:

> As acknowledging thy stress
> On my being and as seeing
> Something of thy holiness.

But the self in carrying out the task of consciousness is free not to acknowledge the source of its being, the divine self-definition of self, for the energy of selfness is a freely determining energy as to its direction, purpose, and end. Moreover, as the *kerygma* of scripture reveals, self-energy became ancestrally disordered so that there occurred an imbalance in its powers, making the strong energies of desire and choice inharmonious. Fallibility entered into personality to the level of a structural fault. The key disordering feeling in the consciousness here is that of pride, the archetypal source of defective selving—sinning—about which Hopkins wrote, "Pride lies in the claiming a high rank in this scale [that is, the "self of things"], and the pride which is in all sin is essentially the matching of the sinner's self with God's and for himself preferring it, setting it higher in that scale; not his nature against God's, which even Satan could not do, but his bare self."[15] By "bare self" Hopkins meant one's "I-ness, the very distinctive, abrupt self that each of us is.

We are bound, then, as God's creatures, to offer, give, and assign our selfness in and through the very enactments of our self-being back to God. Never did Hopkins put this duty more clearly than in his poem "The Leaden Echo and The Golden Echo"; using metallic imagery of golden and leaden sound, he depicted how humankind should sound God in the music of their selving. The Golden Echo says:

> Cóme, then, your ways and airs and looks, locks, maidengear,
>   gallantry and gaiety and grace,
> Winning ways, airs innocent, maidenmanners, sweet looks,
>   loose locks, long locks, lovelocks, gaygear, going
>   gallant, girlgrace—
> Resign them, sign them, seal them, send them, motion
>   them with breath,
> And with sighs soaring, soaring sighs, deliver
> Them; beauty-in-the-ghost, deliver it, early now, long
>   before death
> Give beauty back, beauty, beauty, beauty, back to God,
>   beauty's self and beauty's giver. (156)

"Beauty-in-the-ghost" is made up of two instresses or energies. One is the "I-ness" of the self; Hopkins described the bare self in another poem as "The selfless self of self," poised before the choice of denying or affirming some self-expression, the yes or no of the energy of its nature that is the inscaping of self-energy.

Hopkins acknowledged that creaturely inscapes "vanish away," but he pointed out that in conjoining the energy of self with divine energy "mortal beauty" can be reprieved, the inscape of selfness can be transformed into the care and concern of God who is the center of all being-energy.

"Beauty-in-the-ghost" also tells us of another kind of beauty—moral beauty. Hopkins placed great emphasis in his epistemology of selfness on the energies of the volitional powers as the key determiner of self-reflected "I-ness." Human persons, possessing the powers to choose their self-representations in and through their natures, selve their selfness, that is, identify self, distinguish self, assert self through and by energies that are theirs only. This human array of powerful energies makes the distinguishing of our authentic selves dependent upon an ethical inscaping of these energies; that is, the inscaping of selfness through our choices becomes self-structuring formulations that uphold and support every external manifestation of our selfness. Behind every intellectual, emotional, or physical self-scape lies the volitional inscaping of the will as choosing either moral beauty or ugliness.

Everywhere, Hopkins pointed out, one sees what he called the spectacle of the wicked will, free choice abusing good, the moral beauty potential in its nature:

> And what is Earth's eye, tongue, or heart else, where
> Else, but in dear and dogged man?—Ah, the heir
> To his own selfbent, so bound, so tied to his turn,

(Not only do human beings become "selfbent"; they vent their distortions on the rest of the world)

> To thriftless reave both our rich round world bare
> And none reck of world after . . . . (157)

As here in "Ribblesdale" Hopkins describes human destructiveness, just so elsewhere in his writing he repeatedly laments the misuse of human energy. In "Binsey Poplars," for example, he sorrows over trees being felled:

> All félled, félled, are áll félled;
> Of a fresh and following folded rank
> Not spared, not one . . .

> O if we but knew what we do
> When we delve or hew —
> Hack and rack the growing green! (142)

Another striking instance, reflecting Hopkins' sense of the destructive will, is recorded in his notebooks. "April 8—The ashtree growing in the corner of the garden was felled. It was lopped first: I heard the sound and looking out and seing it maimed there came at that moment a great pang and I wished to die and not to see the inscapes of the world destroyed any-more."[16]

Every person lists towards being "selfbent," an inclination that is fostered by evil powers that lurk and lure all around, so that the personal susceptibility towards internal destructive energy seems matched with external evil. The will, flawed in its division between choice and desire, seems systematically determined to choose badly, decide destructively. In his poem "On a Piece of Music," ("How all is one way wrought") Hopkins declares that we are our own off-key tune, the cacophonous music of the fallible selving of self:

> Nor angel insight can
> Learn how the heart is hence:
> Since all the make of man
> Is law's indifference.

> Not free in this because
> His powers seemed free to play:
> He swept what scope he was
> To sweep and must obey.

> Though down his being's bent
> Like air he changed in choice,
> That was an instrument
> Which overvaulted voice.

What makes the man and what
The man within that makes:
Ask whom he serves or not
Serves and side he takes.

For good grows wild and wide,
Has shades, is nowhere none;
But right must seek a side
And choose for chieftain one. (145-46)

"What makes the man and what / The man within that makes": this is the mystery of selfness and selving. While we cannot penetrate this mystery very far, according to Hopkins, we do know the human results of the radical freedom of our self-tastes. They are frequently self-accusation, guilt, and disconsolation. And these sufferings are not alleviated in any curative way in reflecting upon those great myth symbols which emanate from the narration of tragic myth or the sacral darkness of the Adamic myth. The injured self of every person hurts deep down and mourns its fracture. Hopkins created some of the most powerful symbols ever made of the stress-energy of suffering. These symbols clearly locate the wounded "I" of the self as self-victimization, but the making of the unholy self has deeper meaning than self-torment. The deviant action by which evil enters into existence is an individualization of a world evil become a world-sorrow—alienating the wonderfully rich energies of the inscape of selfness from their connection with the source of its common Being-energy—God. The springs of this sorrow lie at the heart's core; in "My prayers must meet a brazen heaven," Hopkins wrote: "Nor tears, nor tears, this clay uncouth / Could mould, if any tears there were." (74)

Part of the mystery of the fallible self is hidden in the structure of selfness. Inscaping the "I-ness" of the self can, indeed, be non-destructive in the sense that no harm is done to nature or to the natural self. But still the self "sours," as Hopkins put it, because the self inscapes its "I-ness" as if it were self-sufficient, self-determined, self-ended in doing something good. Such actions of self-taste turn sour because the self relies on its own energy exclusively, as if finite Being-energy were somehow on a scale of divine Selfness. Such pride falsely finds the *ego* of the *ego cogito* an apparent good which more and more discovers its choices less and less satisfying in its representations of the self. As the self confronts more and more the distorted and inadequate representations of its "I-ness," it descends into loneliness and sorrow in experiencing its self-deception, disconsolation. Guilt begins to become self-accusation. In one of the great poems of religious psychology, "I wake and feel the fell of dark, not day," Hopkins described this abject state of guilt as God's judgment of the sin of pride which corrupts the order of creation into the hell of me-ness:

> I am gall, I am heartburn. God's most deep decree
> Bitter would have me taste: my taste was me;
> Bone built in me, flesh filled, blood brimmed the curse.
>
> Selfyeast of spirit a dull dough sours. I see
> The lost are like this, and their scourge to be
> As I am mine, their sweating selves; but worse. (166)

Mankind, so "selfbent, so bound," inscapes selfness that makes "The times that are nightfall." Pride has become destructive to the self, as for Carodoc, the killer of St. Winefred in Hopkins' unfinished drama, *St. Winefred's Well,* who cries the cry of the murdering self, "my other self, this soul, / Life's quick, this kínd, this kéen self-feeling, / With dreadful distillation I of thoughts sour as blood, / Must all day long taste murder. . . . " (164). In such self-distress, we become strangers to our own selfness in our very estrangement from others; we become threatened by our own tormenting visions; we can be driven to madness, which Hopkins depicted as falling from mind mountains, "cliffs of fall / Frightful, sheer, no-man-fathomed" (167). We begin to lose the desire and the will to sustain any energy of selfness, so that the "I" seems to untwist and fall into the emptiness of despair while fear shakes the self as even the selving of nature turns threatening; "beakleaved boughs dragonish" in the dark loom like hungry beasts ready to devour us, body and spirit. No poet has ever exceeded Hopkins in depicting in poetic symbols this deepest felt agony of the doomful dark of self-adoration.

Selfness as self and God are major symbols in the religious consciousness of Hopkins; part of their mysterious illumination in the reflective consciousness is the order of justice that the scale of common Being enjoins on Creation and the terrible penalty that has entered into the world when that justice was, and continues to be, breeched, setting up the terrifying moment when sin's injustice must be rectified. Hopkins wrote: "And the true position of things between man and God appears by an immediate light at death, when man's self is set face-to-face with God's."[17]

The other great symbol which emerges out of the master symbol of the self-texts of selfness in Hopkins' writings is Christ. Perhaps the self-text of Christ is the center of everything Hopkins wrote. Hopkins' understanding of Christ is centered in his notion of selfness. We recall that, according to Hopkins, God made everything that is as existing, distinct selves. Everything shares in the common Being-energy of God save only infinitude. Hopkins' famous poem "Pied Beauty" opens with the line: "Glory be to God for dappled things." The poet then goes on to list the order of piedness of everything and everybody. All are different, yet all in their difference share a sameness in the instress-energy with God. Therefore, they are in their sameness and difference both the one and many of the universe and at the same time are an expression of the undifferentiated oneness of God. The finite beauty of the world changes, of course, but the infinite beauty of God is past change. Because everything that is is an expression of God, everything that is temporal, spatial, individuated, and changing is what Hopkins called "news of God"; that is, acts as a sacramental for God's eternality, unity, and changelessness. The poem ends with the doxology "Praise him," which is to say praise God in his marvelous multifarious expression of Himself in Creation.

But human persons can know God only through His piedness, for humankind knows selfness only through individualized other selves. The fact that the omnipresence of God in all things can be experienced only in finite selves, however, is not a deficiency in Creation. Each of us knows our selfness and all other selves, according to our created natures as God intended, and thus He meant to be known in all of His glorious unity through the beautiful diversity of selving Creation. Still it seems that God was not satisfied with expressing Himself at the scale of existence of the universe we know. He also created an angelic world on a different scale, yet still He was not finished. He expressed his Selfness in a perfect reflection of his Self-being in the person we know as Christ, who from all eternity would be God's highest reflection of His "I-ness." By this theological notion Hopkins meant that in Christ God subsumed all created orders—angelic, human, and natural. This is what Hopkins meant in his poem, "As kingfishers catch fire": "For Christ plays in ten thousand places, / Lovely in limbs, and lovely in eyes not his / To the Father through the features of men's faces." (129)

But in the story of Creation, as we know in the *kerygma* of scripture, angels and man interfered with God's gracious work. Lucifer rebelled and human beings were disobedient. Evil entered existence, discord became common, death certain. The result of this calamity was a new manifestation of God's love for the goodness of His created Selfness. The highest expression of His "I-ness" would take a created nature, even a human nature, and show the way back to the proper sharing of God's Selfness expressed as love. This willingness to take a finite form in Creation, a form of infinite sacrifice to the Father Creator, is the meaning of Jesus who was the Christ. Hopkins called his act "The Great Sacrifice," insisted that Christ's humbling of Himself in the selfness of human nature became the paradigmatic act for all the selves in the world to be reconnected to the energy of divine order. Self-sacrifice in imitation of Christ, then, became the moral base of all human choice. In a beautiful prose passage Hopkins described the notion of Christ's sacrifice as a stress in God's selving:

> The first intention then of God outside himself . . . outwards, the first outstress of God's power, was Christ. . . . Why did the Son of God go thus forth from the Father not only in the eternal and intrinsic procession of the Trinity but also by an extrinsic and less

than eternal . . . one?—To give God glory and that by sacrifice, sacrifice offered in the barren wilderness outside of God, as the children of Israel were led into the wilderness to offer sacrifice. This sacrifice and this outward procession is the consequence and shadow of the procession of the Trinity, from which mystery sacrifice takes its rise.[18]

The mysterious shadow of Christ's sacrifice was inscribed, then, on all creation, thereby making the norm of all selving the emulation of Christ's actions of self-humbling, self-giving, self-offering. Everything that started as selving in God's energy now was changed into selving in Christ's incarnational stress. This sacrificing selving especially applied to human beings, who now are called to selve themselves in Christ's image. Only in this Christic election can human beings deal with external evil as well as reform the structural flaw in human volitional powers. Hopkins did not declare that, in virtue of the fall of God's original kingdom, nature became evil, nor did he assert that human selving is always or even normally an evil self-destruction. What he did affirm was that human selves, left alone to experience the consequences of this aboriginal disablement, see nature's inscapes vanish; moreover, the inscape of every individual human nature, and every inscape created by every human nature, vanishes away into nothingness unless some radical change in selving energy is obtained. In "The Wreck of the *Deutschland*," he personified death as saying, "'Some find me a sword; some / The flange and the rail; flame, / Fang, or Flood goes Death on drum, / And storms bugle his fame'" (112).

Against the distress of death flows the Christic energy, the stress of grace, a new, freely given energy from God which He offers through Christ to every existing thing—a continuing creation of fresh selving—except in the case of human selving. Each person must be open to His new energy, be open to accept it and its consequences, which means placing the "I" of the self in ready and willing acceptance of whatever God wills the self's destiny to be. Self-taste of self is to be ready to accept freely Christ's "calls" to giving, offering, sacrificing in, and through, the mysterious graces which He brings to everyone who loves

Him. Christ's graces started to flow from all eternity, but, in consequence of the bafflement of disobedient human choices, they became temporal in the life of Jesus, and remain temporal in the continued sacrifice of Christ in His living Presence in the Blessed Sacrament, the sacred grace food of His Holy Eucharist. The image of self-tasting, human and divine, remains Hopkins' image for ingesting the energy of God so that it becomes inter-fused with the self-stress of the self-receiver. The energy of grace lifts us back up to our original self-destiny, the end of all the instress of selfness, which is our self-sacrifice to God, our salvation.[19]

But God in His justice respects His order of creation. Human selves either accept or reject God's activity according to the nature of their own selving—choosing or not choosing. Grace could, but does not, force a restructuring of human nature; rather it calls out for correspondence to this new energy to move the self to a better self, to that self which will unite with the selfness of Christ. In this self-sacrifice in imitation of Christ's "Great Sacrifice," each self can regain its destiny, which is to share fully in God's energy. Hopkins allowed for a good deal of mystery regarding the direction of human choice. His mature perspective about the nature of human choice was expressed in a Christmas poem written three years before his death, "On the Portrait of Two Beautiful Young People." In this poem he contemplates the beauty of a young brother and sister he observed in a photograph in the home where he spent the Christmas holidays. Seeing all their beauty, he wonders what would become of it. Their individual destinies, he asserts, would be significantly their own doing and nonetheless myste-rious for such being the case, for selving lies hidden in the springs of personality, what he calls "the selfless self of self":

> Man lives that list, that leaning in the will
> No wisdom can forecast by gauge or guess,
> The selfless self of self, most strange, most still,
> Fast furled and all foredrawn to No or Yes. (176)

Of course, what makes Hopkins' insights—regarding choice and grace, the crucial issues in human selving— live with great staying power is the the energy of imagination by which Hopkins created self-texts in his religious poetry. He left us with many wonderfully poetic expressions of those moments when the self accepts Christ's grace. Donald Walhout in his article on "Modes of Religious Response in Hopkins' Poetry" has catalogued the range of responses and has noted that Hopkins' great ode "The Wreck of the *Deutschland* " contains most of those modes.[20] Certainly the poem contains all the classes of religious response that Walhout cited.

Let us briefly examine in sequence some key instances in the ode, not only to find evidences of how rich the religious experience in Hopkins' first great poem is but also to appreciate the metaphoric brilliance with which Hopkins symbolizes selving his religious consciousness.

Stanzas 2 and 3 in "The Wreck" have been read by many as expressions of religious conversion. Whether conversion or transformation, the stanzas are replete with images of change in the self. The images Hopkins uses are those which express misdirection and struggle accompanied by terror. Yet it is not the "fire of stress" in stanza 2 which determines the aura of the experience, nor is it the "frown of his face" in stanza 3 that best expresses the religious experience. Rather the dominant expression is the imagery that instresses the poet selving himself in Christ's grace. As striking as God's lightning and Christ's terrifying call are, more astonishing are the poet's self-affirmations: "I did say yes," which opens stanza 2 and is picked up again three times in stanza 3: "I whirled out wings that spell / And fled with a fling of the heart," "My heart, but you were dovewinged, I can tell," and "I am bold to boast, / To flash from the flame to the flame then, tower from the grace to the grace." Hopkins is saying here that conversion is grace, but he is as well selving saying yes, whirling out the self, and affirming the consequences of such an election in the very ascendence of the self to a new order of being. Conversion is the beginning of an aboriginal new selving. Such is the self-text of conversion.

Or take stanza 4 where the poet describes his selfness as the sand in an hourglass, and, in the extension of the figure, details the flow of grace into his selfness which "ropes" his consciousness, however it drifts, to God's providence, Christ's gift, his grace connection. This faith-awareness calls forth religious responses of consolation and devotion. Hopkins' image for these responses is that of blown kisses: "I kiss my hand" to the inscape of God's stress in the stars, in thunder, in a sunset. This image is strikingly personal, sensuous, and loving. Of such intimacy is the reception of grace, the poet asserts, which results in a unique religious exchange with God—greeting and blessing. In such passages, the poet insists that the instressing in the consciousness of God's presence everywhere is intensely personal, indeed, in the very reflective form of the selving self: "For *I* greet him the days *I* meet him, and bless when *I* understand [emphasis mine]." Such is the self-text of loving God.

From this selving in God arise powerful feelings of adoration, an adoration that lies in the recognition that behind the surface ways the world works—"the stress felt" and "the stroke dealt" in Hopkins' words—is the mystery of God's providence, the inscrutability of the human personality, and the play of graces released through the incarnation of Christ. All of these are the imponderable factors that are realizing the destiny of everything and everybody. Yet again Hopkins emphasizes that, in his poetic expressions of these subtle religious moments of great significance, the selving self remains the enabling factor by which a major alteration of personal destiny occurs: "only the heart, being hard at bay, / Is out with it!" (stanzas 7-8). Only the individual self can selve God-Christ or unselve in the oblivion of death. And the poet tells us that even this selving, often sudden and dramatic, occurs in the maze of grace that is beyond understanding: "To hero of Calvary, Christ's feet— / Never ask if meaning it, wanting it, warned of it—men go" (stanza 8). Hopkins sums up selving the triune God of Christianity in the most personal of terms: "Thou art lighting and love, I found it, a winter and a warm; / Father and fondler of heart thou hast wrung; / Hast thy dark descending and most art merciful then" (stanza 9). Such is the self-text of instressing God, our almighty Father.

Or take the self-texting of depression which can be a form of religious disconsolation. In "The Wreck," of course, this disconsolation lies at the heart of the second part of the poem. At issue is that dark mystery of evil chance that results in terrible destruction, here in an horrendous shipwreck. Death, the poet points out, is the prime disconsolation in the consciousness: "But wé dréam we are rooted in earth—Dust! / Flesh falls within sight of us, we, though our flower the same, / Wave with the meadow, forget that there must / The sour scythe cringe, and blear share come" (stanza 11). Sensing this fate, knowing its inevitability, each of us lives each day fatefully. When it happens to others, we often ponder the event with shuddering bewilderment.

This is what Hopkins did in his poetic instressing of the wreck of the *Deutschland*. The tragedy entered into his awareness in a particularly ironic time. He had chosen to become a Catholic, and now had elected to become a Jesuit priest under the inspiration of St. Ignatius' *Spiritual Exercises*. He had experienced the lows of such radical choices in his life's direction (family shock and career alteration) and now was enjoying the elation of commitment to his new vocation. Into this joy came news of God in the form of a horrible shipwreck. Hopkins' poetic nature, which he had put by as part of his effort to enter into his priestly vocation as purely as he was able, reasserted itself, and he attempted to instress the *Deutschland* tragedy as a major instance of the drama of God's grace. In some way, to Hopkins this shipwreck represented all the storms of external evil beyond the walls of the seminary as well as, perhaps, the dragons that lie in the dark places inside the self however externally secure. Little did he know of the "wrecking and storm" which would lay in his way throughout his life. Perhaps the second half of the ode is really about Hopkins' premonitions of his own shipwreck.

Whatever spiritual and psychological forces were working in him, Hopkins was often inspired to struggle with the public disconsolations of such world sorrows as the *Deutschland*. The self-texts of this catastrophe he left us honestly attempt to face the nature of the tragedy; moreover, they depict his efforts to find in the terrible event the stress of God. The poet exhibited powerful verbal energies in attempting to symbolize the graces attendant to the wreck, the nuns, the tall sister, and trust in God's providence. Those passages in the ode which are the most dramatic, compelling, and finally transforming, tend to overshadow the pervasive disconsolation that lay deep in Hopkins' consciousness, the consciousness of a morally and religiously sensitive man.

Three times Hopkins interrupts the flow of his narration of the tragedy to ponder himself pondering the sad event. Part of his intrusion is wonderment, but I submit that the main part is his effort to instress "God's cold," that is, all the death that ices all the world all the time. Six stanzas into the second part of the poem, the poet makes his first interruption. Overwhelmed by the horror of the wreck as he reconstructs it in his poem from details in the newspapers, he stops aghast. In stanza 18, he reveals how deep are his feelings of sympathy for those on the *Deutschland*, so moved that he becomes tearful. These must be considered tears of regret and sorrow for those lost in the tragedy, but the poet also proclaims a certain joy in the honesty of his feelings in that he feels the tragedy so deeply. So the sadness of the wreck and his tears over it are very disconsoling, but at the same time, he reveals his capacities to be truly empathetic. The central image in the stanza is his "mother of being in me, heart" which rejoices and cries as the poet celebrates his empathic ability to sense the ultimate spiritual implications in the wreck. He does not understand the collision of the two patterns of emotions in him. He asks, "What can it be, this glee? the good you have there of your own?" How did such grief produce this joy in him?

Six stanzas later, the poet interrupts his narrative again, this time an extended intrusion of three stanzas. In the first, stanza 24, perhaps the dramatic and religious personal center of the ode, Hopkins opens the stanza with an allusion to the security of his own person in Wales while the shipwreck was taking place, when the tall nun was calling to Christ at her death. There is the sense of disappointment and regret in these lines where he describes his own safety—in a pleasant place, under a protecting roof, and resting in a warm bed—while the nuns were undergoing their ordeal and, in doing so, in Hopkins' interpretation of what was happening, were perhaps experiencing, amid all the trauma, an apparition of Christ Himself. Was this youngish member of the Society of Jesus hoping for, even anticipating, some heroic moment of religious epiphany such as he felt the tall nun might have had? Was her joy really his regret? Or maybe his fearful future?

In stanza 25, the intrusion continues. The poet wrote this and two more stanzas about what the nun's predicament and reactions really meant: "The majesty! what did she mean?" The poet conjectures several possible answers. One might be that the nun was moved to imitate Christ's sufferings. The poet notes that this was not the mood of the disciples in the boat with Christ on Lake Gennesareth when it seemed they were about to suffer a wreck. Another possibility might be that the nun simply wanted death to come to end her terrible ordeal. It is interesting that each of these conjectures pivots around two exclamations. Both are calls for inspiration in the manner of an epic poet: "Breathe, arch and original Breath," and "Breathe, body of lovely Death." Hopkins seems to be seeking here the consolations of the true meaning of the wreck and the nuns from either the spirit of life or death.

The quandary continues in stanza 26. In this passage the poet envisions through the use of natural imagery a kind of religious apotheosis wherein the true meaning of the nun's aspiration would come clear, like the dissipation of grey clouds on a dull day when the heavens turn a clear bright blue again. Still the poet is not satisfied, for he feels left with the same question that seemed imponderable to St. Paul: "What by your measure is the heaven of desire, / The treasure never eyesight got, nor was ever guessed what for the hearing?" The poet is still unhappily brooding over the religious meaning of the wreck.

The poet's disconsolation hits bottom in stanza 27. He dismisses all of his previous conjectures and tries some new ones. Was the nun's action simply the culmination to a long life of "Time's tásking" which she was happy to abandon? He dismisses danger as a motive for giving up because danger usually makes us cling to life. And the tendering tenderness that arises from quiet and peaceful prayer could not be the nun's motive amid the tumult of the storm and the torment of the wreck.

So Hopkins gives up trying to understand the character of her motives. However, this three-stanza intrusion is important, for these self-texts reveal to us how strongly Hopkins felt that heightened religious consciousness was partly dependent upon some kind of choice or election, however opaque, that corresponding to God's grace involves the counterpart of some personal selving energy which responds, if its elevating action is to be accomplished, in some transforming way. Just what the nun meant by her actions and words would remain unclear, and this obscurity represents a spiritual disconsolation to the poet because his admiration is undercut by his wonder over the mystery of selving grace.

Stanza 28 is perhaps the most famous intrusion by the poet, famous because Hopkins seems to have overleaped his spiritual bewilderment and attributes a miracle answer to the meaning of the tall nun's experience—an apparition of Christ—whatever her motives. Contrary to many readers, I do not see the need to read this text as Hopkins' poetic effort to express what he hoped and believed the nun "saw"—Christ coming—walking towards her on the stormy sea. Rather I read the stanza as the last, but best conjecture in Hopkins' poetic mind, the conjecture in faith that, in some fashion, Christ answered the nun's call—whatever her motives. This being the case, then, the stanza is really about the incapacities of the poet to express the climax to that fitful scene on the ship. Thus when the poet writes "How shall I . . . make me room there," he hopes for an imaginative transfiguration which would put him imaginatively beside the nun, perhaps inside her consciousness, so that he could really grasp the religious meaning of what was happening to her. But, as we have seen in the earlier intrusive stanzas, such an elevation of insight did not happen, so he is left with, "Reach me a . . . Fancy, come faster—." Hopkins is poetically speechless in the face of what he in faith hopes for the nun. All he can do is reiterate Christ's names, and in his belief that Christ answered her call, assert that whatever her needs, spiritual and temporal, Christ would respond fully. Hopkins still holds on to the mysteriousness of the nun's rule in this awesome event, but obscure as her motives were, they brought her to Christ, Hopkins believed, and thus he writes "Let him ride, her pride, in his triumph."

In these passages I believe the poet's disconsolations, both religious and aesthetic, are matched with those on shipboard, particularly those of the tall nun. Both represent the mysterious quandary of selving one's destiny. Hopkins was to get his chance to look directly into the actual heart of deep spiritual jeopardy and disconsolation during the last part of his life in Dublin. As we know, from these wrenching experiences he wrote some of the most powerful poetry of despair for which the key self-text is "No worst, there is none. Pitched past pitch of grief, / More pangs will, schooled at forepangs, wilder wring." His poetic prayers in this early ode asking for insight and aspiration, were to be answered in perhaps the most dreadful inspirations any poet has experienced: "written in blood," he said later of these dark sonnets. One cannot help recalling at this point his wonderful poem "Spring and Fall: to a young child" about the child Margaret's intuition of death and apply it to his own life:

> Ah! as the heart grows older
> It will come to such sights colder
> By and by, nor spare a sigh
> Though worlds of wanwood leafmeal lie;
> And yet you *will* weep and know why. (152)

Of all the poetic passages in which Hopkins depicted selving, none are more memorable than those which express union with the selfness of Christ. And I mean here more than poetic brilliance, though there is much brilliance as well. I am here speaking of Hopkins' profound insight into the subjective character of Jesus' Selfness. Hopkins looked into the Christic tradition and was dissatisfied with that part of the tradition which interpreted following Christ to mean a behavioristic imitation of Christ. If, as he held, God is original Selfness and Christ the first and fullest expression of that Selfness, then the same Selfness came into Jesus as a human being living a particular, historical existence. To Hopkins this was the essence of the incarnation, the "Great Sacrifice" of deific Selfness with a capital S becoming human selfness with a small s.

What then in terms of the phenomenology of selfness did Jesus' life on earth mean? Jesus Himself answered this question when he spoke to the disciples about what it meant to follow His path by living as He lived:

> Jesus then said to his disciples, "If anyone wishes to be a follower of mine, he must leave self behind; he must take up his cross and come with me. Whoever cares for his own safety is lost, but if a man will let himself be lost for my sake, he will find his true self. What will a man gain by winning the whole world, at the cost of his true self?"[21]

Hopkins knew the Christological tradition of attempting to follow Christ by copying His life. But gradually in his spiritual life, as we know from his religious and devotional writings, he came to believe that following Christ had deep phenomenological implications in the reflective act of the consciousness selving one's self. As he pondered the Gospels, especially as he encountered them in Ignatius' *Spiritual Exercises*, he began to understand that following Christ meant the realization of how, through the grace of the Holy Eucharist, the Christ-Self entered into, and became part of, his personal self. This understanding comes down to interpreting what Jesus meant, in his injunction, by the symbol "the cross."

In terms of the phenomenology of the self, Hopkins' understanding of "the cross" might be called self-texting the psychology of the Christ-Self in the Gospels. In his reading, the key was self-sacrifice, which did not mean self-destruction, but rather recognizing the primacy of choosing out of the felt motivations of love of others rather than choosing out of love of self-pride. To Hopkins, Jesus' life was, and is, the paradigm of every self selving, that is, the model for the way each of us should individuate our selfness. Time and again in his ethical directives, Jesus stressed the inner state of conscience in any behavior as the crucial determinant of goodness, not the outward conformity to formal moral modes. Jesus summed it up in some of his harshest language when speaking of murder and anger. He said murder is evil and must be brought to judgment, "but I tell you this: Anyone who nurses anger against his brother must be brought to judgment. If he abuses his brother he must answer in court; if he sneers at him he will have to answer for it in the fires of hell" (Matt: 5:21-22). Public abuse answers to positive law, but hidden hatred is a deeper disorder of the self, an evil of the personality, that can be morally lethal to true self-fulfillment. For hatred comes of self-pride that distorts the harmonious order of love of both self and others.

In terms of selfness, taking up the cross of Jesus as Hopkins understood, practiced, and wrote about it, means locating one's "I-ness" in the self by acts of reflective consciousness possessing that integrity and wholeness which keeps the self intact, an intactness that can only be maintained by being true to those highest motivations of giving, loving, offering, sacrificing, and forgiving, out of which each self takes on a radiant fullness of its own individual uniqueness. In terms of the phenomenology of the self of Christ, this is what He modeled in His life, deeds, and words, what He was and is.

This is the self-text of Christ in Hopkins' poetry. It is the Christ who, in selving his Self for love of his Father, renounced his sonship to take on a created nature, then out of the same obedient love became a human being, and then out of an ultimate love for His Father, who "fathers forth" in all things, gave Himself entirely to living and serving his fellow human beings, even laying down his life so that they could be reunited to His Father. The acts, then, by which believers follow Christ, take up His cross, are acts of renunciation. But in phenomenological terms renunciation of what? Hopkins is very clear about this. It is the renunciation of the "I-ness" of that self, that which is most mysteriously, deliciously, but quintessentially the self of selfness, which constitutes the true imitation of the Christ of the Trinity and the Christ of history.

And what comes of this renunciation? If we can enter such renunciation in union with Christ, we are brought to His fulfillment—escape from death, entrance to a new level of Being, a recovered relationship with our Father-Maker, and a transnatural existence. The phenomenological shorthand for all of this hopeful religious promise is that our personal self-sacrifice through His Self-Sacrifice transforms the "I" in the self so that it is able freely and fully to realize its individuality with such radiance that the "I," and everything in the world around it, shines by its own light. The "I am" of self interfuses with the

"I AM" of Christ. Northrop Frye put it this way in speaking of the ultimate revelation that is the meaning of Christianity:

> The apocalyptic vision, in which the body of Christ is the metaphor holding together all categories of being in an identity, presents us with a world in which there is only one knower, for whom there is nothing outside of or objective to that knower, hence nothing dead or insensible. This knower is also the real consciousness in each of us.[22]

The poetry of Hopkins, then, is first of all the self-taste of his own self-texting. But we have seen that absolutely distinctive inscaping of his selfness was not self-utterance for his self's sake, not like Lucifer singing his own song out of unison with the choral masterpiece of God's creation. Rather it is the song of the self exalted through a renunciation out of love of Christ as Christ loved His Father. This explanation is the true understanding of the so-called priest-poet problem in Hopkins. Loving sacrifice is the key self-text in Hopkins' poetry that truly glorifies the "I-ness" and "It-ness" of Creation. His poetry, like all great religious poetry, is the metaphorical unifying of wonderful individual difference into cosmic orders of shining beauty hinting of their divine splendor underneath. But even more radiantly beautiful are the makers of such metaphors, for every self-text is as well an inscape of its creator, the poetic "I-ness" instressed in the very design of the poetic work of art. So mortal beauty is always double-featured—doubly inscaped.

It is notable, I think, that more often than not Hopkins pictured Christ differently from the apocalyptic imagery of the Christic tradition. In that tradition, Christ is imaged as God, Spirit as Flame, Dove or Wind, Trees of Life, Water of Life, Bridegroom, Shepherd, Lamb as Body and Blood, Bread and Wine, Temple, and Stone.[23] Hopkins, of course, used some of these images, more so in his early poetry. However, in the poetry of his spiritual and theological maturity, he tended to use imagery that reflected his own lights about the meanings of Christ. Generally in his mature poetry, Hopkins used Christic imagery which expresses Christ as a person enacting and reacting in His human personality, Christ on earth, in time, in our existential state. While we find Christ expressed in the images of fruit, sacrifice, power, the Eucharist, Savior, martyr, and the cross, we also have Christ as our lover, the Christ to whom we call and who answers, the Christ to whom we personally offer ourselves; Christ, Mary's son, Mary's mirth; a Christ who terrifies, a Christ who suffers, a Christ who Christens; a Christ who is king, head; a Christ who is compassionate, a Christ in His home with His family, a Christ whose relationship with us is clouded by sin, a Christ who is an heir to His Father; a Christ who plays in our play, accomplishes wonderful deeds, cries out, holds out hope, is our brother, can be shut out, comes to us, gives us gifts, minds and cares about us, employs us, charms us, binds us, is mystically us.

These self-texts of Christ in Hopkins' poetry inscape the human Christ, the personal Christ, the individual Christ, the Christ-self of the Incarnation. These inscapes of Christ, of course, are the stress and instress of Hopkins' poetic consciousness—his own self-texts selving Christ.

Moreover, the same Christ imagery occurs in Hopkins' priestly consciousness, as can be seen in his spiritual writings and his few extant sermons. I know of no more beautiful passage in Christian homily than his magniloquent sermon given on November 23, 1879, calling on the congregation to dwell in their minds and hearts on Christ as their personal hero. Hopkins describes Christ in the text in every thinkable guise that makes for heroship, and he links all of these wondrous and admirable attributes under the heading of beauty—the beauty of appearance, the beauty of mind, and the beauty of character, the highest beauty of all. In the sermon, Hopkins dwells most on Christ's personality, that sacred "I-ness" that awed, baffled, frightened, and overwhelmed all who knew Him because of the radiantly perfect wholeness of His selfness. Hopkins ends his moving sermon with a doxology to Christ much of which called for the glorification of Christ's humanness:

> Glory to Christ's soul; Glory to his genius and wisdom; Glory to his unsearchable thoughts; Glory to his saving words; Glory to his sacred heart; Glory to his courage and his manliness; Glory to his meekness and mercy; Glory to his every heartbeat; to its joys and

sorrows, wishes, fears; Glory in all things to Jesus Christ God and
man. If you try this when you can you will find your heart kindle
and while you praise him he will praise you.[24]

Hopkins opened a famous sonnet with a question: "To
what serves mortal beauty I —dangerous; . . . ?" Why "dangerous," we wonder? Was even Christ's beauty dangerous?
Hopkins himself says in the sonnet that "Our law says: Love
what are I love's worthiest, were all known; / World's loveliest—men's selves." Our selfness came from our Maker and in
His image was meant to utter the beauty of our selfness: "Self
I flashes off frame and face." Why dangerous then? Because
we are so highly susceptible to false worship, to inscaping our
"I-ness" into betraying, distorting, destroying images of identity, which Hopkins alluded to in his reference in the poem to
Pope Gregory's sending the angel-looking English boys to
convert sixth-century pagan England, "To man, that once would
worship block or barren stone." How are we to keep pure, in
the sense of truly self-enhancing, the beauty that we are, the
beauty that we encounter, and the beauty that we make?
Indeed, how are we to keep beauty at all? Hopkins wrote:
"What do then? How meet beauty? Merely meet it; own /
Home at heart, heaven's sweet gift; then, let that alone./ Yes,
wish that though, wish all, God's better beauty, grace" (167).
Here is Hopkins' own answer to his own inscapes in his own
self-texts—not denial, not rejection, not destruction—but rather
loving renunciation. Loving because he exhorts us to acknowledge beauty deeply in our hearts as a gift from heaven, and
renunciation because we are urged to offer it back to God
through his grace, that is, through this offering and our other
beautiful acts of love.

These individual acts of renunciation through Christ for
Christ add up to a total offering of the self to God. No Christian
poet has expressed the transformation of selfness into Christ-
ness more beautifully than Hopkins did in his great sonnet
"That Nature is a Heraclitean Fire and of the Comfort of the Resurrection." In it Hopkins portrays in a poetic-prophetic form
the trials of this world each of us must face, the changeful

indifference of nature, the imponderables of time and history, the fading weaknesses of our own wondrous selfness, and the black blotting out of our deaths. Such is the nowness of us all. But at the level of selfness, if the "I" is in grace, there is a promise that, in renunciation of the naked ego in us, roaring to be clothed in its own desires, lies a transforming beatific sunlight which draws up all life into a new order of being. All will be changed, but especially every self will enter into a new beginning. Loving readers of Hopkins all know the famous lines which penetrate so deeply into awareness:

> Across my foundering deck shone
> A beacon, an eternal beam. | Flesh fade, and mortal trash
> Fall to the residuary worm; | world's wildfire, leave but ash:
> In a flash, at a trumpet crash,
> I am all at once what Christ is, | since he was what I am, and
> This Jack, joke, poor potsherd, | patch, matchwood, immortal diamond,
> Is immortal diamond. (181)

After a lifetime of slow time, it will seem to the self most sudden, strobe-lighted, ear-shattering, when the earthly ego of "I-ness," in all of its dying obscurities, will discover hidden in its finite jackness, jokeness (Hopkins may well have used jerkness if writing today), broken-potsherd-pieceness, fool's patchiness, splintering firewood-selfness, the Alph-Omega lettering insignia of Christ shining forth as immortal diamond. I am will become I AM; as James Finn Cotter has shown, every vowel in these last uplifting lines spells out the Apocalypse of Christ.[25]

Hopkins' splendid metaphoric self-text does indeed brilliantly affirm unity in and through Christ. However, I think that the figure might also suggest some state beyond integration and unity, an expanded vision that reaches into the infinite, where the self is not lost in Christ, but rather is freed to be its beautiful "I-ness," that wonderful self-taste that is unlike any other "I am." I cannot imagine Hopkins' vision of Paradise as anything other than the immortal diamond of selfness, free to be its distinctive "I-ness" in the infinite luminous universal "I-ness" of Christ—two diamonds in eternity—"immortal diamond/Is immortal diamond."

Hopkins, Male and Female, and the "Tender Mothering Earth"

Alison Sulloway

A centennial commemoration can be useful not only for reconsidering accepted critical perspectives about a distinguished public figure, but also for discussing any fresh assumptions that shifts in cultural beliefs during the passage of one hundred years have made possible. Merely for instance the various contemporary movements concerned with the complexity of women's needs and values, which in 1988 quietly celebrated their first quarter of a century, have now fully established new forms of scholarly illuminations that would once have been thought to contain nothing pertinent for the study of Gerard Manley Hopkins.

Among Hopkins' scholars, it is a frequent covert assumption, hardly ever examined for its consequences to Hopkins' vocation and his poetry, that he possessed an archetypally feminine self as well as his obvious masculine self. The evidences of Hopkins' archetypally female self—but seldom the self itself—are sometimes praised as benevolent and sometimes condemned as destructive, not, in either case, necessarily according to the soundness of the poet's doctrine or the quality of particular poems, but rather according to those hidden critical agendas that commonly shape most of our first impressions, no matter how wary we struggle to be.

As scholars who feel responsible both to Hopkins' priestly vocation and to his poetry, we have already learned not to separate Hopkins the Jesuit from Hopkins the poet. We now need to heal this second critical disjuncture, so seldom recognized as such: we need to recognize the place of Hopkins' two archetypally gendered selves, the male and the female, in his priesthood and in his poetry.[1] Sometimes these selves blended easily and thus they served both his profession and his poetry without strain. Sometimes they were in conflict and therefore they shared in the genesis of his well-known periods of distress.

Hopkins' celebrations of both his male and female selves were perfectly consistent with many of the most poignant and pedagogically sound and compassionate moments in *The Spiritual Exercises of St. Ignatius*. Furthermore, a very significant but largely neglected characteristic of socially conscious Victorian males was the ease with which they had taught themselves to accommodate both their male and female selves, no matter how often they deplored, just as Hopkins did, the same evidences of androgyny in women. These "Tory radicals" were all anxious to ameliorate the worst brutalities of the industrial revolution through slow and gentle persuasion rather than through legislation, and unconsciously they adopted some of the softer social habits and language usually thought appropriate for women. Hopkins' letters to his poet friends read like the letters of many another Victorian artist, poet, or social thinker to his friends. In these letters, one finds such linked adjectives as "tender, manly verses," "sweet and strong discourse," "deep feeling and masterly execution," "wonderfully felt, wonderfully thought and argued, my dear." This artless oxymoronic praise of each other's work appears again and again, without any sense of gender anomaly.

Since the sexual ontology of each human being is one of the principal shapers and paradigms of that individual's cosmic ontology, and in turn, since the prevailing sexual ontology in any culture mirrors and characterizes everything else, a study of Hopkins' gender assumptions would hardly come amiss. But since the investigation of gender archetypology has only recently been accepted as a fruitful study, when most scholars first approach the gender archetypes and symbols, they seem to slide at random from one to another, because as yet the investigators have only considered these matters preconsciously, if at all. Careful attention to them will soon reveal their own logic, as they move almost predictably from small pardigms in groups and individuals to large and even larger examples of these paradigmatic patterns. In Hopkins' case, when he was thinking as a male Jesuit, he often moved from ideas of himself as an English priest, to ideas of other English Catholics and non-Catholics, and then to the whole endangered human species. In these moments, he thought of himself as Moses preaching in the wilderness, or living and working in "Christ's company" among God's warriors, and then, by implication, of all faithful Catholics anywhere, past and present, attacking Satan and human descendents or cleansing the world's temples. In his feminine mood, his poetry and his journals reflect his vision of himself as selfless nurse or mother, protecting his nurslings, individually or collectively, from sin's mortal stamp.

This feminine archetype also extended to Hopkins' tenderness, his counter-mothering, of the pastoral world "all through" the "mothering earth," that "country . . . so tender, / To touch, her being so slender." A lovely and characteristic example of the way Hopkins' gender archetypes move from one discrete symbol to another, so as to create a paradigmatic whole, occurs in Hopkins' archetypally feminine associations between the "mothering" or "nursing element," and even the fresh, clean "Air we Breathe" —when it is uncontaminated with industrial wastes—and Mary, the virgin mother. For example, whether he is grieving over the industrial rape of the "mothering" land and its inhabitants, or whether he is rejoicing over the uncontaminated landscapes that had somehow escaped the pillagers' bulldozers, he usually responds to these feminine archetypes or their co-mother, the Virgin Mary, with his "heart in hiding." For just as the private, domestic, and selfless virtues of the Virgin were the first paradigms of a human being without stain, in the same way, for Hopkins, unspoiled nature, where "lives the dearest freshness deep down things" hidden from industrial contamination, symbolized human purity, especially feminine purity, of which the virgin mother was the first model.

There is also, for Hopkins, a circular counter-system of images signifying characteristic types of sin, which he associates with other archetypes of each sex. In women, Hopkins' images connect any articulate and independent woman with a slut or a "hussy." On the other hand, the aristocratic rapist, Caradoc, who dispatched the virgin Winefred with his bloody sword," shares a world of sin with the greedy industrialists who have left the "tender mothering earth" "all . . . seared with trade, bleared, smeared with toil."[2]

Hopkins' deep and poignant gratitude for protected and private domesic interiors peopled with hospitable families or affectionate colleagues also exemplifies his artless feminine self. His images of lay friends welcoming him with food and open companionship, and of colleagues in the various Jesuit houses leaving flowers in his room, holding his hand when he was sick, or making kind and supportive remarks when he first arrived at a new Jesuit station, appear again and again in his poetry, his letters, and his journals. These revelations of some of his deepest needs reveal how often his feminine self yearned to give and to get the safe and inopportunistic love that he associated with the sacrificial love exhibited by Christ and his mother.

One of Hopkins' most appropriate and most attractive gender shifts emerges in his treatment of Christ. God the Father, as the Father, is always masculine; Christ the Son is sometimes male and sometimes female. In referring to Christ, Hopkins might call him his "Hero" or his "master." He prayed to Christ the Hero to return to errantly Protestant England like a "kind" husband forgiving a penitent wife and "royally reclaiming his own."[3] But Christ also lived in Hopkins' vividly personifying imagination as a divine prototype of a kind Oxonian don or tutor to the vulnerable and exploited Oxonian young, thus partly as a masculine mentor to those in subordinate positions and partly as a selfless and protective mother. Christ, he said, "is interested in all our undertakings," and like a good mother, "he is more interested in them than we are," and far more interested in us than in himself.

Human worshippers respond appropriately to the royal Christ, since human love is like the love of "subjects" for a "ruler." But Hopkins instinctively sensed something incomplete, not fully selved or authentic in the love of many archetypal subordinates for dominant figures, for he remarked that "this is a cold sort of love." A healthier form of love for Christ, he thought, imitated one's "enthusiasm for a leader, a hero, love for a bosom friend, love for a lover."[4]

Hopkins' expansive list of personifications and typologies for Christ clearly suggests the relaxed permission he often gave himself to think of Christ and of himself as both male and female. For him to undertake the *imitatio Christi* was to adopt one of the archetypal roles historically assigned to women, whereas to function as a Jesuit theologian and an assertive preacher and missionary was to perform tasks then considered appropriate only for men. Some strain between the two types of functioning was therefore inevitable, considering the time in which Hopkins lived.

When Hopkins was working, praying, and writing most successfully, he called up many archetypes of male and female, in himself and in his consideration of the world, and he did so without strain. But during his times of distress, one of the symptoms of these agonizing crises was his sense of himself as an abused, abandoned, or unloved child, begging protection either from his surrogate mother, the Virgin mother, or from his hero and master. In 1959 Christopher Devlin pointed out what a distinct emphasis Hopkins placed upon Christ's sacrificial role and the "perception of Christ adoring the Father." Attractively affectionate and yet judicious as this essay is, it is understandable that Father Devlin could not then make the connection between Hopkins' vision of Christ, who "annihilated himself, taking the form of a servant," [5] and the same Hopkins who believed that a woman should adore her husband as men adore Christ, because the husband "*is* her lord," and that one of the functions of marriage is to enforce a "wife's lowliness," for she is the divinely ordained subordinate of her husband.[6]

Hopkins was very preoccupied with the ancient problem that our modern consciousness now calls *sexual identity*. To a considerable extent he was influenced by the sexism in Victorian England that mandated divisive spatial, educational, and economic distinctions between the sexes. His comments to Richard Watson Dixon describing artistic achievement as purely a male gift and comparing art by women to infertile hens' eggs, suggest some of the difficulties that he was bound to encounter when he followed the sacrificial *imitatio Christi*.[7] It is one thing for an imperious embattled Oxford undergraduate to want to follow the sacrificial way, but it is quite another for him to undertake without stress the role of Christ's handmaiden.

When one considers the pervasive Victorian devaluation of women, Hopkins' courage in tackling the richness and the contrariness of his own gentle and imperious selves in all their internal needs and external requirements is all the more impressive. Most readers are aware of Hopkins' affection for the concept of "selving" and its connection with "inscape." But nobody has asked as yet what "inscape" and the process that he thought of as the selving of the self meant to Hopkins:

> I find myself both as man and as myself something most deter-
> mined and distinctive, at pitch, more distinctive and higher
> pitched than anything else I see; I find myself with my pleasures
> and pains, my powers and my experiences, my deserts and guilt,
> my shame and sense of beauty, my dangers, hopes and fears, and
> all my fate, more important to myself than anything else I see.

Hopkins' comment about the miracle and the trap of selfhood has never been better described. He called the miraculous sense in the self's discovery of itself a "selved self-being" or a "selving" of the self, and he considered it a great and generous gift from the creator, who required its tempered use in return. Hopkins perceived this divine permission to selve the self as particularly generous because the creator had allowed human creatures to become rich and complex in their individuation; yet humans, who were finite in their apprehensions of divinity, could not possibly imagine the creator to be as complex as they knew themselves to be. Often, their greed, their lust,or their intellectual self-absorption prevented them from perceiving the selfhood of other human selves, as well. For Hopkins as for all serious Christians, it was clear that to ignore or abuse creation was to despise the creator.

Hopkins' illumination did not end with praise for the creator in allowing humans this rich complexity. In order to keep faith with the *imitatio Christi*, he worked his own sympathetic imagination outward from himself to the world of natural and human creation, just as his creator bent benevolent eyes upon him: "Nothing," he said, "explains or resembles [the divine permission for human individuation] except . . . this, that other men to themselves have this same feeling. But this only multiplies the phenomena."[8]

Hopkins' coined noun "inscape" usually signifies fully selved living things throughout the natural world, including humans, as well as the artifacts created by male artists and thinkers. "Instress," another coined noun, typically describes a Christian's grateful response to the divine inscapes bestowed upon fallible humans. But humans can bear joyful witness to the world's glorious inscapes in each object, created either by the creator or by *his* creations, only if they have momentarily given up even prayerful self-absorption in order to concentrate upon praise of external objects as selflessly as the creator concentrates upon all creation.

The second quatrain of the sonnet "As kingfishers catch fire" most clearly celebrates the connection between pastoral inscapes and human inscapes, and the delicate balance between self-destruction and self-aggrandizement that constitutes the mortal necessity for both selving and selflessness:

> Each mortal thing does one thing and the same:
>   Deals out that being indoors each one dwells;
>   Selves — goes its self; *myself* it speaks and spells,
> Crying *What I do is me: for that I came.*

The sestet provides a religious conclusion, similar to an Ignatian colloquy, which suggests what each must give back to God: the feasts for the eyes and nostrils become snares unless something is lovingly returned by acting "in God's eye what in God's eye he is — /Christ." This offering is made "To the Father through the features of men's faces."[9]

In all Hopkins' poems celebrating the "grandeur of God," the concepts of inscape and instress include both male and female archetypes. Hopkins takes great pleasure, even pride, in naming and describing inscape after inscape, with its exact pitch and properties, just as Hopkins himself and the scribe of Genesis 2 perceived God to have given Adam the gift of naming things and creatures, including Eve herself, but denied that gift to Eve. In these poems Hopkins also invokes the feminine archetype of selfless adoration that women have traditionally lavished upon men and that Christ so generously offered to God.

Hopkins also combines the impulses of both genders when he is functioning as a Victorian environmentalist, mourning the disappearance of nature's inscapes. For when this ardent celebrant of all God's glories looked on with helpless yearning while the greedy industrial rapists of Victorian England subjected vulnerable humans and tender landscapes to unrelenting pillage, readers are not yet aware how closely his own maternal promptings are entwined with forceful masculine outrage against sinners—archetypally male in this case —who "do . . . not reck [God's] rod," and who "Hack and rack the growing green!" with callous indifference to God's gifts of pastoral beauty. "God's Grandeur" deliberately contrasts the sin of industrial ravage with "the dearest fresness deep down things" that elsewhere he called the "mothering earth" or "Nature's motherhood." In "Binsey Poplars," the speaker mourns over his "aspens dear" whom the ubiquitous pillagers had "Not spared, not one." But these poems and his journals also often express an archetypally female and futile anger of the powerless over the "Strokes of havoc" that "unselve the . . . Sweet especial rural scene" all over England.[10]

When Hopkins adapted his version of Scotan *haecceitas*, or thisness, to the male sex, readers are already pre-consciously aware of how neatly his version invites and leaves room for the healthy androgyny that should be natural to all human beings under unforced conditions. Again, we need to stress that Hopkins' permission to grant adrogyny to himself and to other men, but not to women, was entirely consistent with Victorian assumptions. In any case his stress on the complete and yet tempered selving of landscapes and the male sex in all their rich and complex diversity and specificity led quite logically and psychologically to the flexible blending and separation of male and female archetypes in himself and in other men, and in his own case to the flexible blending and separation of priest and poet, male and female, the public preacher and professor and the private "hidden" worshipper of God's three persons. Although some early Jesuits believed that Hopkins' ardent espousal of Duns Scotus did his vocation scant service,[11] modern hindsight may allow us to modify this assumption. He knew what he was talking about when he said that Scotus was the theologian "who of all men most swayed [his] spirits to peace."[12] Even as an undergraduate at Oxford, he had already anticipated Scotan insights, as his fine essays "On the Origin of Beauty" and "Poetic Diction" should indicate.[13] But his scrupulous attention to the needs of his vocation required sanction from a Catholic authority, no matter how obscure.

Duns Scotus's stress upon *haecceitas*, or *thisness*, of all natural and human creation was bound to reassure a man who described himself as selved with abundant complexities, guilts and glories all pitched as tightly as we know them to have been.[14] Scotus was particularly useful to Hopkins' gendered selves not only when he studied his own idiosyncratic selving but when he described the selving of the Trinity. His frequent distinctions between God, the masculine wielder of the authoritarian rod, and Christ, the tender young tutor, half older-brother and half maternal-protector, and the Holy Spirit, which he imagined as the bird of peace, are traditionally sound. But his tendency to separate them as he did was both stressful and beneficial, and in any case, he emphasized gender archetypes to an unusual extent, as well as pastoral and scriptural images. To him, each member of the Trinity was usually individuated, and each required different responses from him, just as women serve different members of their families in different ways according to each member's needs and demands.

It is equally crucial that Scotus confirmed Hopkins' right, as priest and poet, to pour admiration upon the great panorama of natural and human beauties and masculine talents, as long as he worshipped the creator rather than creation. It is no wonder that Hopkins, who so dearly craved the nourishing support and affection of peers and superiors, even beyond the needs of most professional men, should have appointed Scotus, the dead Oxonian philosopher, as his silent mentor, although Scotus was not in favor with other Jesuits.

After Hopkins had digested the implications of Duns

Scotus' works for his own *selves*, he began to shape radiant, imaginary visions of circles and spirals to describe the close and loving reciprocal relationship between God and his creatures, and between one creature and another when one teaches the other, through art, work or prayer, how to acknowledge the divine giver through his gifts. This concept is circular because it asks Christians to return to the creator what had first been granted them. Through the medium of beauty and goodness, love flows from the creator to his creatures, who then cause it to flow back to the divine source from which it originated.

This concept is also spiral, and under ideal circumstances, the spirals can be as endless as the original flow of love between the creator and his creatures. Each artist or worker whose work is known to others as an oblation to God, creates inscapes of love and praise for the originator of all human inscapes, and the inscapes created by these human acts of oblation serve as promptings for more prayers and celebrations in other Christian workers and artists, who may in their turn create yet more inscapes for yet other Christians.

Hopkins solved one theological problem with his vision of infinite circles and spirals. His concept of pastoral beauty and lovely masculine artifacts acknowledges the creator as the primary instigator of a loving *primum mobile,* which initiates this healing and teaching flow of mutual recognition between creator and creatures. Yet Hopkins' own candid admission of human fallibility and his own brilliant awareness of his own *selves*, or, as he would say, his *instressing* of his own *inscapes*, drove him to admit in both his prose and poetry that finite humans are aware of God's gifts to them only after *they* have instressed the divinely bestowed inscapes. As far as anthropomorphic minds first understand such matters, their minds' instress, that is to say, their joyous acknowledgment of these inscapes, always appears to have taken place before the inscapes were created, since humans cannot know what the creator has done for them until they see what they see, and feel what they feel, and finally analyze its implications. But Hopkins turned even this human fallibility into a divine forgiveness, since inscapes were so obviously put into the world for human rejoicing in the only ways available to imperfect humans.

Once again it is helpful to stress that Hopkins divided human acts of acknowledging divine inscapes into two distinct forms, one natural and theologically appropriate for men under the right circumstances, and the other natural and theologically appropriate for women under almost all circumstances. In theory, gratitude for God's generosity is not only possible but mandatory for both sexes, but Hopkins' consuming Pauline fear of articulate, independent women and vain women, always one and the same creatures, he thought, hampered his own exquisite vision of divine and human unity. His letters contain frequent discussions with men, about men living or dead, concerning vigorous intellectual, theological or artistic apprehension of God and the divine inscapes, but women are almost totally absent from these masculine speculations so crucial to the selving of his own self. However his poems and prose contain one lovely allusion after the other to the Virgin's maternal role and her modest and self-sacrificing life, as women's safest model.[15]

Hopkins' circular and spiral concepts are feminine in other ways as well. Women's minds and lives are often described as fluid and circular, moving in and out of states of being without the desire to acknowledge clear-cut boundaries between causes and effects, between the self and other selves or between beginnings and endings. Nowadays many alert women are struggling with destructively "soluble selves" that render them incapable of effective service to others because they are unable to practice legitimate self-preservation. St. Ignatius, that canny and compassionate psychologist, understood how serious this trap could become for postulants with an unusually ardent temperament. Some of Hopkins' superiors obviously understood that this tendency was particularly troublesome for so zealous a convert as Hopkins. His journals and his letters to friends and family indicate that from time to time, *his* penance was to undergo no penance at all.[16]

In moments when Hopkins' feminine self is in the ascendant, his perspective on inscape and instress brilliantly foreshadows modern insights about women's psychological conditioning. In his vision of divine and human reciprocity, once an ardent and worshipful creature is aware of beginning the

process of adoration, the circular current of love running between creature and creator theoretically has no end and no
beginning.   Nor does this process separate the act of the
worshipful onlooker from the divine gifts, nor the gifts from the
giver.   Hopkins' concept of the benevolent outward-flowing
and highly "pitched" spirals—or inscapes—that become instresses, is also peculiarly feminine: women's native talents
and earned achievements are archetypally assumed to be properly subordinate to their services to others, and their services
are expected to move in spirals according to the external needs
of their societies and eventually to encompass larger and larger
social groups.   This archetype is perfectly consistent with
patriarchal Victorian concepts and with much of scripture,
particularly the New Testament.

According to fresh studies in gender archetypes, one would
expect Hopkins to turn to images of the Virgin Mary or of other
sanctified women when his feminine self is in the ascendant or
when he is seeking Christian confirmation for it.   Readers who
believe that Catholic doctrine spoiled the poet, or that the poet
altogether spoiled the Jesuit, must account for the unforced
feminine serenity in many of the Marian poems.   For instance,
the opening stanzas of "The May Magnificat," with its lovely
pun that suggests both the Virgin glorified and the pregnant
Mother-to-be glorifying Christ, possess the marvelous prosodic simplicity of medieval poetry:

> May is Mary's month, and I
> Muse at that and wonder why:
>   Her feasts follow reason,
>   Dated due to season—

> Candlemas, Lady Day;
> But the Lady Month, May,
>   Why fasten that upon her,
>   With a feasting in her honour?

According to familiar archetypes, Christian, pre-Christian,
and non-Christian, the male sex is cerebral, whereas the female

is closer to silent and inchoate nature in her beauty and in her functions of childbirth and domestic management, and both roles are associated with the earth, with stains and with services to the species. "The May Magnificat" confirms some of these archetypes, but it eliminates the idea of the Virgin with blood and stain. Furthermore, for a moment, Mary takes on the attributes of the heroic nun in "The Wreck of the *Deutschland*": she is the subject of a theological celebration and she is a "mighty mother." And she is also momentarily permitted the male role in that the speaker asks her to solve the logical, theological and archetypal conundrum that he has posed for himself: how can May be her month?

> Ask of her, the mighty mother:
> Her reply puts this other
> Question: What is Spring?—
> Growth in everything—

"The May Magnificat" celebrates "Nature's motherhood" and "All things rising, all things sizing," all things that "blossom" and "swell / In sod or sheath or shell." Just as Christ sees and sympathizes with human achievements, archetypally male for Victorian-bred Hopkins, Mary, who was allowed to "Magnify the Lord" when he was "in her stored," always

> . . . . sees, sympathising
> With that world of good,
> Nature's motherhood.

And just as Mary, the mighty mother, assists the speaker in the Socratic way that she leads him to answer his own question, and thus takes on the attributes of an Oxonian don or a Master of novices, so Hopkins, the speaker, also momentarily trades gender roles in that he also "sees, sympathising" like a caring midwife, with all this divinely permitted pastoral fecundity. But the poem ends with the note of dominance of male over female, of Mary's son and his divine father over the stainless but nonetheless human virgin mother.[17]

In an earlier poem called "Spring," Hopkins once again assigned this season to Mary, the maiden mother. But because this poem includes a "girl and boy" as well as the "flesh, fleece fur and feather" of "The May Magnificat," the principle of regeneration is fraught with danger. Although it is a "strain of the earth's sweet being in the beginning / In Eden garden," the human condition is now such that generation is all too likely to become "sour with sinning." No matter how "Innocent" the allegorical young couple may be, these descendants of Adam and Eve cannot grow and bloom without the fear of sin. The poet's reflection expressed in the sestet urges this Everycouple to dedicate the female principle of gestation to Christ, the royal Son, in his exemplification of the male principle: he personifies the hero for whom the chastening of human instincts should be accomplished, if the couple is to escape damnation. Yet so swiftly does Hopkins dart in and out of gender archetypes, as though he possessed the quicksilver purposes of the radiantly speckled trout in "Pied Beauty," that Christ, the one to be adored, becomes the helpless innocent "maid's child," a divine infant whose very mother chose to worship him and thought the sacrifice "worthy the winning."[18]

In "The Starlight Night" there is a deliberate contrast between the glorious inscapes of the stars' "bright boroughs" in their flaming "circle citadels," and the internal, cozily domestic spaces below, which are usually allotted to women. The stars occupy an awesomely elevated height that emphasizes their public spaces open for all ardent Christians to gaze upon. The women's domestic spaces and functions are not at all sublime: they are spatially low and socially humble, even during those times when men are in them. They are "in hiding," to use one of Hopkins' favorite phrases for self-sacrifice and service. The stars, for all their actual and symbolic brilliance, are only silent witnesses to God's bounty, and since they are not human, they do not risk aggrandizing their own dazzling celestial fire. In more human terms, the Ignatian-like meditation in the sestet invokes "Prayer, patience, alms, vows," and these penitential methods are symbolically associated with a "May-mess" or a feminine Mary-mess of lush spring blooms "like on orchard boughs." The speaker's imaginary progress downward, from the celestial spectacle so near heaven, to the stars' reflection on earth, to the humble male territory of a "farmyard" and a "barn," which are still outdoors and visible to the passerby, and finally to the women's quarters, the "withindoors house," quietly but definitely confirms the Medieval and Cartesian dualism between achievement, usually masculine, and serene confinement, archetypally feminine. The spatial differentiations, all theologically blessed, nonetheless replicate the association in the great chain of being between heights and human superiority and dominance, and low spaces, human inferiority and consequent subservience. But because a "piece-bright paling shuts the spouse / Christ home, Christ and his mother and *all* his hallows," the speaker has combined in Christ the double archetype of male and female. His royal home is above the stars. His human home as a man in nature is often humble, homely, and reassuring, and his presence there is comforting in the feminine sense.[19]

"In the Valley of the Elwy" reverses the placement of male and female archetypes. In the octave, the speaker first affectionately describes "a house where all were good / To [him], God knows, deserving no such thing." He badly needs the "Comforting smell" of fresh firewood that caresses his nose "at very entering." The second quatrain of the octave completes the archetypal chain of gentle feminine allusions to anatomical and floral "growth in everything": the householders assume the metaphoric protection of "a hood / All over" the speaker, as "the mothering wing" will cover her "bevy of eggs," or as mild spring nights will cover the "new morsels" of growth.

Once again the sestet contrasts the benevolent world of nature with the tainted world of human nature. In the last three lines the speaker returns to the dominant male principle, to God, the "lover of souls," "Being mighty a master, being a father and fond."[20]

"Rosa Mystica" is a serene but theologically quite complex poem in which the speaker's imagination scans back-and-forth between pre-Edenic and post-Edenic time and between the time of Christ's birth and the crucifixion. The speaker imagines a divine *exemplum* of the archetypal human triad of mother, father and new-born child. Into this triad of God as father, Mary as mother and Christ as both infant and mature martyr, the speaker has gently insinuated himself with the welcoming permission of the human Virgin Mary as "Rosa Mystica." He imagines himself as a fully human foster son of the divine father and the human mother, and foster brother to the divine son. If the divine family cannot be an exact paradigm of the human family, in that any allusions to daughters and sisters are missing, Hopkins can be excused for following scripture, history, art and tradition.

"Rosa Mystica" has an attractive italicized anapestic couplet that is repeated at the close of each stanza. Except for the last of the eight stanzas, the first line of the couplet invoking "God's gardens," the speaker's imaginary modern prototype of Eden is deliberately paired so as to contrast it with the couplet's second line, which celebrates an earthborn Virgin, whom the speaker always addresses as *"mother of mine."* The first of the eight couplets, which Hopkins calls a "refrain," sets the gently rocking rhythm in motion, as though to summon up, by aural effects, images of an infant's cradle in motion:

> *In the gardens of God, in the daylight divine*
> *Find me a place by thee, mother of mine.*

In keeping with the deliberate couplet pairing of the celestial father with the earthly mother, and with the doctrinal teaching that God's essence is changeless, Hopkins repeats the first line of the couplet—"In the gardens of God, in the daylight divine"—in every stanza except the last of the eight. But in each couplet there is a shift in the speaker's assumptions about Mary's appropriate responses to him or to Christ, his imaginary foster brother. Mary is altogether human, however stainless she may be, and her inscapes will vary to the extent that the speaker perceives the roles of women to vary. The last line graciously focuses altogether upon her, whose poem this is; for despite the speaker's acknowledgment that Mary's feminine status is subordinate to that of the father and son, he wishes to say with as many prosodic felicities as his fertile talents can command: "Hail Mary, full of grace." Mary's rose, and Mary *as* rose, are both "Sweet unto God" and her "sweetness is grace," and its very fragrance even "bathes great heaven above." She pours out of her what the speaker craves: it is "grace that is charity, grace that is love." The last stanza directs readers to Mary's earthly maternal functions:

> *To thy breast, to thy rest, to thy glory divine*
> *Draw me by charity, mother of mine.*

The repetition of the refrain's first line—"In the gardens of God, in the daylight divine"—is bound to stress the masculine principle, because divinity in Christianity is always masculine. Also, the speaker stresses the masculine sense of property and entitlements: the gardens belong to God, not to Mary, whom he addresses as carrying out her maternal functions there. But the couplet pairs the divinity of the masculine Godhead with the femininity of the woman who exemplifies "grace that is love," and who functions as a mediator between humans and divine wrath. Her assistance in this role is second only to Christ's. The speaker begs her to save him a place by her; her *"loveliness"* becomes a legitimate target for his proprietory masculine gaze; he and she are to keep human time together; and she symbolizes the parched spirit's *"home"* for which he yearns. She is the maternal caretaker of her divine son and the bereft mother mourning his brutal death. The speaker asks whether he may join her, as her foster-child, in the family ritual of grief, which is oddly muted, since Christ's wounds have miraculously become "blossoms," as though he had given birth, or perhaps rebirth, to his divine self upon the cross.[21]

It is entirely appropriate that Hopkins' Marian poems are his most serene. Yet some of these poems, for instance, "The Blessed Virgin compared to the Air we Breathe" and "The May Magnificat," represent a slightly more varied, more vigorous Marian figure than Medieval iconography and even some fairly lush Renaissance paintings allow the Virgin. Hopkins' Mary is no Victorian prude: she has undergone labor and birth herself; she has been a "mighty" mother, and Hopkins' delightful puns on the adjective "mighty" and on "May" or "Mary Magnificat," or magnified, suggests both her enormous moral stature which led to a form of sanctification and to the miracle of her pregnancy. Her own example of fecundity combines an almost erotic lushness with innocence as she pours out selfless love that envelopes the speaker "With mercy round and round." Her concern for suffering humans offers the "needful, never spent, / And nursing element" that soothes fretful humanity. Although the speaker calls her "Merely a woman," she functions as a silent and gentle model for his own struggles with his imperious self.[22]

One of the critical commonplaces about Hopkins' poetry is that the Marian poems are too obviously doctrinal, but the fact is that the Welsh sonnets such as "The Windhover" and "Pied Beauty" are fully as doctrinal. The secret of their universal attraction lies in their accommodation to Hopkins' many selves, whereas the Virgin's comparatively static roles and the relatively quiet, understated diction and symbols, attractive as they all are, cannot appeal to the most complex human yearnings for the combined archetypal peace of feminine status and the energetic masculine urges to achieve and to experience the selving of many selves. In the Welsh poems, Hopkins' diction, subjects, symbols and metaphors all richly accommodate Scotan diversity, change and individuation, as the Marian poems are not so well designed to do. In the more complex poems, Hopkins rescues the concept of sanctified *stasis* without sacrificing human *kinesis*.

Hopkins' acceptance of all his sanctioned roles and selves in their proper time and place is never more apparent than in "The Windhover," and it radiates the sense of a complete human being who has found a rare and precious blending of human authenticity and commitment to values that smoothly transcend the birthright of his secular selves, without crushing them. In this sonnet, the feminine "heart in hiding" and the humble earthly function of the plow are deliberately contrasted with the free-wheeling falcon's archetypally masculine "achieve of, the mastery of the thing!" as he strides the sky-walks and "rebuff[s] the big wind." The opening octave is a frank celebration of masculine power, no matter how one interprets the symbolic meaning of the falcon *as* falcon or as analogue for anything else.

The hidden onlooker stresses both his private self and perhaps a wistful echo of one of Hopkins' past public roles as a brilliant Oxford undergraduate with a double first in honors. The opening clause—"*I caught* this morning morning's minion"—suggests the assertive action of reaching out and grasping the significance of the bird's "mastery," as an outfielder rushes toward an oncoming ball rocketing off the bat, and leaps toward it, reaching out his arm to its greatest distance as he runs to capture it. Yet this reaching and grasping action, which has archetypally been forbidden to women, is also fraught with some moral danger to the priestly onlooker. The moral resolution of this difficulty takes place as usual in the sestet. For the priest, the humble tasks "in hiding" are "a billion / Times told lovelier, more dangerous" and therefore more acceptable to God than all the falcon's brilliance.

"The Windhover" is full of benign paradoxes. The falcon's very spatial placement, high above the onlooker, archetypally symbolizes superiority and dominance. But the onlooker, who functions as prosodic theologist, Christ's servant and lover, and, in the very shaping of this dazzling sonnet, a quintessentially achieving Victorian male, places all his selves at the service of both an art and a vocation, each demanding great talents and unconscious acts of unselfish yet vigorous commitment.[23]

"Pied Beauty," a ten-line curtal sonnet, combines oblique allusions to both male and female archetypes and to a public and a private life, and it does so with a stunning richness of economy. The exuberant voice of the speaker is masculine, as it is in most of these Welsh poems, and the first six lines celebrate fast, dazzling active things in motion. The darting trout, glorified by the "rose-moles," the "finches' wings" skimming through the air as the trout skim through the brook, "And all trades, their gear and tackle and trim," are obviously masculine, free to move about at will in their natural habitat.

The opening stanza offers one allusion to a feminine archetype: the "brinded cow," a simile for "skies of couple-colour," moves slowly through pastures as an obvious analogue for the nourishing functions Hopkins always associated with the female. In the concluding quatrain, which does duty for a sestet, the speaker summarizes the whole of creation, and the masculine archetype of "swift" and dazzling things, as well as the female archetype of "slow" and "dim" things or things "in hiding," are benignly contrasted with the father who created them all. The varied movement of things in the natural world symbolizes change, and this permission for movement and change is a gift from the father of it all, "whose beauty is past change."[24]

"God's Grandeur" is another Welsh poem that spatially separates male and female archetypes, but here the gender inscapes are benevolent only in the tender female world of pastoral creation. The archetypally male world of industrial "trade," "toil," "smudge," "smell," and the contamination that men have caused in the bare soil is placed in symbolic contrast to untouched "nature" that is "never spent;/There lives the dearest freshness deep down things," fragile young growths hidden, like women's selves, which the industrial rapists have not yet managed to damage. The Holy Ghost appears as a nestling and broody mother bird, who tries to protect the remnants of God's pastoral inscapes with her own "warm breast," even as she shifts gender roles within the twinkling of a contiguous symbol and becomes a masculine archangel with splendid "bright wings."[25]

Since this discussion of Hopkins' Welsh poems is intended to suggest the poetry that most comfortably and brilliantly accommodates either one of his kaleidoscopic selves or all of them, I have not spent time upon the terrible sonnets, because these have already received such brilliant yet such varied interpretations from *Immortal Diamond* onward.[26] But if I am to plead that Hopkins' selves harmoniously coalesced as often as they threatened to crush one another, I need to look at a poignantly brilliant and tender moment during one of Hopkins' agonizing Irish crises, where the conjoined archetypes of male and female rescued him from his particular form of masculine despair.[27]

The octave of Sonnet 69, "My own heart let me more have

pity on," opens with the speaker's tortured plea that some internal or external resource will make him "hereafter" more "charitable," more "kind" to his "sad self" and his "tormented mind." Twice he invokes the archetypally feminine noun "comfort," once in the octave and once in the sestet. Its appearance in the octave signifies its frightening absence in the speaker's life. Its appearance in the sestet represents a self-created miracle. The speaker's self reaches way down into his darkest roots, which are paradoxically his brightest. He is able to obey himself and "leave comfort root-room." He advises himself to "let joy size," that is to say, to let joy grow large, to let himself be impregnated with joy, so that he can give birth to the blossoms of love and fine work. At that moment, the eyes of his imagination are rewarded: they see God bending an unforced, almost maternal smile upon him, just as Medieval and Renaissance artists pictured the Virgin Mary bending a post-natal smile upon her infant, who has safely negotiated the dangerous journey out of the womb and down the birth canal. Hopkins' symbolic association between the maternal world and the virgin pastoral world now partially rescues his sanguinity: God's smile also reminds him of those brilliant Irish moments when the fog lifts and the sun benevolently pierces the floor of a valley between imposing mountains, and in so doing "lights a lovely mile."[28] Even God the father can take on the tender gestures of a mother when his servant is in deep trouble, just as the Virgin Mary can become a "mighty mother," and Mary's earthly surrogate, the tall nun in "The Wreck of the *Deutschland*," can become a lioness and a prophetess, roles not then normally considered appropriate for Eve's descendants.

From his schoolboy days, Hopkins was in love with love. As a Christian, and most distinctly as a Jesuit, he learned to transform his imperious needs and his demands upon the world into the Christian principles of *agape* or *caritas*. The Welsh poems are paradoxically disciplined effusions of a man in love with his Lord, his Jesuit vocation, and his capacity to serve them both. At the same time, he was exhilarated with the varied inscapes of the Welsh countryside and with his own capacity to make and to shape brilliant poetry which paid tribute to all these blessings. In these poems, the inscapes of priest and poet, male and female, scholar and artist, city sophisticate and observant countryman all coalesced into an ecstatic but unfrenzied reverence toward the divine harmony that created such generous and such copious room for natural and human diversity. The hearts of his readers might in witness to Hopkins' work be "Stirred for a [man],—the achieve of, the mastery of the thing!"

The Choices of Two Anthologists: Understanding Hopkins' Catholic Idiom

In memoriam **William A. M. Peters, S. J.**
April 16, 1911 — June 16, 1988

Frans Jozef van Beeck, S. J.

What first gave rise to this essay was the publication, in 1981, of *The New Oxford Book of Christian Verse*, edited by Donald Davie. A quick comparison of this volume with its predecessor by more than forty years, Lord David Cecil's *The Oxford Book of Christian Verse*, served to reveal the surprising extent to which it was still possible, in the eighties, to call into question Gerard Manley Hopkins' standing, both as a poet and as a Christian poet.

Cecil's selection had comprised as many as nine poems—a remarkably generous gesture. After all, Hopkins' small volume of poetry had hardly entered the bloodstream of the body of generally received English literature in 1940, and the man behind the poetry was still a virtual unknown. But there it was: Cecil had included the entire first part of "The Wreck of the *Deutschland*," five sonnets interpreting the "inscapes" of scenes taken, respectively, from the natural world ("God's Grandeur," "The Starlight Night," and "Spring") and the human world ("The Lantern out of Doors" and "The Candle Indoors"), the long "The Blessed Virgin Mary Compared to the Air we Breathe"—a piece as Catholic as it is idiosyncratic, and two of the "terrible" sonnets ("Thou art indeed just" and "Carrion Comfort").[1]

By comparison, Donald Davie turned out to have included only four poems, and short ones to boot: one of the more telling juvenilia ("Heaven Haven") and three mature sonnets, one interpreting a natural scene ("As kingfishers catch fire"), one interpreting a human scene ("In the Valley of the Elwy"), and one a "terrible" sonnet ("I wake and feel the fell of dark").[2] Davie's anthology as a whole, it must be noted at once, is much leaner than Cecil's, but then again, it is implausible that limitations of space alone account for the less than two pages he has allotted to Hopkins, as against the more than eleven pages in Cecil's anthology.[3]

We have all come to understand and accept the half century of relative obscurity that followed Hopkins' death. We have also come to understand why the light should have broken, in the thirties, when Hopkins' originality was first recognized by critics like F. R. Leavis,[4] and in the next decade, when studies multiplied and when the breadth and subtlety of Hopkins' talent was first established by scholars like Professor W. H. Gardner[5] and the Dutch Jesuit William Peters.[6] In our own day, however, after half a century of vigorous critical and scholarly interest on every side (sometimes bordering on an industry), a firm consensus about Hopkins' place among the poets, and among the Christian poets in particular, might have been expected to be *in possessione*. Such a consensus, if indeed available, might also have been authoritative enough to put pressure on Professor Davie's curiously scant appreciation of Hopkins and forced the inclusion of a more generous *and* more representative sample in his anthology.

But there it is: *The New Oxford Book of Christian Verse* features Hopkins as a minor Christian poet. And while Professor Davie's admirably explicit criteria, explained in the introduction, invite an argument, he cannot be accused of bigotry. For this reason, we must let his selection raise questions about Lord David Cecil's generosity. And even if Cecil's decision of almost fifty years ago should turn out to have the support of the majority of appreciative and critical opinion today, Professor Davie, while judged mistaken, must still be allowed to raise doubts about criteria: did Cecil, perhaps, for all his good taste, do the right thing for the wrong reason? And what are the right reasons in the case of Hopkins?

The present essay is written to argue that both Cecil and

Davie appear to have partly misjudged Hopkins—misjudged him as a poet, but especially as a Christian poet in the catholic tradition, and specifically in the Roman Catholic tradition.[7] Curiously, in my analysis, Cecil and Davie will turn out to have one decisive feature in common, contrary to the impression created by their considerable differences in appreciation.

Central to the analysis proposed in this essay is the issue of *idiom*. By an idiom I understand a loosely coherent system of shared, public usage: the whole panoply of available linguistic and literary expedients that have authoritatively served, and continue to serve, a particular cultural group in expressing its vital concerns, in the interest both of living by them and bearing witness to them before the common culture. Poets and other writers, to be memorable, must exploit idioms to the full as well as stretch them in the exploiting. To the extent that they do so successfully they will achieve two things: they will manifest the originality of their talent, *and* they will help carry forward as well as transform and enrich both the idioms they exploit and the traditions of concern embodied in them. In this way poets will also advance as well as invigorate the communities that live by the traditions, much to the enhancement of the common culture.[8]

Both *The Oxford Book of Christian Verse* and *The New Oxford Book of Christian Verse* assume, by their very existence, two broad sets of norms. First of all, both books (their titles notwithstanding) assume that true Christian poetry—as against mere verse[9]—exists, and that it is at least one of the ways in which the Christian idiom is handed down, carried forward, and developed. For that reason, Christian verse is beholden to generally received literary standards, even if other utterances of the Christian faith are not. Secondly, both books assume that there exists a broadly normative Christian idiom. Both Cecil and Davie are aware of the fact that not all religious poetry is Christian poetry.[10] In addition, Davie is keenly aware that the very concept of Christian poetry is at least partly based on an abstraction—a decision "to *pretend*."[11] The Christian faith, after all, makes "the claim . . . to govern and encompass all of human behaviour." Consequently, poetry dealing, say, with the particulars of sinfulness could well be claimed as "Christian." The exclusion of such poetry from the realm of "Christian verse," therefore, while practical, is to some degree artificial and casts doubt on the very concept of "Christian verse."[12]

Still, in practice it is legitimate to say that, to earn recognition as a Christian poet, an author must face the cross examination that results from the application of two broad norms, distinct, but not entirely unrelated: poetic artistry and Christian faith. Needless to say, Cecil and Davie understand and apply the norms in characteristically different ways, with significantly different results in the case of Hopkins.

Let us begin with Davie's criteria. On the literary front, he states that thanks to a "persistent strain of asceticism . . . in every age Christian poets . . . have fallen in with those theories of poetry which, from the Ancients to the present day, have put a high value on what is called 'the *plain* style.'" Let us hasten to observe that Professor Davie at once goes on to earn his absolution from this curious statement of alleged fact: he confesses that he—like all anthologists—may be deceived by prejudice, and freely admits that he is himself "specially drawn to the plain style."[13] Still, the plain style does have a significance apart from the tradition's alleged devotion to it and Professor Davie's literary tastes: it has *congregational* potential. The memories of generations of plain people, Davie touchingly remarks, have been "stocked . . . . with scraps and tags (if no more) from some very sturdy and admirable poems." Thus the justification of the artistry of plain-style Christian verse partly occurs on "democratic" grounds.[14]

Professor Davie is as articulate when he comes to the issue of content, where he explains his interpretation of what is meant by "Christian" verse. Specifically Christian poetry "appeals . . . to . . . one or more distinctive doctrines . . . : to the Incarnation preeminently, to Redemption, Judgement, the Holy Trinity, the Fall."[15] To the recognition of this doctrinal element must be added the fact that the Christian faith "rests also, and perhaps preeminently, on a narrative . . . of historical events." But here a caution is introduced. To qualify as Christian poetry, verse narrative must reveal its "doctrinal implications," for "the narrative of Christ's life gives us doctrines, for instance, Incarnation and Atonement, in narrative form." Hence, narrative (especially if it draws on the Old Testament for its subject matter) merits inclusion only if it is doctrinal, and not, for instance, purely "picturesque or pathetic." Davie concludes: "a Christian poem . . . must treat of scripture to show how scripture embodies doctrine, and of doctrine to show how it has scriptural authority."[16]

This position has an interesting side effect: "Principles of Christian ethics [astonishingly, Professor Davie clarifies: "such as Hope or Charity"—where have the theological virtues gone?] can be called specifically 'Christian' only when they are espoused or practised for specifically Christian reasons . . . which take us back immediately to matters like Incarnation or Atonement or Redemption." In other words, "stringency in understanding what is Christian and what is not"[17] requires that faith alone—apparently understood as explicit, manifest[18] doctrine and narrative, professed in their mutual relatedness—qualifies as the content of Christian poetry.

From a theological point of view, Davie's commitments are far from arbitrary. Even though he is not, nor does he claim to be, a theologian, in developing his criteria Professor Davie has in fact made a coherent theological decision. This decision, I wish to argue, reflects the commitments, both doctrinal and literary, of what can be fairly called the "liberal Evangelical" tradition.

With regard to content, Davie's selection of the salvational themes of Incarnation, Fall, Atonement, Redemption, and Judgment (and in this salvational context, of the Holy Trinity) as simply determinative of the Christian faith goes back to the dawn of the Reformation.[19] So do his emphasis on narrative,[20] his apparent plea in favor of "faith alone," to the exclusion of ethical practice, and his interpretation of sacraments in doctrinal terms.[21]

In the area of content as well as style, Davie's preference for plainness and congregational appeal and his reluctance to draw "ethical" themes into his definition of "Christian verse" recall the mid and late seventeenth century, with its Arminians, Latitudinarians, Quakers, Cambridge Platonists, and associated types of quiet agnostics. Theirs was a calm but resolute protest against the fulminations and mutual excommunications of the established churches and congregational sects, and against the complicated orthodoxies and disciplines enforced by them, all of which had resulted only in unprofitable and often murderous debates, carried out amid the devastation and confusion of religious wars.[22] Relying on the Atonement and the assurance of salvation as the core of the gospel, they opted for a simple, uncomplicated, Evangelical biblicism, in which the links between biblical text and professed doctrine were immediate and obvious.[23] This type of Christianity (which a variety of dissenters brought with them to North America) took its stand on simplicity and sincerity of heart as the basis of all profession of faith, and combined it with an ardent, often even mystical trust in the authority of reasonableness. It came to be commended as the only way to anchor this tumultuous life in assurances not of this world, in the interest of recovering the serenity promised to those who believe.[24] Eventually, in the course of the eighteenth century, when the prevailing religious climate turned into cool, ethical common sense, especially among the educated, this tradition renewed itself by generating a popular, congregationally oriented wave of fiducial piety and fervor centered, of course, on the present experience of Atonement.

It is consistent with his apparent theological-literary commitment to the doctrinal and literary antecedents just outlined—even though it still comes as a bit of a shock—that Professor Davie can read more than twelve centuries of Christian poetry in English as a tradition in which the central, normative story is told in a period not quite two centuries long: George Herbert, Henry Vaughan, Christopher Smart, and William Cowper wrote between 1610 and 1800. One is, incidentally, also led to wonder if the leanness of Davie's anthology as a whole does not owe a debt to the same theological-literary creed.

The problem with this creed lies not so much in its untruth as in its selectiveness. It is one thing to value particular doctrines as belonging to the core of the Christian faith, or even to live by a preference for such doctrines; it is something else to propose one particular set of doctrines as determinative and to treat them as normative for the coherent understanding of the Christian faith-tradition as a whole. Here, stringency in understanding what is Christian and what is not has turned into constriction.[25] At the literary level (where doctrinal commitments are ordinarily more easily counterbalanced by artistic impartiality) this yields a flagrant and unnecessary reduction of the totality of available Christian idiom to an assortment of idioms proposed as *normative*.

This is why Professor Davie and Hopkins are bound to clash. Hopkins, both the Christian and the poet, owes no allegiance to either Christian doctrine or Christian idiom so narrowly defined; he acknowledges as authoritative a range of doctrines and idioms much broader than Davie allows.[26] Consequently, it would appear to be a mere postulate, necessitated by theological-literary narrowness on Professor Davie's part, to put Hopkins' "honesty" as a poet (which Davie recognizes) down to "the romantic individualism that is inherited by the Victorian Father Hopkins";[27] Hopkins operates from a much broader base than individual experience coupled with verbal talent. It is the enduring merit of F. R. Leavis to have shown how evocative, allusive, and stirring, and, thus, how un-Victorian, Hopkins' diction is. It is unwarranted now to jump to the charge that the *content* of his poetry is the product of Victorian individualism. Not that Hopkins is entirely innocent of individualism; he himself admitted to plenty of oddness and singularity as integral to his poetic talent, and there may well be even more there than Hopkins admitted to. But simply to call him an individualist is to miss the (clearly intentional) breadth of his idiomatic reference as a Catholic Christian poet.

In the context of the present essay, this insight yields a first conclusion: if Hopkins is to be adequately understood and appreciated, the entire range of his idiom must be recognized, including those sectors that express the Catholicity of his doctrinal commitment. The narrowness of Professor Davie's

idiomatic commitments has provided us with a first, if negative, norm to judge Hopkins by.

🌱

If Professor Davie provides us with a measure by which to
gauge the breadth of Hopkins' idiomatic reference, Lord David
Cecil, I wish to argue, furnishes us with a yardstick—again, a
negative one—by which to appreciate its objectivity.

In his preface, Cecil has much more to say about Hopkins
than Davie does in his. Comparing him with Christina Rossetti,
he writes:

> Hopkins is also a virtuoso. A natural juggler with words,
> intoxicated by the fertility of his own invention, he sometimes
> strained the resources of language beyond their strength; in his
> efforts to extend the bounds of expression he becomes obscure. But
> at his best, his verbal invention has a Shakespearean boldness and
> felicity. And he conveys with extraordinary fire and immediacy
> the more full-blooded religious emotions; the ecstasy of the rapt
> worshipper, the black night of the soul cut off from its vision of
> God. Like Christina Rossetti he had nothing very unusual to say.
> He voices the typical feelings of a Roman Catholic devotee as she
> voices those of a high Anglican. But this gives his poems a general
> appeal of which their eccentricities of expression might otherwise
> deprive them.[28]

These comments contain three statements. The first involves
Hopkins' verbal artistry—its limits and its strengths. The
second acknowledges Hopkins' power as a religious poet. The
third concerns Hopkins' Roman Catholicism. All three invite
reflection.

Let us begin with the second. To understand Cecil's
characterization of Hopkins, we must go back to his understanding of religion *and* poetry in general. His preface opens
with a magnificent statement of principle: "Religious emotion
is the most sublime known to man." Almost immediately, his
statement is joined by two declarations of comparable weight:
"A writer's best poetry is usually the expression of his keenest
feeling," and: "Poetry should be the spontaneous expression of

the spirit; the poet lets his personality burst forth without concealment."[29]

As the preface develops, however, these stirring statements get dull and discouraging company. By reason of its very loftiness, the religious sentiment is experienced with strength and continuity by only very few; even fewer can express the "spiritual experience" in its original purity. Hence, "most poets" are forced to settle for the derivative and the secondary: they "fall back on the traditional symbols of the orthodox liturgy." In addition, the New Testament's lofty conception of God makes any real spontaneity inappropriate.[30] In this way, the Christian poet is, by the very dynamics of the Christian faith, forced away from originality, into "unexceptionable sentiments," and even into "what he thinks he ought to feel," which, of course, will eventually tempt him to become "insincere."[31]

It is not difficult to recognize, in Cecil's analysis, the fundamental creed, *both theological and literary*, of high romanticism. In the romantic worldview, religion is, at bottom, a matter, neither of knowledge (that is, doctrine), nor of action (that is, ethical commitments), but of irreducibly original, self-authenticating, individual "feeling," "emotion," "sentiment." Friedrich Schleiermacher summed it up when he explained that "piety cannot be an instinct craving for a mess of metaphysical or ethical crumbs."[32] The authentic sense of God is given exclusively in an individual person's basic identity experience. Any concrete structures of religion, such as doctrines, devotions, and practices, are essentially derivative; to the extent that they are alive (and Schleiermacher, for one, thinks they frequently are[33]) they are so only because they feed off the deep wellspring of authentic religiosity that is each individual person's native blessing.

In this framework, does religiosity not make a person the prisoner of subjectivity? Far from it, for the authentically religious, "God-conscious" experience of self-identity is also the ground upon which the person is natively related to what is most original as well as objective: the universe in its pristine majesty and beauty, and, in and beyond the universe, God. Not surprisingly in the romantic frame of reference, therefore, the wellspring of authentic religiosity is identical with the source from which all authentic poetic experience and expression flow: sublimity and originality of feeling ultimately coincide. However, amidst the wearisome ordinariness of adult life (Wordsworth took a lifetime to explain and reexplain it as he wrote and rewrote *The Prelude*), authenticity is covered over by the alienating accretions of the life of thought and action. Only to the extent that the poet could retrieve the blessings of childhood—that is, his native contact with God and his original, immortal self—could he also see and appreciate the world in its true, native state, and express his vision, not in conventional, long agreed-upon truths, but in language as fresh and vivid as the experience that prompted it.[34]

Wordsworth, of course, is clearly not a Christian poet. In fact, the question arises if, on these romantic terms, a Christian poet is a possibility at all: Is the freshness of natural language not, by definition, denied to the orthodox? Yet with perfect consistency, Cecil finds his hero: William Blake, "gifted with the power to forge new and living symbols for the cosmic mysteries of spiritual experience."[35] But what entitles Blake to a place in an anthology of Christian verse? Not orthodoxy, Cecil concedes,[36] but the fact that Blake made original, creative use of the Christian idiom. To rank as the premier Christian poet, it suffices for Blake to be "soaked through with Christian thought," to be "exquisitely responsive to certain phases of Christian sentiment," and (most importantly in Cecil's eyes, it would seem) the fact that "more even than Donne or Vaughan, he had the spiritual eye." The Christian poets (beholden to the derivative idioms of orthodoxy?) have only "glimpses of the mystic vision; Blake seems to have lived for hours together at the heart of its ineffable light." In a climax like this, one wonders just at what point a critic's admiration will turn into credulity.

Given these commitments, Cecil has little difficulty finding both the original and the derivative in Hopkins. The former consists in individual experience, which certifies his standing as a *religious* poet: the "extraordinary fire and immediacy" with which Hopkins conveys "the more full-blooded religious emotions; the ecstasy of the rapt worshipper, the black night of the soul cut off from its vision of God." The latter involves Hopkins' *profession of faith*—what he has to say. That part involves "nothing very unusual": just the "typical feelings" of a Roman Catholic, just as Christina Rossetti voices those of a high Anglican. In Hopkins' case, however, this undistinguished element is to some extent redeemed by its social function: it "gives his poems a general appeal of which their eccentricities of expression might otherwise deprive them."

If Cecil's theological and literary commitment to romanticism has its weaknesses, we should not underrate its basic merit as a critical theory. Ironically, thanks to his highly questionable dismissal of all religious structures and their attendant idioms as a mere matter of conventionality, Cecil's taste is broadly catholic.[37] In his view, it would seem, Christian poetry can never attain to any fullness of originality and purity; with the lone exception of heretical Blake, Christian poets, of necessity, have to be compromisers. Nevertheless, pure, original religious and literary genius has often enough leavened the otherwise dull dough of orthodoxy to have produced a long, wonderfully varied history of Christian poetry in which there is much to admire. Cecil's appreciative survey of English Christian poetry shows that its author does not dream of using the yardstick of normative doctrinal commitments to push, say, florid baroque poetry of the meditative or emblematic kind to the periphery of the tradition of Christian poetry, let alone beyond it.

Still, Cecil's romantic theory must be challenged, especially on structural (or rather, "structuralist") grounds. The respective roles of individuality and community cannot be so statically defined and told apart and apportioned as Cecil assumes; the two are structurally interrelated. It is naive to think that individuality represents nothing but pure identity experience and the flight of originality and the urge to emerge, and that community amounts to nothing but alienation and pedestrian conventionality and the call to compliance. Individual originality and creativity are not self-generating, and to the extent that they are they tend to lose touch with reality and go to seed. Nor are shared tradition and convention by definition dead. Rather, they are ensouled, or at the very least dormantly so: being the treasury and the embodiment of a community's experience, they are waiting to be valued and activated and quickened and expanded. Thus tradition harbors a potential inaccessible to the isolated individual. For the individual, being fostered on the tradition means being welcomed to the community and its shared experience; but also, having the community's experience grow on one means being awakened to growth oneself. Thus the tradition is capable of introducing individuals, both to the community and its shared experience and to their own creativity, and it is in virtue of the latter that individuals can do for a community what no community can do for itself: move beyond its limits. Needless to say, all of this is a matter of a dynamic whose success is by no means assured; hence, it is never achieved without conflict and struggle, cultural and individual.

Cecil's appreciation of Hopkins' originality, therefore, must be called suspect. When he admires the "extraordinary fire and immediacy" with which Hopkins conveys "the more full-blooded religious emotions; the ecstasy of the rapt worshipper, the black night of the soul cut off from its vision of God," the question arises if Cecil has recognized, not just the music, but also the words—*the objective reference.* Or is he, perhaps, simply warbling—a thrilled mockingbird returning a different bird's call but failing to respond to it in kind, unable as he is to recognize its meaning?

As a result, Cecil appears to misinterpret Hopkins' preoccupation with language as well. In his view, Hopkins "had nothing unusual to say," even though he said it in extraordinarily original ways. The latter is said to be proof of his original talent; the former blandly ensures a "general appeal" that his eccentricity might otherwise have jeopardized. But all of this is far too pat and easy; Cecil's romantic preconceptions prevent him from seeing that both Hopkins' insistent preoccupation with language and his insistence on shared idioms are based on experienced meaning.

Hopkins, in other words, had an agenda in exercising his indomitable verbal skills and fertile invention to the point of eccentricity, and in straining the resources of the language at the risk of obscurity. (The latter, incidentally, as F. R. Leavis first pointed out, is often an integral part of the meaning.) He was seeking to *exercise and test and exhaust and expand, in the light (or often, the darkness) of his own experience, the idioms that sustained him.* What gives his poetry its rare credibility is that Hopkins was doing so in the process of capturing the ways in which *he was having his own commitments—and, indeed, his very self—exercised and tested and exhausted and expanded.* Margaret R. Ellsberg has given us an impressive account of one part of this exacting process: Hopkins' struggle to come to terms with his two apparently incompatible vocations.[38]

At its best, therefore, Hopkins' poetry is the record of a gifted individual struggling both with his own integrity and with the integrity of the communities he is part of and whose idioms are his own. In this regard he resembles Odysseus: his painful inner struggles on the high sea serve the twofold purpose of securing his own life and leading his associates to where they belong.[39] The strength of his best poetry, in other words, lies in its being both personal and impersonal, as one of the century's most reliable judges of Christian mysticism observed when the first edition of Hopkins' poems was barely two years old.[40]

In the meantime, the result is clear: Hopkins' poetry has the ability to enlighten and regenerate those idioms for others who recognize and cherish and seek to understand them as well as the concerns and experiences they represent. This element of objectivity of idiomatic reference, therefore, is integral to Hopkins' poetry. For Lord David Cecil not to have recognized and tried to understand it—or at least, not to have suspended his disbelief in its regard—is to have failed, in a crucial area, to appreciate the poetry.[41]

The theme of objectivity of idiom raises another issue, pivotal to the understanding of Hopkins' poetry: the source of its commitment to objective reference. This is where both Cecil and Davie have a blind spot; in an unthematic way, the critical approaches of the two editors of the *Oxford Books of Christian Verse* share a decisive preconception. This preconception, I wish to argue, is an anthropocentric conception of faith.

In the case of Donald Davie, this takes the shape of an implicit conviction that flows from his tradition's choice of Atonement as the Christian faith's central doctrine. Ever since sin and redemption were turned into the Christian faith's determinative themes (as evident, for instance, in Melanchthon's firm reduction of the Gospel to the forgiveness of sins[42]), the Reformed tradition has tended to believe in God predominantly, and often exclusively, as the Savior of humanity. This move had two related results. First of all, it favored the separation between the natural world and humanity; the former came largely to be viewed as no more than the stage on which the salvation of the latter is enacted. Secondly, within this special, unworldly relationship between God and humanity the Protestant tradition has tended to limit the focus of faith to the area characterized by the opposition between human sin and divine holiness.

For all their devotionality, and indeed their relative truth, these views run a dreadful risk of constriction. For what is placed at the heart of faith is not the adorable glory of God's transcendent majesty, nor the God-made, God-telling glory of creation, nor the glory of humanity made in the divine image and likeness, nor humanity's ineffable privilege of being called to live in familiar partnership with God, nor humanity's vocation to be God's responsible representative in the world, but wounded humanity's need for wholeness and redemption. In this way, God's ability to meet the human need for redemption has tended to become the measure of the divine greatness, and human weakness and sin, and the deliverance from them, have moved to the center of the faith experience. The literary expression of religious anthropocentricity of this kind shows in the Evangelical tradition's preference for devotionality: Christian poets witness to the happiness that flows from the inner assurance of salvation, in which they invite others to share.

Cecil's implicit endorsement of the romantic tradition of religious anthropocentrism is well demonstrated by the consistency with which he discusses faith in God in terms of immanence—"feeling," "emotion," and "sentiment." His characterization of the content of Hopkins' and Christina Rossetti's poetry is in the same vein: "He voices the typical feelings of a Roman Catholic devotee as she voices those of a high Anglican."

In the religious world of romanticism, anthropocentricity is not based on awareness of sin and salvation, but on its secularized permutation: the loss and recovery of human authenticity. In Schleiermacher's *Speeches*, not encounter with God but piety and self-consciousness are the decisive categories: "True religion is sense and taste for the Infinite."[43] In Schleiermacher's view, it is axiomatic that "the Infinite [. . .] we cannot be conscious of immediately and through itself."[44] The Infinite is attained only indirectly, *in* the depth experience of the finite self.[45] Now given that the sublime and the authentic ultimately coincide, the sense and taste for the infinite is also salvational: in their spiritual communion with Christ, whose knowledge of God was so singular and so original as to amount to a decisive "power . . . to communicate itself and awake religion,"[46] Christians acquire a new and higher God-consciousness. In this way, they are also reborn and restored to their better, more authentic and spiritual selves. All of this implies, of course, that true worship is impossible, for worship implies awareness of the living God as the term of an *other*-directed, responsive act. A modern commentator has aptly summed up the tradition embodied by Schleiermacher by writing: "God is out though godly attitudes may be in."[47] The literary preference of this romantic tradition of religious anthropocentrism is the *oracular*: Christian poets are the unquestionable, romantic witnesses to a better, purer, more interior world of human consciousness, into which they wish to initiate others.[48]

Both traditions, the liberal Evangelical and the romantic, embody an anthropological reduction of the Christian faith. In this reduced world, faith in God is centered on immanence rather than transcendence, on the experience of the reconstitution of human integrity rather than on the revelation of the reality of God and the reality of the world, which have moved to the periphery.

This has important consequences. The characteristic feature of all revelation is that it involves a call to ecstatic, responsive encounter, in which the respondent is also inwardly renewed in virtue of the fresh identity acquired in the encounter.[49] This is the core of the Catholic tradition. In that tradition, what is at the heart of the faith experience is mutuality of encounter, in the awe and the intimacy of worship and prayer, in response to the revelation of God's merciful glory, ultimately in the person of Christ as the source of rebirth. Immediately connected with this is the call to appreciation of, and responsible care for, the world, in response to the disclosure of the divine origin and destiny of all creation manifested and promised, ultimately again, in the person of Christ. Both revelations and both responses, along with the idioms that convey them, are as integral to Hopkins—a Catholic by resolute determination and a poet by irresistible talent—as they are to the Catholic tradition.

It is an ill paper that does not, in the end, make a point. It is high time to turn to the main theme, the Catholic idiom in Hopkins' poetry, lest we get mired in criticism. Still, the preceding reflections may have served to sharpen the realization that, in T. S. Eliot's words, "you must in the end come to understand every part in order to understand any part."[50] Hopkins' poetry does not settle for either the devotional or the oracular; it is broader and more objective, and in that sense, more universal and Catholic. Its author meant it that way. The Catholic idiom and the faith tradition it represents (Hopkins accepted both out of conviction, in a culture marked by anti-Catholicism) are so integral to his poetic intentions that they demand to be understood, both in their breadth and their objectivity. Like all matters of commitment, they can be dismissed or rejected as matter for belief; but critics and other interpreters, whether Evangelical or romantic, cannot afford to overlook or ignore them on ideological grounds, lest they misinterpret what they read.

Least of all, it must be added, should it be suggested that Hopkins would have been better off without the idiom and the Catholicism—that he would have had less inner suffering to cope with, and that he would have been happier and less neurotic. In this way to wish to protect Hopkins, after the event, from the struggle resulting from his own convictions is condescending as well as facile. After all, the thesis that complete freedom of self-expression assures the recovery of inner harmony remains to be proved. That it is the chief norm for individual fulfillment, in the writing of poetry as in everything else, amounts to a shallower version of the anthropocentric creed, and one more self-indulgently applied. Hopkins' admirable if painstaking certainty of literary and theological purpose stands in no need of pity.

Recognizing the Catholicity of Hopkins' idiom is all the more urgent since his Catholicism was so admirably attuned to his individual literary talent. This remains true, despite the fact that the pains he suffered in forging the two together were considerable and not always fruitful; also, that his work was often marred by his myopic insistence on being particular and different; also, that he was to an extent himself the cause of the embarrassing incomprehension with which even his best work was greeted by his few confidants and friends.

Still, his knack for visual detail, his astonishing lexical breadth, his exquisite ear (especially for assonance, rhythm, and the fetching colloquialism), the synaesthetic intensity of his sensibility, the daring of his diction, and the strength of his kinaesthetic instincts were favored by the Catholic tradition of analogical experience and the idioms that convey it. It moved him away from mere edification and moralizing, and encouraged him to focus on the reality of the world in itself and to appreciate it in all its original detail, yet at the same time to "read" it in a typological, emblematic, sacramental, and ultimately liturgical, doxological perspective.

In a similar way, the Catholic tradition of meditative and mystical prayer enabled him to recognize and suffer through the labyrinthine ways of his self-conscious, painfully self-captivated mind as well as the native instincts of his undomesticated heart. The secret of his success in capturing the experience of mental prayer and its idioms of consolation and desolation, self-examination, self-acceptance, and attempted surrender to God lies both in his fierce precision and his delicacy.

Thus he can be easily recognized as a companion by all those who have come to rely, for their own life with God, on the accumulated wisdom of the ascetical and mystical tradition.[51]

Finally, less rhetorically than John Donne, but as keenly, and certainly in no less Catholic and objective a vein, Hopkins succeeded in confronting and accommodating failure, corruption and conflict in humanity and the world: nuns hated and banned from their land; a row of fine poplars pointlessly cut down; the fact that his family were "in Christ not near"; the countryside and Duns Scotus' beautiful Oxford equally blighted; the ugly predicament of the unemployed; the sickness and death of a smith; people everywhere cheerless and dulled, and children's innocence threatened by the souring presence of sin: all of it, all of them estranged from their natural goodness and beauty, yet all of it, all of them Christ's "choice and worthy the winning." In this third area especially, the catholicity of Hopkins' Christian poetry is obvious—it is not the fruit of any decision to "pretend." Hopkins does not show the slightest worry about "stringency in understanding what is Christian and what is not," for his perspective is universal enough to include the world, including the particulars of sin.

Freedom and Necessity in the Poetry of Hopkins

"From my necessities deliver Thou me."

—St.Augustine, City of God

"Hereby, I may tell you, hangs a very profound question
treated by Duns Scotus, who shews that freedom is compatible
with necessity."

—Hopkins to Bridges, 4 Jan. 1883

Donald Walhout

In this essay I want to explore a theme that I believe is significantly present in Hopkins; namely, the way in which we are subject to various kinds of necessity and yet at the same time are simultaneously free to respond to them. It seems to me that Hopkins is among a small number of writers who hold steadily in balance the tension and the reality of both conditions. Certainly there may be those who from their convictions may exceed him in proclaiming the unassuaged control of necessity, fate, or destiny, just as there also may be those who exceed him in celebrating the existentialist claim to unmitigated freedom. But when it comes to acknowledging the impact of the interaction of both freedom and necessity and when it comes to perceiving the mystery of their interaction—then, that is a different matter. My contention is that in Hopkins' work we have an outstandingly significant presentation of this balance of the two conditions.

Necessity and freedom in this context involve what I believe is, in Gabriel Marcel's sense, a mystery rather than a problem.[1] A problem can be intellectually formulated and in principle solved, whereas a mystery can be only somewhat illuminated, not fully understood. Therefore, I shall approach our subject—the interaction of necessity and freedom— as a mystery worth probing, not as a problem to be disposed of. In a typical Hopkinsian inversion, Hopkins begins "Rosa Mystica" by referring not to the mystery of the rose but to "the rose in a mystery." In like manner we ask:

The rose in a mystery—where is it found?

Even though we are not likely to learn exactly *how* necessity and freedom operate together, we do hope to show that they *do* and *can*.

It may be helpful to our discussion to have formal definitions of necessity and freedom. Therefore, let us define necessity as follows: a person P is necessitated with respect to any life circumstance C if and only if C has some causal or restricting influence on P and it was not or is not within P's power to prevent C from having this influence And let us define freedom as follows: a person P is free with respect to an action A if and only if it is within P's power either to perform A or to refrain from performing A.

Notice that these definitions do not define necessity and freedom as contradictories. Of course, there would be a contradiction *de facto* if the action or circumstance in question were the same one in both cases, for then we would be speaking of necessity and nonnecessity or freedom and nonfreedom, which *are* contradictory. And on this point Hopkins would undoubtedly agree with Scotus: "Scotus saw the problem in terms of a contrast between an order or system of nature and an order or system of liberty. A single human act with a single object cannot belong to both of these orders at the same time."[2] But with our general definitions we can speak of certain circumstances in life as being necessitated without denying that there may be at the same time opportunities (within a certain scope) for the exercise of free responses. In this broader sense, it is possible to speak of necessity and freedom as constituting not a contradiction but a mystery.

As another preliminary to Hopkins' poetry it might be well to survey the various kinds of necessity that occur in life and that Hopkins wrestled with both personally and poetically:

Logical Necessity. This refers to the laws of logic. Although we are free to make statements or not, it is not within our power to construct them to be contradictory or not. They do this by the truth or the meaning which they have.

Ontological Necessity. This refers to the fact that being has certain properties or structures not of our making. Although being includes our freedom, we are not at liberty to make the entire realm of being into whatever we want. Especially obvious examples would be existents that are eternal, such as divine existence, natural numbers, or possible worlds.

Epistemic Necessity. This refers to necessary truth of propositions rather than to necessary modes of being. Such truths are often described as self-evident truths or a priori truths. It is not within our power to make them false. We can only become cognizant of their truth.

Natural Necessity. This term, sometimes called nomological necessity, refers to the causal laws of the physical universe. These are the familiar laws of nature we take for granted in daily life and thought. Their necessity is assumed in such epithets as "deterministic," "inexorable," or "iron-clad." We live always under the sway of these regularities, and sometimes they cause unprovoked disasters or natural evils.

Biological Necessity. This kind of necessity is part of the laws of nature, of course; but its particular significance is felt in the three inherent conditions to which all life is subject: aging, disease, and death. Human choice is shaped in part by the conditioning of these biological factors.

Physical Necessity. By physical necessity I mean to emphasize the ways in which our bodies are restricted by spatial limitations and by other occupants of space, either human or nonhuman. Some of this necessity is socially induced, such as imprisonment or urban crowding, but can be considered physical constraint nonetheless. Three common circumstances which highlight this kind of necessity are accidents, confinement, and separation.

Psychological Necessity. This is the type of necessity in

which the mind is molded, controlled, inhibited, elevated, or depressed by outer or inner circumstances. Though we may reject behaviorism and determinism, we must recognize that some aspects of our psychic life are part of "the given" of human existence. A common experience in this area is one that I have discussed elsewhere under the heading of encagement.[3]

Historical Necessity. This is the necessity of the past, called by William of Ockham accidental necessity.[4] Although human acts at the time of occurrence can be said to be free, once they have been performed they cannot be undone. We cannot undo the past, which thenceforth brings about inevitable effects on persons, generations, and times. For good or for ill, we must accommodate to the past.

Aesthetic Necessity. If one is to appreciate beauty or seek artistic excellence, some aesthetic requirements must be followed. Although a current trend emphasizes maximum subjective construction or deconstruction in the aesthetic arena, there are restrictions in this area as in any endeavor. We are not at liberty to do absolutely anything and still have aesthetic merit.

Existential Necessity. This is the situation we sometimes face in which we must choose one way or the other. We may be free to choose among alternatives but not be free to avoid choosing altogether, at least in those situations where not choosing is tantamount to making a choice of a certain kind. This is the human situation which existentialists emphasize, the demand for choice.

Moral Necessity. Unlike Sartrean existentialists, however, common moral tradition acknowledges some real distinction, however specified, between right and wrong, good and evil. In choosing, therefore, we confront a moral order in which there is some necessity about what is right or good. This point is summarized in the notion of moral requirements or moral law. We are free to follow or not follow the moral requirements, but we are not free to make them into something other than what they are.

Spiritual Necessity. Finally, for those with religious convictions, there is the impingement of divine action on human life which is not of our own instigation. We can only acknowledge and respond to this initiative; we do not create it. It comes down to the mystery of freedom and grace, a mystery to which we will return later.

Now each kind of necessity mentioned here can be classified, it seems to me, as either a cognitive state, an affective state, or a volitional state. Not that I am ranking these necessities as subjective mental states; but I am suggesting that in terms of the impact they make upon us in our daily living, it is possible to speak of them as cognitive necessity, affective necessity, and volitional necessity. For example, the first three necessities mentioned above—logical, ontological, and epistemic —seem to appeal to our cognitive interest. For example, we think about the laws of logic but do not really lament them (an affective reaction) or undertake campaigns about them (a volitional reaction). The next five necessities—natural, biological, physical, psychological and historical—seem to have their influence primarily on our affective life; that is, how we experience life phenomenologically. Since affective states also have ramifications for volition states, and cognitive states cannot be totally removed from the other states or be totally uninfluenced by them, we should not pretend that the compartments exist in complete separation one from another. The last four kinds of necessity—aesthetic, existential, moral, and spiritual—are more directly related to our decision making. They set the framework for our aesthetic decisions, personal decisions, moral decisions, and spiritual decisions.

I realize that much of what I have said so far might be challenged by pragmatists and relativists. Their challenge, however, might be more about metaphysical interpretation than about the phenomenological elements of necessity which we do in fact confront in human life. In any case, I have given what may be called a common traditional account of Western realism, a tradition which Hopkins would certainly espouse.

We need not give a similar rundown in the case of freedom. Freedom is a common capacity in us, a single psychic trait, in contrast with the various kinds of necessity that seem to characterize our existence. Of course, there are many contexts in which freedom operates, and the above list would do well enough for a classification of those contexts. But with freedom we are mainly interested in whether this common human capacity can function effectively under the impact of all these necessities. I now want to illustrate that Hopkins does indeed take into account, and sometimes silhouettes, the necessities that swarm in upon us.

Necessity in Hopkins

We can hardly expect to find much direct evidence of the cognitive necessities—logical, ontological, and epistemic. These are highly abstract concepts and not the stuff of poetry. We may assume that Hopkins took the laws of logic to be objectively necessary. So too with structures of being. Once in a letter he identified himself with traditional realism.[5] And realism accepts the objective givenness of logic and reality. There is an interesting reference to an epistemic necessity in one of the early poems. Comparing the plethora of modern doctrines to musical fare, Hopkins writes:

> I have found my music in a common word, . . .
> And know infallibly which I preferred. (19)[6]

Philosophers would call this an incorrigible truth, a direct awareness of our own mental states not subject to correction. We may assume there are many other truths which Hopkins would regard as necessary truths.

The prime examples come, however, from the next category, the affective necessities we feel. Here we have abundant illustrations. Explicit reference to nature's regularities is found, for example, in "The Silver Jubilee," where Hopkins speaks of "Nature's round"; in "The May Magnificat," where he speaks of "All things rising, all things sizing"; in "The Blessed Virgin Mary Compared with the Air We Breathe," where he speaks of "This air, which, by life's law,/My lungs must draw and draw"; and in "That Nature Is a Heraclitean Fire," where he says that "nature's bonfire burns on" and that "time beats level" everything human. Even more obvious are the implicit references to nature's regularities in the innumerable allusions in Hopkins' nature poems and journals. Nature's laws lie behind his accounts of stars, planets, winds, rainbows, birds, flowers, trees, rivers, fields, skies, seasons, and so on. To illustrate this rich vein, I choose fragment 84, where nature's round is seen

> During the eastering of untainted morns,
> In the ascendancy of rainbow's horns,
> In the first signals of the several drops
> That lick the shelly leaves which floor the copse,
> In the quick fragrance of tall rolling pines,
> Under the cloister-light of greenhouse vines.

Nature's regularities are also the cause of mishaps and disasters, which deeply moved Hopkins, as with the *Deutschland* and the *Eurydice*. Verses 13-15 of "The Wreck" give a vivid description of how "the sea . . . in the regular blow" and "the combs of a smother of sand" necessitate that "lives at last were washing away."

Biological necessities are also evident in Hopkins. The inevitability of the aging process is hauntingly depicted in "The Leaden Echo": "O is there no frowning of these wrinkles, . . . no waving off of these . . . sad and stealing messengers of gray?— No there's none, there's none, O no there's none." In "Morning, Midday, and Evening Sacrifice," three stages of life calling for different responses are identified.

The grip of sickness and disease, often so unexpected and so crippling, and something which Hopkins himself encountered at an early age, is dominant in "Felix Randal." Randal, the "mould of man," was reduced to

> Pining, pining, till time when reason rambled in it and some
> Fatal four disorders, fleshed there, all contended . . .

And, Hopkins adds succinctly: "Sickness broke him."

Death, that inescapable theme of life and poets, is so frequently alluded to by Hopkins that we can only mention a small sample of the illustrations. The simplest, but one with great pathos, is in the lines "to a young child" in "Spring and Fall," that begin "Márgarét, áre you gríeving/Over Goldengrove unleaving?" and ends "It is the blight man was born for,/ It is Margaret you mourn for." Some other illustrations are: "all

/Life death does end," from "No worst, there is none"; "our night whelms, whelms, and will end us," from "Spelt from Sibyl's Leaves"; and "death blots black out," from the Heraclitean poem. Clearly, death is an engulfing necessity which conditions human decision.

Physical necessity includes accidents, already mentioned with the shipwreck poems. It was not within the power of the crews, under the immediate circumstances, to avoid the shattering physical accident, though they might have done so earlier. The same is true of personal accidents, although we do not find these cited in the poems.

Accidents often bring not only debilitation but physical confinement, as in the case of the crews and passengers in the above poems. A poignant symbolization of what confinement can mean is found in Hopkins' fragmentary poem on Pilate (80), who is banished to an icy isolation.

Another physical necessity that grated on Hopkins is that of spatial distance, which separates a person from other people or from a preferred locale. In "To seem the stranger," he laments his own distance from England. In "The Lantern Out of Doors," he regrets having to walk by strangers, never getting to know them, until "death or distance soon consumes them." In "The Candle Indoors," physical barriers prevent him from knowing anything about the Jessy or Jack behind the window. Clearly, we must cope with the separation of distance.

Psychological encagement comes when, despite effort and will, we feel ourselves trapped, deserted, or despairing. This is a theme, of course, in the familiar desolation poems. A paradigm of this affection, however, occurs in "The Caged Skylark," which depicts a bird that longs to be in the open but is closed in instead.

Encagement was a lifelong concern of Hopkins and not a latter-day encroachment. In a youthful poem (18), he uses necessitarian images to express this feeling:

> My heaven is brass and iron my earth:
> Yea iron is mingled with my clay,
> So harden'd is it in this dearth
> Which praying fails to do away.

In a mid-career poem, "Peace," the helplessness of the feeling is rendered thus: "When will you ever, Peace, ... /Your round me roaming end, and under be my boughs?" Even the desolation poems carry not just outcries but necessitarian images, for example: "God's most deep decree / Bitter would have me taste" (67); or "why wouldst thou ... / ... lay a lionlimb against me?" (64); or "My cries ... / ... on an age-old anvil wince and sing" (65).

The influence of the unchangeable past is also evident in Hopkins. Historical necessity comes about from free actions of past generations which later generations cannot alter but must live with.

> Generations have trod, have trod, have trod;
>   And all is seared with trade; bleared, smeared with toil;
>   And wears man's smudge and shares man's smell. (31)

This theme in Hopkins usually comes in the form of past misdeeds and travesties, as in the felling of trees at Binsey or Ribblesdale, but occasionally in the form of past glory, as in the persistence of the Church in "Andromeda." The past sin of man was not only a doctrinal but a poetical interest of Hopkins. In "The Sea and the Skylark," he writes: "We, life's pride and cared-for crown, / Have lost that cheer and charm of earth's past prime." But past misconduct, reaping its inevitable effects, can be individual as well as generational, as in personal sloth; for example, "the waste done in unreticent youth." (17)

Historical necessity means that the past is an inescapable pressure on us. Hopkins refers to this in "Ad Mariam" as "the pain of the past's unrest." "To His Watch" notes our necessary temporality and suggests that through it we must find "comfort's carol" or "woe's worst smart." We can use the past; but we cannot alter the fact that we are conditioned by it.

Turning now to what I have called volitional necessities, it is clear that Hopkins holds to the objectivity of aesthetic requirements for aesthetic appreciation and for artistic creation. Referring to the majesties of nature in "Hurrahing in Harvest," he says: ". . . these things were here and but the beholder / Wanting." Likewise, music has an "O-seal-that-so-feature"

(62), presumably some objective essence, found especially in Purcell. In the poem entitled "Henry Purcell," this feature is identified as something like the Aristotelian universal in art, "the very make and species of man." Though we can make little of these aesthetic tidbits as formal theory, they do point to objective requirements, "not mood in him," to which the artist must submit. The best citation, however, is Hopkins' own lament in "To R. B.," where he says he lacks the poet's essentials: "the fine delight that fathers thought," "the strong spur, live and lancing," the incubation of ideas, "the one rapture of an inspiration," "the roll, the rise, the carol, the creation." This is not an aesthetic theory but an acknowledgment that there are artistic requirements if one is to create art.

Existential necessity—the life situation in which we are forced to choose—is taken for granted by Hopkins inasmuch as he frequently urges moral and spiritual choices, and such urgings would be pointless without the reality of choice and the need for choice. Both of these factors—free will and the necessity of choosing—are sounded in the seventh stanza of "On the Portrait of Two Beautiful Young People":

> Man lives that list, that leaning in the will
> No wisdom can forecast by gauge or guess,
> The selfless self of self, most strange, most still,
> Fast furled and all foredrawn to No or Yes.

In "Spelt from Sibyl's Leaves," he uses the metaphor of sewing, a common image of necessity, as when the Fates sew the threads of our destiny. He sees "life wind off . . . on two spools." These spools represent the need to choose one way or the other.

The same image shows the objective necessity of moral law in Hopkins' convictions. For the two spools are in fact "black, white; right, wrong"; and we are enjoined to "mind but these two." There is an objective rightness and wrongness that we can choose between but do not invent. In "To What Serves Mortal Beauty?" he refers explicitly to moral law and gives one of its precepts: "Our law says: Love what are I love's worthiest, were all known." In "As kingfishers catch fire," he says "the just man justices," suggesting that one can only be morally just by embodying the essence of justice. This justice, like all moral law, is, for the Scotist Hopkins, rooted in divine will. And this source Hopkins acknowledges when, in the same poem that he ends with "send my roots rain," he begins the poem with "Thou art indeed just, Lord." (74)

This brings us to spiritual necessity, the impact of God upon us. We can respond to, but do not determine, this impact. It may come in the form of "God's most deep decree" (67), of "Thy terror, O Christ, O God" (28), of one's "first, fást, last friénd" (40), or in many other forms. But more of this later under freedom and grace.

All of these necessities surround, pervade, and condition our human lives. They forge the anvil against which we must live and choose. But can we choose at all under all this weight of iron, or, to modernize the metaphor, this operant conditioning?

Freedom in Hopkins

The answer is, for Hopkins: "I can; /Can something." (64) Despite all the binding necessities—and they are powerful in, for example, the desolation poems—one still has it within one's power to

> Not untwist—slack they may be—these last strands of man
> In me or, most weary, cry *I can no more.* I can. (64)

Let us now illustrate this theme in Hopkins, namely, how freedom can operate despite necessity. And what we need to siphon out is not just any sorts of human actions, which in general might be said to be free because humans are free, but specific cases where some necessity seems to dominate or override the self but in which the self still acts from its deep reservoir of freedom. As usual, we cannot expect Hopkins to coincide with our categorial neatness. But our verificational interest will be satisfied if we can find some significant illustrations. They will confirm our theme.

As with so many other themes, "The Wreck" is a point of arrival. The freedom-necessity paradox, or FNP for short, as we may call it, is found especially in stanzas 16-17. Crew and passengers are trapped by the inexorable working of nature's laws. But one crewman makes a decision:

> One stirred from the rigging to save
> The wild woman-kind below,
> With a rope's end round the man, handy and brave.

However, he did not succeed:

> He was pitched to his death at a blow,
> For all his dreadnought breast and braids of thew.

But before his death he could still make a decision, and did make a decision, of right intention. The next verse begins with a summary of the FNP in five words:

> They fought with God's cold—

Then the wind and the waves crushed them all or broke their hearts

> Till a lioness arose breasting the babble,
> A prophetess towered in the tumult.

The "call of the tall nun" was a final decision to call upon Christ. We do not know what calm or final thoughts it brought to others; but the implication is that she was a vehicle of some comfort to those below deck and perhaps even "to the men in the tops."

"The Loss of the *Eurydice*" presents a similar situation. Here also we find some heroic decisions in the face of physical necessity. The captain, Marcus Hare, following voluntary rules of the sea, decided to stay with his ship and in fact "Kept to her—care-drowned and wrapped in / Cheer's death." Another sailor, Sydney Fletcher, against all odds, "takes to the seas and snows," is kept afloat by "a life-belt and God's will," and is finally rescued by a schooner. These acts occurred even as "Death teeming in by her portholes / Raced down decks."

"Felix Randal" shows freedom in time of fatal illness. "Impatient, he cursed at first," a reminder today perhaps of Kübler-Ross. But then he "mended / Being anointed and all."

"The Caged Skylark" obviously symbolizes psychological encagement. But even within the grip of this necessity, freedom is acknowledged: "Both sing sometimes the sweetest, sweetest spells" even though both can "wring their barriers in bursts of fear or rage." Barriers are fearful; but singing is possible.

"The Candle Indoors" begins by showing that darkness can separate people without being penetrable. But then the poem declares that one can use a realization like this to strengthen one's resolve to mend one's internal life, i.e., to rekindle that "vital candle" within.

"To seem the stranger" also deals with distance. Here it is called a "third remove," a strong image of separation. Nevertheless, freedom to overcome the loneliness of distance is possible; for "in all removes I can / Kind love both give and get."

In "Peace," although the poet is constrained in a condition of no peace, he states that patience is still a good that is available. However, patience must be voluntarily sought. Yet we can be assured, as stated in "Patience, hard thing," that "bid for, Patience is."

In "My own heart" (69), desolation is likened to other necessities. For example, the poet can no more find comfort than blind eyes can see the day. Yet, despite this fact, it is still within his power to outmaneuver the grip of desolation:

> My own heart let me more have pity on; let
> Me live to my sad self hereafter kind.

Again, one can "call off thoughts awhile / Elsewhere"; one can "leave comfort root-room"; one can "let joy size." Even under desolation, one maintains the will to counteract it.

If we take the unemployed Tom Garlands of the world to be fixed in a kind of social necessity, a "low lot," which may not be literally true but may be felt to be so, we still observe spontaneity of action, as symbolized by the worker who "rips out rockfire homeforth" and even by the troublemakers who "infest the age." (70) Similarly, "Cheery Beggar" may reflect a person forced into a state of poverty and homelessness but one who can still live with some cheer.

As far as biological aging is concerned, "The Silver Jubilee" celebrates someone who chose to grow older with serenity and dignity. And let us not forget Alphonsus Rodriguez, who did so also in a lowlier office.

An example of historical necessity is our cultural upbringing. We do not choose and cannot alter "the land that bred me" or the "homes and fields that folded and fed me." (156) But we must still choose to be loyal and patriotic rather than rebellious. More typical of Hopkins in other places is the historical necessity of past human evil and of past misjudgment. Yet there is always the sense that the will is not destroyed and that redeeming decisions are open. Conversions do take place; reforms can be initiated; proper loyalties can be adhered to; even "death with duty" (156) can be chosen.

Hopkins seems often to have a brooding despair about the way in which this historical weight has corrupted and rendered irremediable modern life. The words "The Times are Nightfall" symbolize this attitude, and the opening lines of the poem express it:

> The times are nightfall, look, their light grows less;
> The times are winter, watch, a world undone:
> They waste, they wither worse.

And yet, despite this seemingly ultimate pessimism, Hopkins can say there is something more: "There is your world within." And he summarizes our current theme in a nutshell when he declares: "Your will is law in that small commonweal." And that will can make a difference, in oneself first, and possibly even in the times we inhabit.

I find in "On a Piece of Music" a marvelous statement of the simultaneous operation of freedom and necessity, the FNP, in the aesthetic sphere. First comes a testimony to the freedom of the artist:

> Nor angel insight can
> Learn how the heart is hence:
> Since all the make of man
> Is law's indifference.

"Law's indifference" makes possible, I believe, free artistic creativity. And yet, simultaneously, there is aesthetic necessity to be obeyed, since the artist is

> Not free in this because
> His powers seemed free to play:
> He swept what scope he was
> To sweep and must obey.

This example of the artistic situation is, to my mind, the sharpest statement of the paradox and mystery of freedom and necessity. I venture to claim, however, that it is no less real in other cases.

Finally, regarding moral freedom, let us turn again to "Carrion Comfort," with which we began this section. In the opening stanza, there is the suggestion of a necessary, either-or choice between being and not being. Shakespeare's "to be or not to be" can refer, we might say by extension, to existential and not just physical suicide. That is, one can choose to live one's being and actualize one's potentiality, or one can choose nonfunctionality and settle for unfulfilled potentiality. This is an either-or, right-wrong choice that cannot be avoided. Moreover, there is a right way that is morally necessary under moral law. And it is within one's power to "not choose not to be," which means, logically, that one chooses being, the moral requirement. This is the moral affirmation Hopkins makes, despite the attraction of "carrion comfort."

As a transition to the next section, let us look for an

archetypical symbol for the height which freedom can reach despite necessity. I suggest the windhover. Not that the bird is free in itself; but it is a symbol of freedom. Against the backdrop of necessity, its swings and glidings are spectacular, beautiful, ecstatic, and graceful. This is not surprising, given what the windhover represents for Hopkins.

God and Nature

We come now to the realm of spirituality, always, I think, the *telos* in Hopkins poetry. The omnipresence of God is not something that is within our power to create, to engineer, to govern, or to avoid. We can only confront it and respond to it. The specific impingement of this omnipresence may be felt as a controlling or challenging necessity which we cannot flee from or escape. At the purely spiritual plane, this experience will embody the paradox of freedom and grace. But at a more mundane plane, Hopkins has a good deal to say about the workings of God in nature relative to man. Is there a preliminary insight we can gain by first considering this plane?

A clue to an insight is found in "The Wreck," stanza 5, where Hopkins says, "His mystery must be instressed, stressed." In other words, though God is real and eternal, "tho' he is under the world's splendour and wonder," he will not be known unless divine self-communication takes place: "For I greet him the days I meet him, and bless when I understand." Now this self-disclosure must involve, it seems, at least as far as nature is concerned, structures and processes that appear to be regular, permanent, and necessary. Otherwise, we would encounter changeability, fickleness, and uncertainty in nature. We could never count on a divine-human encounter being genuine. So our preliminary insight is that necessity in nature has the function of facilitating free responses which have the prospect of being truthful, abiding, redeeming.

We may ask next what are the forms in which this divine necessity appears to us. I suggest that in Hopkins there are three principal forms of this self-disclosure or what he came to call instress. First is the constancy, the regularity, the lawfulness of nature. We find this theme expressed, for example, in stanza 32 of "The Wreck":

> I admire thee, master of the tides,
> Of the Yore-flood, of the year's fall;
> The recurb and the recovery of the gulf's sides,

and so on. And "throned behind" all this matter in motion, with its regularity and lawfulness, is the "Ground of being, and granite of it: past all / Grasp God." We cannot grasp God; but we can know that the steadiness of nature discloses the steadiness of God.

Second, God is instressed in the form of superlative valuational quality, variously called *glory*, *grandeur*, *beauty*, or *majesty*. These are celebrated especially in the nature poems. Consider in turn the predicates mentioned:

glory—
> Glory be to God for dappled things, . . .
> All things counter, spare, original, strange; (37)

grandeur—
> The world is charged with the grandeur of God; (31)

beauty—
> Nothing is so beautiful as Spring— . . .
> A strain of the earth's sweet being in the beginning; (33)

majesty—
> And the azurous hung hills are his world-wielding shoulder
> Majestic— (38)

Third, and most mysterious and baffling for Hopkins, God's instress is felt in natural disasters and the truncation, suffering, and death they sometimes bring. Natural disasters happen to us as part of the lawful regularity that is not within our power. And yet, at the end of his meditation on the shipwreck of the *Deutschland*, Hopkins can still refer to "lovely-felicitous Providence," even though his explanation has to be put in the form of a question, not an answer: "is the shipwreck then a harvest, does tempest carry the grain for thee?"

With this insight, namely, that for Hopkins the necessities of nature can have the function of facilitating free responses that are vindicated and lasting, we come now to personal encounters with spiritual necessity. And here we arrive at the traditional paradox of freedom and grace, for the divine impingement upon us which is inescapable but yet providential can only be the operation of divine grace.

Before our concluding remarks on this theme, it is well to remind ourselves of a traditional view on the subject, as summarized in the *New Catholic Encyclopedia:* "The way in which the fact of man's free choice is reconciled with the fundamental Christian truth of his total dependence on the grace of God is, ultimately, a mystery. The Catholic Church has always believed and taught both truths while allowing its theologians full liberty to attempt their compatibility."[7] And, we might add, its poets as well. The paradox has got to involve an apparent necessity, for a grace on which we are totally dependent, which is not ours to control, and which must be a determining cause even for us to make a free response, must strike us as a necessity, at least phenomenologically.

There are many places in which Hopkins expresses this union of freedom and divine necessity, or freedom and grace. "The Wreck of the *Deutschland*" begins with this paradox. The opening lines are:

> Thou mastering me
> God! giver of breath and bread.

The poet is clearly under subjection. But the stanza ends:

> Over again I feel thy finger and find thee.

The second stanza opens with an even more succinct joining of freedom and necessity:

> I did say yes
> O at lightning and lashed rod.

Yet that necessity is nothing other than what allows the heart to "tower from the grace to the grace."
"In the Valley of the Elwy" the poet urges God to

> Complete thy creature dear O where it fails,
> Being mighty a master, being a father and fond.

The creature may choose to fail but can be made to choose aright by a mighty master. There again is the FNP in stark form. Fragment 155 expresses divine necessity in the first stanza:

> All dáy long I like fountain flow
> From thy hand out, swayed about
> Mote-like in thy mighty glow.

But the fifth stanza expresses freedom and its prerequisite of grace:

> I have life left with me still
> And thy purpose to fulfil; . . .
> Help me, sir, and so I will.

In "The Bugler's First Communion," Hopkins says that "this child's drift / Seems by a divíne doom chánnelled." This clearly suggests a salvation by the necessity of grace. And yet free choice must be available, for Hopkins can immediately petition: "May he not rankle and roam / In backwheels though bound home?"

Margaret Clitheroe, in martyrdom, was throttled by earthly powers. But Hopkins also presents her as a brilliant example of grace and freedom. "God's counsel," he says, "Had always doomed her down to this." And yet she is described as freely accepting her destiny: "Her will was bent at God." ("Margaret Clitheroe," #145).

In "The Half-way House," Hopkins refers explicitly to the paradox:

> Hear yet my paradox: . . .
> To see Thee I must see Thee.

Freedom and grace are also intertwined in such passages as the following: "the just man . . . acts in God's eye what in God's eye he is ("As kingfishers catch fire," #57); "What do then? . . . Merely meet it . . . heaven's sweet gift ; . . . / . . . wish that though, wish all, God's better beauty, grace" ("To what serves Mortal Beauty," #62); and "forge thy will . . . but be adored" ("The Wreck of the *Deutschland*," #28, verse 10).

Now is there anything we can say that will help illumine that paradox? A suggestion from the Scotist voluntarism of Hopkins may provide the key we need. Such voluntarism desires above all to preserve the superiority of divine will over any subjection to reason that might be conjectured. Divine freedom is ultimate in God's being and therefore in the world he creates. Could it be, then, that the very necessities that bind us are but the workings of freedom of a higher kind? Could it be that what we experience as necessary constraints are but the outer resoluteness, regularity, and persistence of an ultimate freedom? If so, the following quotation commenting on Scotus would be admirably pertinent:

> If one asks which is the higher faculty, he will find, according to Scotus, that it is the will, for it is by the will, "rational will" to be sure, that man achieves what he exists for—the love of God. We saw how much Scotus wants to protect the freedom of God against all necessity, so that His will is the pervasive force of creation, and the highest expression of His will toward man is His love. In return, the highest expression of man's free will is in loving God. In a sense, the love of God for man and the love of man for God is a mutual union of freedoms.[8]

Could it be, then, that underneath the gnawing clash between freedom and necessity is the deeper interaction between freedom and freedom?

We cannot expect to find such ontological explanations detailed in Hopkins' poetry. But this view is consistent with what we know externally about his thought and with what he constantly appeals to internally in the poems. By external knowledge of his thought I mean his Scotism. By internal appeals I mean the way in which, even after acknowledging necessities, he constantly pleads, prays, challenges, and exhorts God to triumph nonetheless. This would make good sense if in fact the very necessities, just cited, were the resilient and malleable workings of a free agent. Hopkins' assumption would then be that God could mold, relax, melt, vary—or even harden if need be— the necessities through which he is fulfilling his purpose.

We cannot claim, as in a detective story, to have solved the mystery, for in a sense freedom against freedom is a greater mystery than freedom and necessity. But we can claim with more certainty now to be pondering a mystery of compatibility rather than a contradiction.

Let us allow Hopkins, in his "The Habit of Perfection," to have the last words, doing what he does so well, namely, what we might describe as pleading freely for a freely given and providentially controlling necessity:

> Elected Silence, sing to me
> And beat upon my whorlèd ear,
> Pipe me to pastures still and be
> The music that I care to hear.

Giving Beauty Back: Hopkins' Echoes

Agnes McNeill Donohue

Happily, the interest in Gerard Manley Hopkins of professional literary critics, scholars, students, and people who love poetry has increased and multiplied since the early thirties. Fortunately, some of the first questions that preoccupied critics have either been answered or dropped as truly meaningless. John Pick in 1942 in his excellent *Gerard Manley Hopkins: Priest and Poet* tackled head-on the following aimless speculation: Think how much more, and what better, poetry Hopkins would have written if he had not converted and, irreparably worse, joined the Jesuits. Pick showed convincingly that "priest and poet" were not antithetical epithets for Hopkins, but complementary descriptions of him. Most critics have stopped patronizing Hopkins' Jesuit superiors (and there were many superiors) who from time to time sought a suitable situation for him: as a teacher of novices, as a parish priest (from the urbanity of the Farm Street parishioners to the poor and desolate of Liverpool) and finally as a Professor of Greek in Ireland, which meant as Hopkins put it "examining a nation" at "a third remove." I am sure my passion for Hopkins and his poetry is as real as anyone's; however, I do feel some sympathy for those superiors who saw Father Hopkins as a brilliant scholar but frail of body and nervous of temperament, and wondered what to do with him. Certainly there must have been some frustration among Ignatius' soldiers of Christ as they tried to fit Father Hopkins into a situation that would be fruitful for them and him.

95

It is a delight that Hopkins would have richly savored to find some critics foundering in his commentary on the "Spiritual Exercises" and his attempts to live his life according to this discipline. For these readers as well as for his dearest friend, Bridges, the "Spiritual Exercises" were some frightful and Spanish relic of the Counter-Reformation, like Torquemada's water torture, no less horrifying than drawing and quartering. For Hopkins, who refrained from taking any fluid until he collapsed as a student at the Highgate school, and who wrote in the "Habit of Perfection" (before his conversion) a magnificent denial of his five senses ("O feel-of-primrose hands") in order to prepare himself in chastity and obedience to take poverty as a bride, mortification and asceticism were as commonplace as self-indulgence would be for the uninitiate.

The circumstances of the publication of Hopkins' poetry, thirty years after his death, and eighteen years into the twentieth century, have presented more problems for critics who like to label and pigeonhole writers. Is Hopkins pre-modern, modern or post-modern? Is he a Victorian poet, who was left languishing by Bridges' long delay only to be thrust into the twentieth century, or was Bridges' hesitation an inspired bit of timing so that Hopkins and T. S. Eliot, separated in reality by nearly half a century, could appear on the literary scene about the same time, each challenging the poetic tradition in their own difficult way —two poets whose best work is devotional poetry, two men who longed to be mystics but were unable to penetrate the Unitive way or to get much beyond the diaspora of the dark night of the soul.

As far as Hopkins' own assessment of his literary contemporaries is concerned, he finally wrote off Tennyson, sickened of Swinburne, made fun of Browning, dawdled a bit with Christina Rossetti, and ignored Arnold. However, it is worth noting that there may be some connection between the grieving in Arnold's "Marguerite" and Hopkins' "Margaret" — between "enisled" by "the unplumbed, salt, estranging sea" and "it is the blight man was born for, / It is Margaret you mourn for"; that Swinburne acknowledged what Hopkins celebrated and fought—"Thou hast conquered, oh pale Galilean; the world has grown gray from thy breath"; and that the Tennyson of the first third of "In Memoriam" whose careful quatrains cannot cover the immediacy of his naked grief is closer than any other poet of the Victorian era to the Hopkins of the "terrible sonnets," those great poems in which his grief and suffering force the reader into participation in his agony. In section 2 of the Tennyson poem, the metaphysical apostrophe to the old yew tree whose fibres and roots net the "dreamless head" and wrap around the bones of the dead until the mourning Tennyson grows "incorporate" into it, is as comfortless as Hopkins' (#65) "Here! creep,/ Wretch, under a comfort serves in a whirlwind: all / Life death does end and each day dies with sleep." In section 6 Tennyson bitterly rejects the commonplaces offered by those who try to comfort him with "loss is common to the race." Just as Shakespeare's Hamlet scorns his mother's insensitive:

> "Thou knowst 'tis common,—all that lives must die."
> "Aye, madam, it is common."
> "If it be, why seems it so particular with thee?"
> "Seems, madam! Nay, it is. I know not seems."

In section 53 Tennyson tries calming himself with the further commonplace—so hurtful to the grief-stricken—"everything that happens is for the best"—"good will triumph over evil—"; Tennyson lets go of his Victorian restraints enough to question—"But what am I? / An infant crying in the night: / An infant crying for the light: / And with no language but a cry." And Hopkins (#67) ". . . my lament / Is cries countless, cries like dead letters sent / To dearest him that lives alas! away." In section 7 of "In Memoriam" Tennyson reaches the nadir of his sorrow and with inhibitions blasted uses all of the poetic devices and music that he has so carefully mastered in a fury of racked torment:

> Dark house, by which once more I stand
> Here in the long unlovely street,
> Doors, where my heart was used to beat
> So quickly, waiting for a hand,

A hand that can be clasped no more,—
Behold me, for I cannot sleep,
And like a guilty thing I creep
At earliest morning to the door.

He is not here: but far away
The noise of life begins again,
And ghastly thro' the drizzling rain
On the bald street breaks the blank day.

And Hopkins—

"I wake and feel the fell of dark, not day.
What hours, O what black hours we have spent
This night! What sights you, heart, saw: ways you went!
And more must, in yet longer light's delay.

One of the great disappointments, at least for me, in "In Memoriam" is the way in which Tennyson so commonsensically, so Victorianly takes comfort in a belief in progress, in blind optimism that scientific determinism will not hurt anything and that the "new" the wild bells ring in will be no more hurtful than the way in which his grief has been dissipated, just as everyone with all their commonplaces said it would. To me the saddest part of "In Memoriam" is section 118 where Tennyson describes his revisit to Hallam's house. Tennyson cannot face the commonplace "Time heals all wounds"—even though section 118 states it faithfully. The sadness of 118 is that human grief is overcome by time—the fallen human condition does not permit seventeen years of naked grief:

Doors, where my heart was used to beat
So quickly, not as one that weeps
I come once more; the city sleeps;
I smell the meadow in the street;

I hear a chirp of birds; I see
Betwixt the black fronts long-withdrawn
A light-blue lane of early dawn,
And think of early days and thee,

And bless thee, for thy lips are bland,
And bright the friendship of thine eye;
And in my thoughts with scarce a sigh
I take the pressure of thine hand.

I am certainly not trying to patronize Tennyson, but when I look back at the prologue to "In Memoriam," written after the seventeen years he spent finishing the poem, and see his pleading to the "strong son of God" to forgive his sin in loving Hallam too much, forgive him his grief at Hallam's death, and forgive him "these wild and wandering cries, / Confusions of a wasted youth," it seems as if the careful politic laureate is speaking, not the great-hearted poet whose passionate death throes of grief we shared. I feel as if Tennyson had betrayed me and I resent his refusal to see the brokenness of the human condition, which allows him to be comforted by commonplaces and to smooth over honest passion with the blandness and phlegm of nineteenth-century moderation. Hopkins in "Carrion Comfort," #64, does not blanch at agony, nor does he pretend his Jacob-like encounters with God are anything else than that:

But ah, but O thou terrible, why wouldst thou rude on me
Thy wring-world right foot rock? lay a lionlimb against me? scan
With darksome devouring eyes my bruisèd bones? and fan,
O in turns of tempest, me heaped there; me frantic to avoid thee and
    flee?

The comparison of Hopkins to Tennyson does not rest on an attempt to label either poet, but rather to compare nakedness with nakedness. No religious scruple could keep Hopkins from truth-telling in his poems; however, Tennyson feels he must apologize for the honesty of feeling that makes his poetry great. The Hopkins' poems that I look at bear out his successful attempts at honesty in poetry.

The unfinished drama "St. Winefred's Well" was worked on by Hopkins in 1879 and 1881. Bridges requested a copy in 1885, just four years before Hopkins' death, to see Hopkins' use of a six-stressed line. What remains are three fascinating soliloquies by Teryth, Caradoc and St. Beuno. Surprisingly, this fragment of 124 lines has not been studied much by critics. Peter Milward, S.J. in *Landscape and Inscape: Vision and Inspiration in Hopkins' Poetry*, whose commentary on Hopkins' poetry is illuminated by Father Schoder's wonderful photographs, treats the fragment in its three soliloquies as having a beginning, middle and end. Lynn Hamilton, a former student of mine in a graduate Hopkins seminar, expands on Milward's observations in *The Explicator* (Winter 1985, pp. 23-24) and sees three different perspectives given of Winefred by each speaker— the father, the lover-murderer, the Restorer— as well as three perspectives in nature.

The legend of Winefred is the story of a seventh-century saint: "Winefred (c. A.D. 650) was the daughter of Teuyth (Teryth) and niece of St. Beuno, who instructed her in Christian piety. According to the legend, the chieftain Caradoc severed her head from her body as she was fleeing, in defence of her chastity, to Beuno's chapel. The saint restored her to life, and the famous spring gushed from the spot where her head fell. Later she became an abbess, and died fifteen years after her miraculous resuscitation."[1] Holywell is only seven or eight miles from St. Beuno's in Wales, where from 1874–1877 Hopkins was doing his theology. He records in his journal on October 8, 1874: "At Holywell, N. Wales: 'Barraud and I walked over to Holywell and bathed at the well and returned very joyously. The sight of the water in the well as clear as glass. . .trembling at the surface with the force of the springs, and shaping out the five foils of the well quite drew and held my eyes to it. . . . The strong unfailing flow of the water and the chain of cures from year to year all these centuries took hold of my mind with wonder at the beauty of God in one of his saints, the sensible thing so naturally and gracefully uttering the spiritual reason of its being (which is all in true keeping with the story of St. Winefred's death and recovery). . . even now the stress and buoyancy and abundance of the water is before my eyes.'"[2]

I would like to show the connection between these three soliloquies and the two parts of the "Maidens' song from St. Winefred's Well," "The Leaden Echo and The Golden Echo," a connection not only of alliteration and assonance but of a vital, organic unity that extends both the chorus and the soliloquies into a more meaningful and less fragmentary poem. Part of this unity is attained by Winefred's martyrdom in which she gives back to God her virginity and beauty. After the miraculous restoration of Winefred, some of the maimed and diseased regain their health and beauty—so they may give it back, and even those pilgrims unaided are praying.

Teryth, the father of Winefred, speaks of her after a short dialogue in which he tells her the news she is waiting to hear— that her Uncle Beuno, her spiritual guide, will arrive shortly and that she must prepare his cell.

After she leaves, Teryth muses about Winefred, her singularity among daughters, and his very real apprehension about her future. "Being a father and fond" he speaks of her uniqueness, the ways her dearness "laces" round and round his heart—(interestingly, "laces" is the only "l"-word in Teryth's soliloquy; it recurs in the voice of the Leaden Echo—"lace," "latch," "long")—but only to be denied "since, no, nothing can be done," therefore "be beginning to despair." In the voice of the Golden Echo, "loneliness," "lastingness," "looks," "locks," "lovelocks," "least lash" are all given back and thus kept. The closer Winefred laces around Teryth's heart the more he feels "some monstrous hand," the adumbration of Caradoc, groping "with clammy fingers," tampering with the laces, the bines, drawing them out and straining them. As the image continues, Teryth hears a voice mocking him, asking him what he will do when "this bloom, this honeysuckle," Winefred, who like the honeysuckle with its bines and laces and its fragrance and beauty "rides the air so rich about thee"; then the metaphor changes and Winefred, the lovely flower, becomes a lamb and "is sheared away, thus!" Teryth sweats "for fear." He further imagines not only the clammy fingers groping at his heart but a funeral or a pageant requiring his tears in which Winefred is carried endlessly, although he is not sure whether she is alive or dead. This funeral "marches thro'" his mind as in Emily Dickinson's poem, "I felt a Funeral, in my Brain, / And mourners to and fro / kept treading — treading"— Teryth then forbids his thoughts, accusing himself of being more the mother than the father.

The "f" alliteration is important in Teryth's soliloquy:

"father," "fingers," "fond father," "fear," "funeral," "foot,"
"feeling," "father," "fanciful," "forbid," "fool," "fears"; it does
not recur in force until "The Golden Echo" where the "f" words
lose their terror: "fresh," "fast flying," "face," "flower," "fleece,"
"fleet," "fastened," "fagged," "fashed," "freely forfeit,"
"fonder," "far," "fonder," "finer," "fonder." The "d" alliteration, so striking in "The Leaden Echo," with the repetition of
"despair" as well as "deep," "down," "do," "do," "do," "done,"
"drooping," "dying," "death," "decay," is adumbrated in
Teryth's soliloquy: "daughter," "deeper," "dearness," "draws,"
"dead." Teryth's thoughts establish his character as a loving
father, genuinely afraid for his daughter whom he sees in her
beauty and dearness as threatened and vulnerable as a honeysuckle or a lamb and doomed to a mysterious, appalling death.
However, no ugly, horrible dream could have conjured up for
Teryth the reality of Winefred's murder. Teryth, the loving
father, is only too aware of that which Hopkins also warns of in
the sonnet "To What Serves Mortal Beauty?" In this sonnet,
"God to a nation I dealt that day's dear chance" when Pope
Gregory, seeing the beauty of the young boy slaves from Britain
("wet-fresh I windfalls of war's storm") perceived them as
angels not Angles and consequently sent Augustine to Chris-
tianize England. In the final tercet, Hopkins answers his own
questions, "What do then? how meet beauty?" His reply,
"Merely meet it; own, / Home at heart, heaven's sweet gift; I
then leave, let that alone." Unfortunately for Teryth, Caradoc,
feeling only his carnal desires, will not leave Winefred. The
danger of mortal beauty that ignites these flames in the lustful
should be, as the sonnet continues, converted to "God's better
beauty, grace." Winefred is full of grace but that does not
protect her beautiful body from the lion, Caradoc.

Caradoc, Winefred's murderer, has a kind of Shakespearean soliloquy, although the seventy lines make it about twice as
long as the usual Shakespearean one. Creating the character of
Caradoc, based upon whatever accurate history one can attrib-
ute to the life of a seventh-century saint, was a new experiment
for Hopkins. The problem of making the antagonist real and
not just a beastly cardboard villain who would appear only
once with his sword dripping blood from the head of Winefred,

have his say and leave, is far from simple. Hopkins makes
Caradoc psychologically interesting by having him go through
a number of stages of denial and justification for his deed. That
he does not repent makes Hopkins' task of truth-telling extremely difficult. That Hopkins met all of these difficulties
head-on and that the character of Caradoc is real and believable
is no small accomplishment.

If we visualize Caradoc rushing out to center stage we see
that he has only one prop, the bloody sword which he thinks he
has wiped clean. Hopkins, always masterly in the use of
rhetorical questions, uses fourteen to forward Caradoc's mood
changes. In the first two lines Caradoc asks four questions that
certainly command attention: "My héart, where have we been?
| What have we séen, my mind? / What stroke has Caradoc's
right arm dealt? | what done?" Caradoc questions his heart
and his mind but answers truthfully and defensively that
"Head of a rebel / Struck óff it has." However, as he recalls the
blood he realizes that her lovely limbs have been soaked in it.
He tries to tell himself that the blood wrote lessons of revenge
on her limbs, that she had gone against him, that she had been
warned "of this work." The image of her own blood writing on
her limbs his lesson of revenge is reminiscent of Teryth's pre-
monition that Winefred will be "all sheared away," as in the
"Wreck of the *Deutschland* " the stigmata scored "in scarlet. . .
on his own bespoken. . . for lettering of the lamb's fleece."
Caradoc now denies, "What work? what harm's done? . . .
Perhaps we struck no blow." However, he is too much the
realist to delude himself long and he rebukes himself for the
"make believe" of thinking that no harm is done. Caradoc now
has the illusion that his sword is still bloody although he had
wiped it clean. His pretense of not having done harm or of
seeing blood on the blade ("Still the scarlet swings | and dances
on the blade") angers him into further defiance. He can wipe
the blade and "sheathe" it "in thy dark lair," a marvelous image
that makes the blade "thou butcher" and also the animal that is
responsible for the murder. There is then a sudden horrid
epiphany as Caradoc realizes that although he can hide the
weapon he can never restore Winefred to life, and he becomes
momentarily a Lear as he rehearses the death of Winefred:

"these drops / Never, never, never in their blue banks again. / The woeful, Cradock." He forces himself to answer the question:

> What have we seen? Her head, | sheared [again the lamb
>   image] from her shoulders, fall,
> And lapped in shining hair, | róll to the bank's edge; then
> Down the beetling banks, | like water in waterfalls,
> It stooped and flashed and fell | and ran like water away.

Here we have an interesting first adumbration of the Holy Well and its healing waters that sprang from the places where Winefred's head touched.

> Her eyes, oh and her eyes!
> In all her beauty, and sunlight | to it is a pit, den, darkness,
> Foamfalling is not fresh to it, | rainbow by it not beaming,
> In all her body, I say, | no place was like her eyes,
> No piece matched those eyes | kept most part much cast down
> But, being lífted, ímmortal, | of immórtal brightness.

The shining hair of Winefred is an image of beauty and sensuousness. The falling head like water in waterfalls foretells the glorious well that will spring up as part of the restoration of Winefred to life. However, there is no eloquence like Caradoc's praise of Winefred's eyes:

> Her eyes, oh and her eyes!
> . . . .
> . . . no place was like her eyes,
> No piece matched those eyes

Hopkins has managed in these wonderful lines to convey Caradoc's horror of what he has done, and because of his passion and terror some empathy begins to be felt by the listener. Our outrage at the dreadful deed, the desecration of the virginal child, and the agony and defiance of the murderer, draws our unwilling attention and in a kind of blasphemous hypnotic trance we watch the criminal to see what he will do next. Caradoc has seen Winefred's eyes "flash towards heaven" and knows her appeal will be answered. He imagines "airy vengeances. . . afoot." Since the death of Winefred, she who outshone the sunlight making it a "pit, den, darkness," a waterfall no longer fresh, a rainbow no more beaming, the world is dark. Caradoc sees portents in "heaven-vault fast purpling"—a favorite image of Hopkins ("dappled-with-damson-west")—and he knows the "first lightning" will be directed at him.

Hopkins, who could have drawn Winefred's murderer in a more sympathetic light, chooses to have Caradoc an unrepentant boor, which makes the task greater of keeping the audience's attention and sympathy. Perhaps, like Shakespeare with Richard III, he appreciates the challenge of making a villain interesting. Caradoc, who knows he has outraged heaven, is determined to continue his defiance: "And I do not repent; I do not and I will not repent, not repent." Caradoc then tries to justify himself as proud, outraged royalty:

> . . . What Í have done violent
> I have like a líon dóne, | líonlike dóne,
> Honouring an uncontrolled | royal wrathful nature,
> Mantling passion in a grandeur, | crimson grandeur.

The assumption by Caradoc of the royal prerogative is impressive and Hopkins is lending to Caradoc for the time being the heroic pride of Lucifer, so that in his crimson mantle of Winefred's blood he becomes an archangel fallen:

> Now be my pride then perfect, | all one piece. Henceforth
> In a wide world of defiance | Caradoc lives alone,
> Loyal to his own soul, laying his | ówn law down, no law nor
> Lord now curb him forever. | O daring! O deep insight!
> What is virtue? Valour; | only the heart valiant.
> And right? Only resolution; | will, his will unwavering
> Who, like me, knowing his nature | to the heart home, nature's
>   business,
> Despatches with no flinching.

Caradoc is carried away with his own self-deception, his defiance, into believing he has fought heroically in some great battle and has triumphed. He forgets that his huge conquest, his valor, the resolve of his implacable will, his knowledge of his own wrathful nature have all been expended in the beheading of a defenseless girl. The boasting alliterative pride, the bold cosmic insolence break down, and he faces his own self-inquisition:

> . . . . But wíll flesh, O can flésh
> Second this fiery strain? | Not always; O no no!
> We cannot live this life out; | sometimes we must weary
> And in this darksome world | what comfort can I find?
> Down this darksome world | cómfort whére can I find
> When 'ts light I quenched; its rose, | time's one rich rose, my
>   hand,
> By her bloom, fast by | her fresh, her fleecèd bloom,
> Hideous dáshed dówn, leaving | earth a winter withering
> With no now, no Gwenvrewi.

Caradoc's impassioned rhetoric now turns against himself as he realizes that he has doomed himself to live in a world bereft of Winefred's light. He has quenched the light of his world, by his hand "hideous" has "dashed down" time's one rich rose, "her fleecèd bloom." The metaphor is potent and moving—Winefred as fleeced rose suggests Mary as five-petalled rose, the dolorous five evoking the bloody stigmata; the fleece, the sacrificed *Agnus Dei*. Earth without its rich rose undergoes "a winter withering" and is "darksome," comfortless, deprived. The monstrous arrogance of Caradoc's next musing: "I must miss her most / That might have spared her were it but for passion-sake" continues the study of a man driven to frenzy, to rash murder and then the necessity of finding excuses for himself since he cannot survive the loss of his victim. He remembers how it was before he murdered Winefred; he hungered, he was foiled at every assault and "deeper disappointed." Yet he acknowledges that the "turmoil and the torment" had in it "a sweetness," a "kind of joy," "a zest, an edge, an ecstasy, / Next after sweet success." But Caradoc, the realist, knows he is merely deceiving himself and faces full on his dire action and its dreadful consequence: "I all my being have hacked | in half with hér neck." In his fury he sees himself divided, hacked in half; reason and choice are "corpse now, cannot change" and his soul, "Life's quick, this kínd, this kéen self-feeling, / With dreadful distillation I of thoughts sour as blood, / Must all day long taste murder."

The imagery is grim and gruesome; not only is Caradoc literally covered with Winefred's innocent blood, but the awful halitus of blood, the "dreadful distillation" of sour blood is in his mouth and he must always taste it. He cannot get rid of the blood—like Lady Macbeth: "Here's the smell of blood still: All the perfumes of Arabia will not sweeten this little hand." Caradoc begins again his self-inquisition: "What do nów then? Do?" But he knows there is nothing to do because "óne deed tréads all dówn here I cramps all doing. What do? Not yield, / Not hope, not pray; despair; I ay, that: brazen despair out / Brave all, and take what comes—" Here is another prefiguring of "The Leaden Echo"—despair, despair. Caradoc, the anti-hero, knows only that he must still resist, take physical action. His tortured exercise of thought has taught him that he lives by the sword and must die by it. It seems a deliverance when he now sees the rabble coming and knows he can fight. He shows a Shakespearean contempt for the mob: "Whose bloods I reck no more of, no more rank with hers / Than sewers with sacred oils." The blood imagery continues, for even though he is weltering in Winefred's blood—it is in his nose, it is in his mouth—he is prepared to rush off and shed the blood of any of the rabble. The bloody imagery changes only in the way he compares the rabble's blood, "sewers," with Winefred's, "sacred oils."

Hopkins' royal lion, Caradoc, is a kind of barbarian, a man of action, a man of blood who is confused, muddled by having to answer his own questions about his motives, about his cowardly deed. Accustomed to having his own way, of not being accountable for his action, he is captured directly after his beheading of Winefred and Hopkins shows him squirming to answer his own catechism. *Why* did he commit murder most foul against a young woman fleeing to protect her chastity? Caradoc writhes in pain as he attempts to be honest with himself, to stop rationalizing and blaming Winefred for provoking him. The effort of thought and the gradual assumption of responsibility for his actions, although not repenting, is more torturous for Caradoc than physical battle. He says over and over that he does not repent; however, his revelation that he has been overwhelmed by Winefred's eyes, that they have fixed him, accused him even, is enough for us to know that he will not survive her long. Tormented Caradoc flies into action at the end of his soliloquy. He puts all of his bitterly learned self-disdain into his last words before action: "Mankind, that mob, comes. / Come!" Death, especially death through battle is what Caradoc wants. Pitched battle, sword on sword, is infinitely preferable to mocking, taunting thought.

Although Caradoc's soliloquy may be overlong, Hopkins achieves a masterly, psychologically authoritative study of a brute who might in less skillful hands be nothing more than a one-dimensional abomination. Nothing that Hopkins has done before, the whining bully of "The Answer from the World" or the Pilate who is going to officiate at his own icy crucifixion, prepares us for this accomplishment.

The insistent "d" alliteration in Caradoc's soliloquy: "dealt," "done," "days," "dances," "dark," "drops," "down," "den," "darkness," "down," "did," "do," "done," "done," "done," "defiance," "daring," "deep," "despatches," "darksome," "dashed," "down," "daring," "deep," "deeper," "disappointed," "disposal," "dreadful," "distillation," "dead," "down," "despair," "despair," tells the story of Caradoc's inverted progression from apotheosis to despair. The "d" words of the Leaden Echo confirm Caradoc's doom: "deep," "down," "do," "do," "do," "despair," "done," "done," "drooping," "dying," "death," "decay," "despair"— repeated six more times.

The third soliloquy is that of St. Beuno, the uncle of Winefred, who has restored her to life. He put her head back on her neck and many representations of Winefred show her with a large scar. Beuno's soliloquy is thirty lines and very different from those of Caradoc and Teryth. Teryth is concerned solely for his daughter; her beauty, her holiness, her virtue make her liable to ravage and destruction, which is similar to the warning Hopkins gives in the first line of a sonnet "To What Serves

Mortal Beauty? —dangerous." In the "St. Winefred's Well" fragment, Caradoc, the despoiler of Winefred, epitomizes such danger to mortal beauty. His concern is the impossibility of living in a world where Winefred is not. Beuno in his soliloquy magisterially speaks of the future effect of Winefred, the influence of her holy well and of its frail pale water adumbrated by Caradoc, who saw Winefred's head roll like "water in waterfalls" and like water run away. Thus, Teryth feels Winefred as a honeysuckle whose vines and bines around his heart are tampered with and strained, occasioning his salt sweat and tears; Caradoc is overwhelmed in her blood; and Beuno sees that the fresh water of her well is her "venerable record," water that becomes the healing water of the maimed and broken. Beuno speaks oracularly and prophetically and his lines are far more a poetic-set piece than the others.

The first seventeen lines of thirty are a single sentence, very highly wrought. The poetic line is divided into two parts, each having two stresses as in Old English with a riot of alliteration and parallelism. Hopkins uses seven "while's" in the first six lines followed by "as long as" (l. 10) and "so long" (l. 11), three "this's" (ll. 11, 12), "with" (l. 13) and three and one-half lines in parenthesis, "for" (l. 14), "but" (l. 15), and "that" twice (l. 16). The parallels extend to the next four-line sentence: "here" (l. 18), "and" (l. 19), "but" (l. 20) and after a break for missing lines, the next five-line sentence is ordered by "what" (l. 22), "on" (l. 22), "on" (l. 23), "or" (l. 24), "hence" (l. 24), "not" (l. 25). The last four lines (incomplete) have "as sure" (l 27), "sure" (l. 27), "sure as" (l. 27), "sure as" (l. 28), "amongst" (l. 29). The poem has a solemn joy as Beuno sets up the echoes which will reecho in the voice of the Golden Echo.

The half lines gather, some in opposition, some in apposition, some in juxtaposition: "now while skies are blue," "while seas are salt," "while rushy rains shall fall," "or brooks shall fleet from fountains." Then from nature's setting Beuno gathers the broken and bent men ("While sick men shall cast sighs I of sweet health all despairing") and particularizes their maladies and afflictions: the blind whose eyes "thírst after daylight," the deaf whose ears desire lost "lípmusic," are marvels of synesthesia; the cripples, the lepers "dancers in dismal limb-

dance," the epileptics, "fallers in dreadful frothpits" and eight
more diseases, saying "what more?" The answer is blithe and
exultant: "as long as men are mortal and God merciful." At this
point in the poem the half lines are quickened, the chiming
becomes louder, nimbler, more agile and the music more un-
mistakable as Hopkins piles up internal rhymes and pelts us
with alliteration and assonance and onomatopoeia until we
and he are breathless and the sentence ends: "sweet spot, I this
leafy lean-over,/ This Dry Dean, nów no longer dry I nor
dumb, but moist and musical,"

> With the uproll and the downcarol I of day and night delivering
> Water, which keeps thy name, I (for not in róck wrítten,
> But in pale water, fráil water, I wild rash and reeling water,
> That will not wear a print, I that will not stain a pen,
> Thy venerable record, I virgin, is recorded).

The plenary, majestic, ceremonial tone is gone. Winefred who
is never named has triumphed over death and disease and all
of the frailties that man is heir to. Her name is writ in water but
unlike Keats it is not on a gravestone but in the wild rash and
reeling sound that calls out "Winefred." Beuno's voice is
peremptory again but he makes no effort to keep the buoyancy
out of it: he asserts that pilgrimages shall be made to the holy
well, not only from "purple Wales" and "elmy England," but
from everywhere—"Pilgrims, still pilgrims, móre I pilgrims,
still more poor pilgrims."

After a space for missing lines, the poem resumes with an
intoxicated playfulness: "What sights shall be when some I
that swung, wretches, on crutches / Their crutches shall cast
from them, I on heels of air departing." The loathsome lepers
will leave "rich as roseleaves" all made clean and more seriously now, those whose boon was "dearer, more divine" in the
haven of their hearts. After some missing lines, Beuno speaks
that which is most sure, the new-dappling of primroses next
spring and "sure as tomorrow morning, / Amongst come-
back-again things, I things with a revival, things with a recovery, / Thy name. . . ." It is difficult to imagine that Hopkins
could have improved on the aposiopesis of the last line, "Thy
name," just as in "Pied Beauty" after the rhapsodic chiming of

dappled things the curtal sonnet concludes, "Praise him!"

The plethora of pealing, ringing sound, assonance, alliteration, onomotopoeia prepares us for the maidens' song, "The Leaden Echo and the Golden Echo." Hopkins was pleased as he should have been by these poems and wrote to Bridges that he had never done anything more musical. He also confided that the poems were dramatic and meant to be popular. Even Bridges admired them and thought that they carried the reader along. Hopkins told Bridges to read his poetry (especially that which is highly wrought and musical) with his ears not his eyes and then it comes right.[3]

"The Leaden Echo and the Golden Echo" echo the fragment "St. Winefred's Well" and then provide magnificent echoes of their own. The last thing Hopkins wanted was for his poetry to echo other poets (unlike Eliot who courts the echoing); he was very disturbed when Bridges accused him of being influenced by Whitman and it surely is a false charge. The good gray poet was many things but he was not a model for Hopkins, who thought he was a great scoundrel. But then Bridges found, he said, "the naked encounter of sensualism and asceticism which hurts 'The Golden Echo'" and for which scholars have been searching in vain since 1918.[4]

Hopkins was mad for beauty, as any poet should be, but the year before his conversion he made a private resolution and entered it in his diary, November 6, 1865: "On this day by God's Grace I resolved to give up all beauty until I had *His* leave for it." Later, he wrote to Bridges: "I think no one can admire beauty of the body more than I do. . . But this kind of beauty is dangerous." Consequently, Hopkins' love of beauty is expressed most often in his poetry through the beauty of the young and chaste: "The Bugler's First Communion"; "The Handsome Heart"; "At the Wedding March"; "Brothers"; "Spring and Fall"; "St. Dorothea"; "On the Portrait of Two Beautiful Young People"; "Spring," the sonnet whose sestet rings with beauty:

> What is all this juice and all this joy?
> A strain of the earth's sweet being in the beginning
> In Eden Garden. — Have, get, before it cloy,

Before it cloud, Christ, lord, and sour with sinning,
Innocent mind and Mayday in girl and boy,
   Most, O maid's child, thy choice and worthy the winning.

And of course St. Winefred and her maidens, who sing the Leaden Echo and the Golden Echo.

The Golden Echo contains one of the Christian paradoxes that make up so much of Christian belief: In my beginning is my end, in my end is my beginning; in order to save one's life, one must lose it; the first shall be last and the last, first; and in this case, in order to *keep* beauty, it must be *given back* to God, beauty's self and beauty's giver. The two Biblical quotations that give spine to the poem are those of John (12: 24–25): "Amen, Amen I say to you, unless the grain of wheat falling into the ground die, itself remaineth alone, but if it die, it bringeth forth much fruit." In the poem it is "What we had lighthanded left in surly the mere mould / Will have waked and have waxed with the wind while we slept." And Matthew (10:29, 30, 31): "Are not two sparrows sold for a farthing and not one of them shall fall on the ground without your Father. But the very hairs of your head are all numbered. Fear not therefore: better are you than many sparrows." In the poem it is: "See; not a hair is, not an eyelash, not the least lash lost; every hair / Is, hair of the head, numbered." When we read "The Leaden Echo" and "The Golden Echo," following Hopkins' directions ("Read my poetry with the ear not the eye"), we should observe his further directions that it be read in a loud voice, chiming and chanting—the Leaden Echo falling, the Golden Echo chiming, and at the end of the Golden Echo the "yonders" sounding like the nightingale of Keats—flying up from the ground farther and farther away, higher and higher.

Read the poem "The Lead Echo and the Golden Echo" as Hopkins instructed—aloud, chanting and chiming, and Hopkins' echoes will become clear.

The Leaden Echo and the Golden Echo
(*Maidens' song from St. Winefred's Well*)

THE LEADEN ECHO

How to kéep——is there ány any, is there none such, nowhere
   known some, bow or brooch or braid or brace, láce,
   latch or catch or key to keep
Back beauty, keep it, beauty, beauty, beauty, . . . from vanish-
   ing away?
Ó is there no frowning of these wrinkles, rankèd wrinkles deep,
Dówn? no waving off of these most mournful messengers,
   still messengers, sad and stealing messengers of grey?—
No there's none, there's none, O no there's none,
Nor can you long be, what you now are, called fair,
Do what you may do, what, do what you may,
And wisdom is early to despair:
Be beginning; since, no, nothing can be done
To keep at bay
Age and age's evils, hoar hair,
Ruck and wrinkle, drooping, dying, death's worst, winding
   sheets, tombs and worms and tumbling to decay;
So be beginning, be beginning to despair,
O there's none; no no no there's none;
Be beginning to despair, to despair,
Despair, despair, despair, despair.

THE GOLDEN ECHO
                     Spare!
There is one, yes I have one (Hush there!),
Only not within seeing of the sun.
Not within the singeing of the strong sun,
Tall sun's tingeing, or treacherous the tainting of the earth's air,
Somewhere elsewhere there is ah well where! one,
One. Yes I cán tell such a key, I dó know such a place,
Where whatever's prizèd and passes of us, everything that's
   fresh and fast flying of us, seems to us sweet of us and
   swiftly away with, done away with, undone,
Undone, done with, soon done with, and yet dearly and
   dangerously sweet
Of us, the wimpled-water-dimpled, not-by-morning-matchèd face,
The flower of beauty, fleece of beauty, too too apt to, ah! to fleet,
Never fleets móre, fastened with the tenderest truth
To its own best being and its loveliness of youth: it is an ever-
   lastingness of, O it is an all youth!

Come then, your ways and airs and looks, locks, maidengear,
    gallantry and gaiety and grace,
Winning ways, airs innocent, maiden manners, sweet looks,
    loose locks, long locks, lovelocks, gaygear, going gallant,
    girlgrace—
Resign them, sign them, seal them, send them, motion them with
    breath,
And with sighs soaring, soaring síghs, deliver
Them; beauty-in-the-ghost, deliver it, early now, long before death
Give beauty back, beauty, beauty, beauty, back to God,
    beauty's self and beauty's giver.
See; not a hair is, not an eyelash, not the least lash lost; every hair
Is, hair of the head, numbered.
Nay, what we had lighthanded left in surly the mere mould
Will have waked and have waxed and have walked with the
    wind what while we slept,
This side, that side hurling a heavyheaded hundredfold
What while we, while we slumbered.
O then, weary then whý should we tread? O why are we so
    haggard at the heart, so care-coiled, care-killed, so fagged,
    so fashed, so cogged, so cumbered,
When the thing we freely fórfeit is kept with fonder a care,
Fonder a care kept than we could have kept, it kept
Far with fonder a care (and we, we should have lost it) finer,
    fonder
A care kept.—Where kept? do but tell us where kept, where.—
Yonder.—What high as that! We follow, now we follow.—
    Yonder, yes yonder, yonder,
Yonder.

"Scope," "Scape," and Word Formation in the Lexicon of Hopkins

Todd K. Bender

In this centennial commemoration of Gerard Manley Hopkins, S.J., (1844–1889), readers have many reasons to express gratitude for his gifts to English literature. Hopkins expanded the possibilities of poetic form and of the English language. His idea of "inscape" and his innovative metrical and formal designs mark the watershed between Victorian and Modernist art, while his vocabulary and lexical selection demonstrate in language the regenerative power of nature itself. Reading his poems is like walking in the woods in early spring "when wéeds, in whéels, shoot lóng and lóvely and lúsh" as the barren earth comes to life and takes on the rich colors, intricate patterns, and startling shapes of the great rebirth. In wonder the reader may well ask along with the poet, "Whát is áll this júice and áll this jóy?"[1] What *juissance*, what play, what imaginative fertility rises from the seed of words long dormant when we read Hopkins' poems?

When Hopkins creates new words, for example his key term "inscape," he forces the reader to ask not only *what* does this word signify, but *how* does it come to bear meaning. The vitality of such a newborn word comes in part from the connection of the word to its roots and ancestors, stretching back to the dim origins of language itself, through generations of mutations and transformations until the fragile blossom unfolds. An organic, genetic process that resembles the evolutionary development of plants and animals stands behind his texts as if they were so many exotic gardens. In truth, where Hopkins said that *"weeds* in wheels shoot long and lovely and lush" in springtide, his readers might well say his *"words* in wheels shoot long and lovely and lush."

Moreover, his ratiocinative process reveals itself in microcosm in his lexicon. The tension, the conflict between opposing possibilities held in balance in his mind, is not only seen in the overall argument of his texts, but in the microcosm of each word. This ratiocinative tension is felt by the thoughtful reader over and above the denotation or signification of an individual word. His web of words is, like a spider's web or the pattern of crystallization in a freezing liquid, an externalization or expression of tensions held in balance which may be sensed aesthetically, not merely understood rationally. Nowhere is this mystery enfolded more lovingly, more cunningly, than in his word "inscape."

Hopkins' letters and notebooks frequently display lists of words related sometimes by etymology, sometimes by sound, sometimes by denotation and connotation. For example, his letters in spring 1887 to Alexander William Mowbray Baillie, his former classmate at Oxford University in Classical Languages, show Hopkins concerned with the words related to *scope* and *scape*. He asks Baillie to look up *scope* in Walter William Skeat's (1835-1912) etymological dictionary. Hopkins asserts that *scope*

> as an English word . . . is primarily nautical and means the play of a vessel at anchor, as the wind, tide, or current may carry her east, west, or all round it; hence 'at a short scope', 'a long scope', that is play or range. And the usual literary sense agrees strictly with this—*freedom of action* or *play*. But I have remarked in Newman and I find the Imperial Dict. quotes from much older writers, Hooker I think, a usage evidently mistaken and got from thinking of *skosos* [Greek word] and the School-Latin *scopus* / *mark, aim*. There even seems a fusion (a real and unfortunate confusion) of these two meanings.[2]

Hopkins goes on to explain that the Imperial Dictionary recognizes only the Greek *skopos* as the etymology and only the meaning of "mark" for the word, although it gives examples which do not support such a limited interpretation of its meaning. In a postscript Hopkins adds on March 11, "I should be glad to hear if there is any other word *scape* than *escape* abridged. I think Skeat says *landscape* is Dutch: the English form wd. have been *landship*."

About a month later, April 6, 1887, Hopkins again writes Baillie that he has now consulted both the Skeat and the Murray dictionaries and that he is going to write Skeat about his error on the etymology of *scope*. "I have doubts about Skeat's treatment of a whole class of words like *scope, cope, scoop, scape, cap*. Though some of these words as they stand (not *scope*) may have come to English from French or low Latin, yet they must before that have got into those same languages from English or some Teutonic one. *Escape* comes from *cape*, but *cape* cannot come from *cope* the Church vestment: *cope* the vestment must come from *cape* or from an older unecclesiastical sense of the word *cope*." Hopkins then speculates that use of the word *cope* for the solemn church vestment must be an example of choir boys' Latin slang. Returning to his argument, Hopkins says, "I suspect that *cope* then comes from the root of *coop* in *hencoop* / and of *shop* (=*scop*)." Here he apparently is thinking of the Anglo/Saxon verb "to make" *sceapan*, which he would most likely have pronounced something like modern "shapen" as he understood Old English in 1887.

Skeat's treatment of the class *scape/scope* in his *Etymological Dictionary of the English Language* (1882) seems, indeed, quite severely limited. *Scope*, he believes, comes from Greek *skopos* (a "mark, a watcher") via Italian *scopo* ("a mark to shoot at"). Greek *skopos*, in turn, Skeat finds "allied to Gk. *skeptomai*, I see, I spy, which is cognate with L. *specere*." A glance at Henry George Liddell and Robert Scott's *A Greek-English Dictionary* under the entries for *skeptomai* and *skopeusis*, which taken together make up more than a page of dense citations, indicates what deep water Skeat is skimming over here. Even more so, Skeat's treatment of *scape* only related to L. *capio*, linking *escape* and *scapegoat*, for instance, and recognizing *scape* only as a shortened form of *escape* seems unnecessarily limited.

Hopkins must have proceeded to address inquiries on several occasions directly to the irascible lexicographer himself

concerning these words. One letter from Professor Skeat survives, dated 27 February 1888:

> I'm very sorry. I received your former letter. But I have not
> the physical strength to answer all letters. It is more toil than
> *all* my other work. — I can't discuss. I'm much obliged. And
> I regret to say I'm not convinced abt. *scope*. All my experience
> tells the other way. There is no French form: so it's all the
> *more* likely that we took it from Greek. Sorry I'm so stupid. —
> No one knows the etymy of *cap* and *cape*. Dr. Murray gives it
> up. *Not* Gothic. — I know *keeve*: quite common. — I take it to
> answer to an A.S. *cefe*, variant of *cyfe*, which is merely Lat.
> *cupa* with mutation, just as our *coop* is Lat. *cupa* without
> mutation. — ... Of course my Dicty requires much amendment.
> But I've no time to do it now. I can't get through ordinary
> work.[3]

Apparently Hopkins had called attention to the dialect word
keeve, a vat, container, or "keeper," in connection with *cap* and
cape.

In a mental constellation, Hopkins links together words
like scape, scope, scoop, cape, cap, cup, coop, with potential ancestors: Gr. *skeptomai* ("to see"), *skopos*; L. *spectare* ("to see"),
specere, scopos; A.S. *sceapan* ("to shape or make"); O. Sax.
skeppian ("to draw water"); and a tangle of vernacular variations. Mentally, we might imagine a "tension" between two
forces in the mind of Hopkins: one struggling to hold together
refractory individual items under one family tree or genealogi-
cal definition, the other counter movement whirling the words
into far separate, unconnected entities. The aesthetic effect of
his language might be imagined as the reader's participation in
such a struggle, feeling afresh the tendency toward variety pull
against the unifying genealogy of the word, replicating in language the struggle between the particular and the universal in
nature.

It was not an accident that Hopkins notices the etymological resonance of scape/scope. A key word in his personal vocabulary, undocumented elsewhere in English, is *inscape*. Since
Hopkins, the word *inscape* has entered the English language,
defying readers to speculate as to its genealogy and denotation.

Perhaps, rather than looking immediately for a definition of the meaning of the word, we should look first at the mental process the word signifies. What contradictory impulses does Hopkins try to yoke together with this sign? Why does his thought crystallize along these lines?

Powerful new tools are available to modern scholars which were denied to Skeat and his contemporaries. Modern computers make it now possible to create in a matter of days or of hours word lists to all the vocabulary employed by an author, to find exactly when a word entered the written vocabulary, to locate all contexts of a given word or of a given sequence of letters within words. Eventually the work begun in the Dilligan/ Bender *Concordance to the English Poetry of Hopkins* (Madison: University of Wisconsin Press, 1970) will be expanded to make available concordances to all of his written records, prose and poetry alike, and to texts by Canon Richard Watson Dixon, Coventry Patmore, Cardinal Newman, Robert Bridges, and related writers as well.

In our lexicographical work with the circle surrounding Hopkins, a printed concordance is useful, but not the central research tool. The computer archive itself, capable of many different manipulations and configurations is the key to future analyses, some perhaps now not even imagined, which allow us to understand the language of Hopkins better and to see more clearly the mental processes signified by his verbal constructions.

The word *inscape* does not occur in the texts of Hopkins' poems. Nevertheless, it is quite simple to create an alphabetical list of all words used in his poetry and to search that list for words in which there is a syllable composed of k or c followed by any vowel followed by p This should provide us with a catalogue of words which might be formed on analogy with *inscape*. The task takes perhaps twenty minutes using a common office computer. We can then perform the same operation with reference to Hopkins' sermons or to the poetry of Dixon and compare the lists of words from these separate sources which may embody some etymological family resemblance.

In the poetry of Hopkins, the most common category of such constituent syllables clearly derives from the Indo-Germanic root we know from Classical Latin *capio,* to take or hold. For example, we find *accept, acceptance, accepted, all-accepting, capable, captivity,* possibly *coop, escape, except,* and *incapable.* Likewise, a number of words clearly fall into the related root we know through Classical Latin *caput, capitis,* head: *capital, captain, precipice, principal,* and *principle.* Several roots relate easily to Classical Greek *skeptomai* or *skopein,* to seem, appear, or to see: *horoscope* and *sceptic.* The root composed of *k* or *c* followed by a vowel plus a digamma, which we know from Latin *cupa,* a container, recipient, or cup, lies behind *acorncup, cup, cupboard,* and *cupp'd.* A similar test of the text of Hopkins' sermons turns up words related to L. *captio* ("to deceive"), captiously; *cupio* ("to desire"), concupiscence; and *disco* ("to learn"), disciple, to add to our list. There are a few words with the correct sequence of letters in the poetry and sermons which seem to fall outside the etymological net we are casting, such as *copying* from Latin *co* plus *ops,* to duplicate the wealth, or one of Hopkins' favorite nouns, *copse,* which occurs eight times, plus once in the plural, all plainly referring to a wooded area, a shortened form of *coppice* from French *couper,* a cutting place for wood.

Of words which show the string of letters *k-* or *c* - plus-vowel-plus-*p,* several interesting sets of words in the poems of Hopkins are not easily accounted for by the *capio, caput, skopein, cupa; take, head, see, hold* origins: (1) *cap, capp'd, caps, plushcapped;* (2) *capes;* (3) *coop;* (4) *coped;* (5) *cypris;* (6) *scoop, scooped, scoops;* (7) *scope;* and (8) *landscape, lovescape, cipher.* If we allow two letters to fall between the k and p sound, we should also add *chips, cusp,* and *sculptured* to this list.

The first group of words refers literally or figuratively to a cap or head covering: Daphne's lover's "cap shall be shining fur" (124,13); Io's "finger long new horns are capp'ed with black" (99, 7); in "May Magnificat" the springtide beauty is complete when "magic cuckoocall / Caps, clears, and clinches all—" (42, 44). In "The Wreck of the *Deutschland* " the climactic moment of faith is compared to:

> . . . How a lush-kept plush-capped sloe
> Will, mouthed to flesh-burst,
> Gush! — flush the man, the being with it, sour or sweet,

Brim, in a flash full! — Hither then, last or first,
To hero of Calvary, Christ,'s feet —" (28, 8, 3).

There are no surprises here, except perhaps the connotation of restraint, sensuality, and completion implied in the figure of the sloe and the cuckoocall.

Hopkins's use of *capes* likewise appears to be straightforward reference to clothing. In poem 104 the invading army is said to "fold the hills with golden capes," where "capes" is a variant of "mantle" in the text.

Coop is used as a dialect term describing a landscape. The stream "Inversnaid" runs "In coop and in comb the fleece of his foam / Flutes and low to the lake falls home" (56, 3). Here a "comb" is probably a narrow valley and a "coop" is a confined place through which the stream flows. A "flute" is a channel, "to flute" would be to form regular channels, like those in a fluted column.

Coped is more puzzling. "Duns Scotus's Oxford" is described as a "Towery city . . . that country and town did / Once encounter in, here coped and poisèd powers" (44, 4). "To cope" here might well mean that opposed powers encounter or join battle, reflecting the Fr. *couper*. Perhaps the reference is architectural, calling attention to the coped roof of the lofty, towery city. Or, yet again, it may be theological, referring to the dress of the ecclesiastical powers established at Oxford prior to Henry VIII and the Protestant Reformation. In all these senses the "powers" would be "contained" or cooped within the landscape.

The etymology of Cyprian Venus is difficult to trace. In "The Escorial" the judgment of Paris tenders the prize to "golden-girdled Cypris" (1, 11, 3), Aphrodite.

The set of words used to signify shovelling or hollowing out, *scoop, scooped, scoops*, appear in three cases. In "Il Mystico" the persona banishes "sensual gross desires" to "Scoop you from teeming filth some sickly hovel, / And there for ever grovel" (77, 6). "Harry Ploughman" is described as "the rack of ribs; the scooped flank; lank / Rope-over thigh; knee-nave; and barrelled shank —" (71, 2). And the cuckoo's song echoes "Off trundled timber and scoops of the hillside ground" (146, 4).

Note here that the "scoops of the hillside ground" are part of what Hopkins calls a "landscape." In all these contexts, *scoop* appears to mean in a "hollow place shaped as if scooped out."

It was the etymology of *scope*, specifically, that Hopkins felt should indicate free play, as the scope of a ship at anchor. In "Morning, Midday, and Evening Sacrifice" the persona speaks of "The vault and scope and schooling / And mastery in the mind" (49, 15). In the fragments from "Floris in Italy," "I have no scope for benefits" (102, 1, 52). Discussing a musical composition, "Not free in this because / His powers seemed free to play: / He swept what scope he was / To sweep and must obey." (148, 15). In these contexts, *scope* appears in all three cases to mean "freedom of play" as in the example Hopkins cited in his letter to Baillie above, although in each citation it is also plausible to see the word as meaning "aim" or "goal."

Landscape occurs five times: "Here in some darkened landscape Paris fair" (1, 11, 1); "And all the landscape under survey" (30, 13); "Landscape plotted and pieced —fold, fallow, and plough" (37, 5); "Earth, sweet earth, sweet landscape, with leaves throng" (58, 1); "The whole landscape flushes on a sudden at a sound" (146, 5).

These occurrences seem straightforward enough, but the analogous formation *lovescape* gives the reader pause, "Lovescape crucified" (28, 23, 4). "Lovescape" is apparently the closest approach in the poetry to the coinage "inscape." So striking is the word, that the reader needs to look at the full passage in which it occurs. The persona in "The Wreck of the *Deutschland*" is contemplating the numerology of the situation in which five nuns were drowned, like the five wounds on the body of Christ crucified:

> Five! the finding and sake
> And cipher of suffering Christ.
> Mark, the mark is of man's make
> And the word of it Sacrificed.
> But he scores it in scarlet himself on his own bespoken,
> Before-time-taken, dearest prizèd and priced —
> Stigma, signal, cinquefoil token
> For lettering of the lamb's fleece, ruddying of the rose-flake.

> Joy fall to thee, father Francis,
> Drawn to the Life that died;
> With the gnarls of the nails in thee, niche of the lance, his
>   Lovescape crucified
> And seal of his seraph-arrival! and these thy daughters
> And five-livèd and leavèd favour and pride,
>   Are sisterly sealed in wild waters,
> To bathe in his fall-gold mercies, to breathe in his all-fire glances.

Note that the "cipher of suffering Christ" employs in "cipher" one of the words in Hopkins's lexicon incorporating the c-vowel-p string, although its historical Arabic etymology appears at first glance to remove it far from the Indo-Germanic roots we have been considering. The reference in these two stanzas is to the wounds of Christ on the cross, which become the cinquefoil token, pattern, the stigmata received by St. Francis, as reported in the footnote to this poem, which in turn is reflected in the death of the five Franciscan nuns in the shipwreck, the cipher of sacrifice.

The historical etymology of "cipher" in English is well established, deriving from Arabic *Cifr*, "zero," which is in turn a substantive use of the Arabic adjective *cafara*, "to be empty," which was the Arabic translation of the Sanscrit word for zero.

The "cipher of suffering Christ" which is his "lovescape crucified" are the five wounds of Christ, the "Stigma, signal, cinquefoil token."

While Hopkins claims to be searching for the historical development of current English words, much as a Darwinian biologist might study similarities in particular specimens of related animals to imagine how species had evolved, at the same time his study reveals words falling into patterns associated in his mind. While we may find his etymological speculations farfetched or amateur, it does not eliminate them as part of the texture of his mind and art. For example, consider his numerology in the stanzas just quoted. A rationalist reader might well observe that it was mere chance that crucified Christ traditionally is depicted with five corporeal wounds and merely by coincidence there were five nuns drowned on the *Deutschland*. Even if it is "mere coincidence," any reader can see that the cinquefoil token is a constellation imaginatively binding together these disparate events in the text of the poem and the mind of the poet.

Likewise, we might observe that "cipher" and "suffer" have historically no etymological connection, merely the coincidental similarity of sound, yet the "cipher of suffering" undoubtedly formed a structural link in the associative mental processes of Hopkins. This unexpected patterning and logically superfluous linkage galvanizes otherwise inert language and gives the reader the feeling that he is participating in an organically developing process.

As for "inscape," when Hopkins finally denominates the word in his letters and papers, it appears very simple indeed, "so design, pattern or what I am in the habit of calling 'inscape' is what I above all aim at in poetry. Now it is the virtue of design, pattern, or inscape to be distinctive and it is the vice of distinctiveness to become queer. This vice I cannot have escaped."[4] "Inscape" refers to pattern, but pattern of such force as that written in the cipher of suffering lovescape in Christ crucified, recalling captain, the head, the principal force, the shaping power, giving full scope to play and choice, while linking together in a single cipher its *capio, caput, skopein, cupa; take, head, see, hold* origins.

It takes but a few minutes to test the poetry of Canon Richard Watson Dixon (1833-1900) to see how he handled the *c* - or *k* -plus-vowel-plus-p string in his word formation. Like Hopkins, he does not employ the word "inscape," but he does use *scape* and *scope* frequently. The eleven cases of the word "scope" all will bear Hopkins' gloss of "freedom of play." St. Mary Magdalene speaks of "in narrow scope / Her narrow hope" and in "Sympathy: An Ode" the speaker observes that "fear can limit all the scope." One of Dixon's most effective poems is titled "The Scapegoat," and additionally he twice uses "scape" as related to "escape." But the remaining occurrence of "scape" in Dixon, in Stanza xx of "La Faerie, or Lover's World," merits our attention. Lovers meet in a "fellowship of beauty" in an enchanted land, where everything is perfectly harmonious, "There was naught / But seemed at one with all things, no surprise / In that vast scape of mingled forms and dyes."

"Landscape" of a beautiful sunset scene, to be sure, but clearly vast "scape" of intricate, harmonious design, shapen by a creator and seen as a cipher of the union of loving souls. Dixon is very near the "scape" of Hopkins' etymological resonance.

Here I must pause and wonder what Hopkins would think, a century gone, to see his delicate and sophisticated texts subjected to computer assisted lexicographical analysis of this sort. Surely in another century, in 2089, God willing, another band of scholars will gather in bicentennial celebration of his great gifts to suffering mankind, the comfort of his fellowship and the glory of his words. They will no doubt view our proceedings today with amusement, much as we view the preliminary and sometimes faltering steps of Skeat, Murray, Liddell, and Scott. But the texts of Hopkins themselves will live for those readers, as they do for us, to make them feel in the rebirth of his language the rebirth of all nature.

Hopkins on "Man" and "Being"

Peter Milward, S.J.

In commemoration of the centenary of Hopkins' death, I wish to address two topics that are at once distinct and yet complementary to each other.[1] The humanism of Hopkins is presented as arising out of his study of the Classics, or (as we say at Oxford) *"litterae humaniores"*; while his philosophy of being is shown to stem not so much from his relatively late enthusiasm for Scotus as from his earlier interest in the pre-Socratic philosophers, to whom he was introduced at Oxford when he advanced from the course of Classical "Mods" to "Greats." Both his humanism and his philosophy of being spring out of Hopkins' classical studies in literature and philosophy, while in each case the Classics are seen as transmuted in the poet's further study of Christian divinity within the Society of Jesus.

Such an emphasis on this dual duality—humanist and philosophical, classical and Christian—in the formation of Hopkins as poet and priest seems particularly appropriate in a contribution to this volume, considering that my association with both Loyola University and the Loyola University Press is indelibly stamped by my long friendship with Fr. Raymond V. Schoder, with whom I published two books on Hopkins for the University Press and for whose Schoderfest, held in his honor at Loyola in April 1986, shortly before his death, I presented a paper on the Classics in Hopkins.

The Humanist

A hundred years after the death of Gerard Manley Hopkins, we are in a good position to look back and appreciate the humanity of a great poet who was overlooked by his own contemporaries. Though he himself died all but unknown, his poetry survived to become an influence upon other literary figures as well as an inspiration to millions of readers. All his disappointment is interred with his bones; his literary and spiritual achievements seem to have survived him. Now that his soul is in the hands of God—according to the saying of Wisdom, *"Justorum animae in manu Dei sunt"*—the humanity and the humanism of Hopkins may be said, like God's grandeur, to "flame out, like shining from shook foil."

"The humanism of Hopkins"—what an attractive word "humanism" is, to be sure, surrounded as it is by an appealing romantic aura! And then, combined with the name of Hopkins, it derives an added charm from the alliteration, not to mention the association. But first it may be well to consider the precise, logical and etymological meaning of the word. Its ending in *ism* is of more recent formation, serving to denote the mental attitude or ideology of the "humanist," which is the older word. As for "humanist," it originally denotes a student of the humanities, or classical literature of Greece and Rome, which is still known at Oxford in the Latin form of *"litterae humaniores."* In this original meaning the "humanist" is ranked with the "naturalist," or student of natural philosophy (or science), and the "divine," or student of theology or "divinity" (as in the title, "Doctor of Divinity").

Even in this narrowest sense of the word, Hopkins may well lay claim to the appellation of "humanist," in view of his undergraduate studies of the Classics at Balliol College, Oxford, at a time when Balliol was leading the world in classical studies under its great Master, Benjamin Jowett. And Hopkins' interest in the humanities did not cease with his graduation in 1867 but followed him through life, as he taught the Jesuit juniors at Manresa House, Roehampton, from 1873 to 1874, coached the boys at Stonyhurst College from 1882 to 1884, and went on to deal with the Irish university students in Dublin from 1884 to 1889— with special reference to the Greek lyric metres. Surveying this thread of classical scholarship, as it runs through the life of Hopkins, one might well put into his mouth the words of Virgil, *"A te principium, tibi desinam."*

Still, when we survey Hopkins' life as a whole, we cannot say that he remained a "humanist" in this sense. Particularly from the time of his entrance into the Society of Jesus in 1868 he follows a line of development from his early "humanism" to a subsequent "divinity," culminating in his theological course at St. Beuno's College from 1874 to 1877. This course he pursued not as an irksome duty or obstacle course on his way to the Catholic priesthood, but as a study that engaged his whole-hearted interest—possibly even too whole-hearted (in his somewhat eccentric manner) to be acceptable to his theology professors. In his approach to "divinity," however, there was no opposition to his earlier "humanism," which is commonly called "man-centered" in contrast to "God-centered"; but for him the one is seen to merge into the other, as the supreme object of his attention in both is God made man in Christ.

Again, Hopkins cannot be regarded as a "humanist" to the exclusion of "naturalism," an interest in nature and natural science. For the humanists of the Renaissance, man may have occupied the foreground of their attention, with nature relegated to the background—as we see in so many paintings of the period. But for Hopkins, as a child of the Romantic movement and the new age of science, nature almost seems to replace man as the object of his poetic attention; and behind his poems we recognize here and there his intense personal interest in the contemporary developments of natural science.

Accordingly, Hopkins may well be regarded as a humanist in the fullest sense of the word: as one who delights to study man not only in himself (where he can only find nothing), but also in relation to the surrounding world of nature, and above all in relation to God within and above him. This humanism of his is revealed not so much in his classical studies or subsequent teaching as in his creative composition. In his poems he looks first on the world of nature, in which he finds the presence of nature's God, and next he looks within himself only to find an aching absence of God. In either case, however, his is a way from man to God, as though following the order of St.

Bonaventure's *Itinerarium Mentis ad Deum.*

To begin with Hopkins' view of nature, what he emphasizes in his early Jesuit poems is "beauty" in general, and "pied beauty" in particular. In his poem with this very title, he gives glory to God "for dappled things . . . / All things counter, original, spare, strange." He is filled with wonder at how from the infinite, unchanging simplicity of the Creator comes such an immense variety of ever-changing forms in the created world of nature. In poem after poem he utters his admiration of "the dappled-with-damson west" ("The Wreck," st. 5), "the dapple-dawn-drawn Falcon" ("The Windhover"), the "drop-of-blood-and-foam-dapple / Bloom" on "the orchard-apple" ("The May Magnificat"), and in general "earth's dapple" ("Spelt from Sibyl's Leaves"). For it is in his eyes the dappledness in form that constitutes the uniqueness and originality of things in nature, where no two objects are precisely alike. This may be contrasted with the artificiality of man- and mass-produced objects that come pouring from factories in our industrial age, as the sad expression of "dear and dogged man" who remains "To his own selfbent so bound, so tied to his turn."

What the poet also emphasizes is the individuality, or "thisness" of things, according to that principle of individuation proposed by his favorite philosopher Scotus in terms of *haecceitas* (or *ecceitas*, with a possible hint at the Latin *ecce*, "Behold!"). This is his particular theme in "As Kingfishers catch fire," where he continues:

> Each mortal thing does one thing and the same:
> > Deals out that being indoors each one dwells;
> > Selves—goes itself; *myself* it speaks and spells,
> Crying *What I do is me: for that I came.*

Here one can almost feel the poet's excited insistence on each word, emphasizing the "one thing necessary" in each thing, as it were in juxtaposition, if not opposition, to the dappledness of things. The emphasis is, of course, on "each" as engaged in doing "one thing and the same" (as if echoing Shakespeare's "all one, ever the same," from Sonnet 76), with the implication that it is intrinsically different from everything else, according to the Aristotelian definition of individual essence as "that by which a thing is what it is and is different from other things." Nor is the emphasis merely on "is," but rather on "does," according to the other axioms, "Does comes after is" (*Agere sequitur esse*) and "Every agent acts like itself" (*Omne agens agit sibi simile*).

Above all, the emphasis of Hopkins moves from the "thisness" which is in all things to the selfhood that is most marked in man. Yet in things, too, in the "kingfishers" and "dragonflies" and "stones" and bells of this poem, he discerns the traces of selfhood, as though granting to things the attributes of persons in a Wordsworthian "pathetic fallacy." It is as if, like Teilhard de Chardin after him, the poet recognizes a "pre-life" in inanimate things and a "pre-consciousness" in plants, which amount to a "pre-selfhood." This is the inner quality of things to which he also gives the name of "inscape," and which for him culminates in the personality of human beings.

Turning now from nature to man, we may consider him according to the two basic aspects of his composite being: as man is essentially dappled with "being," or foredrawn to one out of many, and "non-being," or drawn apart in many directions. On the one hand, man is considered as created by God, the source of all being, whence there arises in him a certain creative tension, which is at the heart of human genius; as the poet puts it in the opening stanza of "The Wreck": "Thou hast bound bones and veins in me, fastened me flesh." On the other hand, man is considered as merely a creature, with an inborn tendency to fall apart and disintegrate into his many constitutive elements, in a series of d's: darkness, despair, decay and death. And this, too, the poet puts in his continuing words from "The Wreck": "And after it almost unmade, what with dread"— where the feeling of falling apart or gaping is aptly conveyed by the open, vocalic syllables.

Not that this disintegration is evil; for it is also, the poet insists, "Thy doing"—the action of him who is both "Lord of living and dead," who brings man down to death in order to raise him up. This is a providential testing of man by means of "lightning and lashed rod," whose terror forces man to come out with an impulsive response: "I did say yes." It is the way God has chosen to renew his work of creation in us since while, as St. Augustine points out, he has made us without us, seeing we were non-existent before he made us, he does not remake us, or redeem us, without us and our free cooperation. In this way out of apparent evil comes real good.

This is what Hopkins, in the second and main part of "The Wreck," goes on to reveal in the case of "the tall nun," when amid the snowstorm and the "endragoned seas" threatening her with despair she cries out, "O Christ, Christ, come quickly!" For then it is as if she imposes a divine name on the natural terror surrounding her; she recognizes Christ himself coming to her over the waters "in the storm of his strides"; she says her "Yes" to him and thereby achieves salvation not only for herself but also for the "Comfortless unconfessed" of her fellow-passengers. And so she arrives at a fullness of personality in him, according to his own word: "Whosoever will lose his life for my sake shall find it" (Matt. 16: 25). For the fullness of personality is in Christ, of whom the poet elsewhere says:

> For Christ plays in ten thousand places,
> Lovely in limbs, and lovely in eyes not his
> To the Father through the features of men's faces.

So from "The Wreck" we may go on to consider how Hopkins delights in the varied selves of human beings, both in general and in particular. In general, we have his sonnet, "To what serves Mortal Beauty?" composed on the very eve of his dark sonnets and his sadness in Dublin. Here he dwells with love on "World's loveliest—men's selves"; and he goes on to remark with wonder how "Self flashes off frame and face." He admires the distinctiveness of human beauty, in which, as in music, "all's to one thing wrought" ("On a Piece of Music"), especially as it stands forth in times of tension, attention, and activity. In particular, we may take his other sonnet on "Henry Purcell," whose music he most admires for its distinctiveness, that in the melody which sets him off from all other composers:

It is the forgèd feature finds me; it is the rehearsal
Of own, of abrúpt sélf there so thrusts on, so throngs the ear.

Then, as Hopkins moves from his bright to his dark period, in his transition from England to Ireland, his approach to self undergoes a corresponding change, adumbrated in "Spelt from Sibyl's Leaves." Here, after beginning with an ominous series of open, vocalic syllables, "Earnest, earthless, equal, attune-able," the poet goes on to note how "earth her being has unbound; her dapple is at end," with "self ín self steepèd and páshed." Everything is paradoxically unselved and yet (in man at least) excessively selved, on a rack "Where, selfwrung, selfstrung, sheathe-and shelterless, | thóughts agaínst thoughts ín groans grínd." Then it is, as Hopkins also adds in the dark-est of the dark sonnets, "I wake and feel," that "Selfyeast of spirit a dull dough sours," whose outcome he finds in hell where it is the scourge of the lost to be "As I am mine, their sweating selves." Thus the end of unselving, when man turns away from God with "No," is paradoxically to be oneself, left entirely to one's own resources, unable to escape from the narrow prison of oneself, as it were in that endless series of mirrors which the poet implies in "My own heart": "This tormented mind / With this tormented mind tormenting yet."

Out of this hell or prison of self, from which God and nature have both seemed shut out, Hopkins emerges in a magnificent poem which stands like a pillar at the end of his dark period as "Spelt from Sibyl's Leaves" had stood at the beginning: namely, "That Nature is a Heraclitean Fire and of the comfort of the Resurrection." Here we find the poet once more able to delight in the prospect of "nature's bonfire" amid all its changes effected by a "bright wind boisterous" upon "yestertempest's creases." Yet in contrast to this delight, he pauses with tragic "pity and indignation" on "Manshape, that shone / Sheer off, disseveral, a star," whom "death blots black out." Here is precisely the contrast, presented in the starkest form possible, between the being and the non-being in man. It is as if, against the background of the eternal recurrence in nature, the conflict in man is seen as ending in victory for the forces of non-being.

But here precisely stands out, all the more vividly against the darkness of despair, "A beacon, an eternal beam" (recalling the "blown beacon of light" in "The Wreck," st. 29): "the Resurrection, / A heart's clarion," as it were the last trumpet, calling men to rise for the last judgment, or rather the final resurrection. Then, in his final response "Yes," the poet finds, "I am all at once what Christ is," in his heavenly glory, "since he was what I am," in his earthly lowliness; and so he is raised with Christ to a fullness of humanity which is also oneness with the divinity, as his "I am" is drawn into the eternal "I AM" of God, in the very sound of the rhyming "diamond."

Thus in the poetic thought of Hopkins, unlike that of St. Bonaventure in his *Itinerarium*, we find two movements: first, as he looks at the "pied beauty" in the world of nature around him and then up to nature's God, with the exclamation, "Praise him"—not without pausing from time to time to lament (with Wordsworth) "what man has made of man," particularly in the industrial age; and next, as he looks at the world of man, with himself in that world, and feels acutely the imperfections of self due to sin and the accompanying absence of God. This, however, drives him all the more impulsively, as at the beginning of his Jesuit poetry in "The Wreck," so in his culminating poem on nature and the resurrection, to confess "thy terror, O Christ, O God," to respond to that terror with "Yes," to stress "the Resurrection" of Christ, and so to find both God and himself again in that Word made flesh who was crucified for him and rose again from the dead. Thus the humanism of Hopkins, while deeply rooted in the world of nature, as that of a Romantic poet reacting (like Carlyle) against the industrial hell of his age, nonetheless impulsively rises up to God in heaven, as "*Ipse*, the only one, Christ, King, Head," and so realizes his fulfillment in divinity.

Despite the depth and complexity of Hopkins' thought, man is for the poet essentially one, a composite rather than a sum. And as a humanist in the older sense of the term, in other words as a student of the classics, Hopkins first encountered this explicit monism in the early Greek philosophers he studied as an undergraduate at Oxford. In exploring the origins of Hopkins' humanistic thought we shall now turn to a study of the ways he drew on two of these philosophers.

The Philosopher of Being

From August 3, 1872, when he came upon a "copy of Scotus on the Sentences in the Baddely library" and felt himself "flush with a new stroke of enthusiasm," we may well say that for Hopkins "the philosopher" *par excellence* was no longer Aristotle (if ever he had been) but Duns Scotus; and we may well think of Scotus as being for him the philosopher of inscape, seeing that, as Hopkins adds in his *Journal*, "just then when I took in any inscape of the sky or sea I thought of Scotus." Later on, when he returned to his alma mater Oxford, on the staff of St. Aloysius' Church, he felt he could breathe the air of his old university with new inspiration, since it was what "he lived on . . . who of all men most sways my spirits to peace."

Yes, but before Scotus came on his intellectual scene, Hopkins had made the acquaintance in his undergraduate days at Oxford of the great Greek philosophers, Plato and Aristotle; but then, apparently, he had been taken not so much with them—in spite of, or perhaps because of their classical preeminence—as with two seemingly lesser, because fragmentary philosophers of the pre-Socratic era, Parmenides and Heraclitus. The ideas of both these philosophers, having entered into his mind from his early student days, may be seen as entering also into his poems at an even deeper level than the ideas of Scotus. Or rather, may it not be said that, if Hopkins was so impressed by Scotus' commentary on the *Sentences*, it was because in the latter he recognized an echo of the former? For then he thought of Scotus "in any inscape of the sky or sea"; but his first use of the word "inscape" occurs in his undergraduate composition on "Parmenides."

In this fragmentary composition we come upon Hopkins' first use not only of his favorite "inscape," repeated no less than four times, but also of his equally favorite "instress" three times and "stress" twice. It is quite extraordinary! He notes, without criticism but rather appreciation, that "His great text, which he repeats with religious conviction, is that Being is and Not-being is not —which perhaps one can say . . . means that all things are upheld by instress and are meaningless without it."[2] This is oddly reminiscent of the sage dictum attributed by the Clown in *Twelfth Night* to an old hermit of Prague, "That that is is" (iv. 1)—to which one is tempted to add the obverse, "And that that is not is not." From one point of view, it is so obvious, if not tautological, it hardly needs to be said; and yet, from another point of view, it is so profound, it needs to be repeated over and over again, if only (as Hopkins later says in another context) to "keep warm men's wits to the things that are" ("To what serves Mortal Beauty?").

Here Hopkins rather associates the thought of Parmenides with the perception of instress in things, as it were a perception of the divine energy at work in the world. For the Creator, according to the Christian faith, remains active in all his creatures; and the creation is not altogether a separation, but that God remains in things by his essence, presence and power, as the inmost being of things. For it is by the being of God that all things less than God have their being; and without God all things would fall into non-being. Moreover, as the being of God is essentially one, so it is the nature of every being to be one, or (as Hopkins puts it) "flush and foredrawn"; whereas it is the nature of many, as many, to be "unforedrawn" or "foredrawing away from one another" into a state of non-being.

It is in this connection that Hopkins moves, in these notes on Parmenides, from "instress" to "inscape," first in relation to his impact on Plato: "His feeling for instress, for the flush and foredrawn, and for inscape, is most striking and from this one can understand Plato's reverence for him as the great father of Realism."[3] Indeed, in his dialogue *Theaetetus* Plato describes Parmenides as a man "to be reverenced and . . . feared" and as one endowed "with an exceedingly wonderful depth of mind." Then, as for Parmenides' impact on himself, Hopkins continues: "But indeed I have often felt when I have been in this mood and felt the depth of an instress or how fast the inscape holds a thing that nothing is so pregnant and straightforward to the truth as simple *yes* and *is*."[4] Here he seems to see the "inscape" of a thing as that which holds its many parts together as one, arising as it were from the depths of its inmost being or "instress"; and this may be compared with his later definition of pitch, in his spiritual writings, as "that by which being differs from and is more than nothing and not being," which, he adds, "is with precision expressed by the English do."[5]

Now we may go on to see how all this philosophizing on

Parmenides comes to a poetic climax in "The Wreck of the *Deutschland*," from the very opening stanza, where we feel "the depth of an instress" and "how fast the inscape holds a thing" in the confession: "Thou hast bound bones and veins in me, fastened me flesh." There indeed we find the unity of being; but it is immediately contrasted with the multiplicity of non-being, which—as Hopkins also states in his notes on Parmenides—"is here seen as want of oneness, all that is unforedrawn, waste space which offers either nothing to the eye to foredraw or many things foredrawing away from one another. . . "[6] And so he continues in the following line of the stanza: "And after it almost unmade, what with dread."

All the same, as he goes on to say, this very undoing of his being somehow proceeds from the being of God, "thy doing," as a necessary preliminary to a renewal of being, a touching afresh by God's creative finger, prompting the emphatic response, "I did say yes," at the beginning of the second stanza— and reminding us of what the poet had noted on Parmenides, "that nothing is so pregnant and straightforward to the truth as simple *yes* and *is*." In such a moment of confession, as it were echoing the archetypal confession of Peter, "Thou art the Christ, the Son of the living God," everything seems to come together in the poet's memory, "the walls, altar and hour and night," when he responded to the divine instress on his being with a corresponding "lace of stress." And so he was inspired, as he also sings in "Hurrahing in Harvest," to "whirl out wings" and to "[flee] with a fling of the heart to the heart of the Host"—to the Sacred Heart of our Saviour.

Another such climax is reached, in more general terms, in the seventh and eighth stanzas, showing the impact of the unselving stroke of "the dense and the driven Passion" on man, as a result of which "the heart, being hard at bay, / Is out with it!" This is precisely the moment of death, metaphorical or physical, the time of testing that finally brings out "the best or worst word," namely yes or no. And it is in this precise way that all men—"never ask if meaning it, wanting it, warned of it"— go to the feet of Christ crucified, as it were in a day of judgment or "day of the Lord." Then the response of "yes" brings men together in the oneness of being, all "flush and foredrawn";

whereas that of "no" reduces them to a "foredrawing away from one another" in endless multiplicity of non-being.

Thus the storm, so vividly described in Part the Second, symbolizes the forces of chaos and non-being; but in the dispensation of "lovely-felicitous Providence" it also serves as a setting for the emergence of "a lioness," "a prophetess," with her "virginal tongue" to "be a bell to, ring of it, and / Startle the poor sheep back," in that "she that weather sees one thing, one; / Has one fetch in her." This is precisely her individual, unique response to the coming of Christ over the waters "in the storm of his strides," as with her "heart right" and "single eye" she "read the unshapeable shock night" and interpreted it correctly by uttering the one Name of Christ, the Name above every other name, the Name of the one "I AM." This is not only the word but also the vision to which the poet leads up as the climax of this second part, when words seem for a moment to fail him, as he stammers:

> But how shall I . . . make me room there:
> Reach me a . . . Fancy, come faster—
> Strike you the sight of it? look at it loom there,
> Thing that she . . .

What he fails to express in words is the "thing," the object of the nun's vision, while it is as yet unfocussed; but once it is focussed on the one "person" of Christ, once he finds himself able to give a name to the vision, he no longer stammers but utters with all assurance—like Peter walking on the waters, after having been raised up by Christ:

> There then! the Master,
> *Ipse*, the only one, Christ, King, Head.

Thus, amid the stroke and the stress of the storm and the shipwreck, Christ is revealed as the One, invested with the fullness of Being, He Who Is. He comes, on His day of visitation, not with "a dooms-day dazzle in his coming," but "royally reclaiming his own"—not to destroy but to save, not only the nun and her four companions, who are "sisterly sealed in wild waters," in the full reality of baptism, but also "the rest of them" who merely seem "comfortless unconfessed," whereas in reality they have received the comfort of her one word which brings them the "finger of a tender of" the mastery, mercy and love of God. And so, in coming to him, as he comes to her, the nun in her unique response is fittingly compared to "the one woman without stain," the Virgin Mary, who was first "conceived" immaculate and then went on "to conceive" Christ as a virgin with her *fiat*, "Be it done to me according to thy word."

Further echoes of Parmenides are to be found in the other poem of shipwreck, "The Loss of the *Eurydice*," where the poet's original feeling "that nothing is so pregnant and straightforward to the truth as simple yes and is" is reproduced in the similar case of a drowning sailor:

> It is even seen, time's something server,
> In mankind's medley a duty-swerver,
>   At downright 'No or Yes?'
> Doffs all, drives full for righteousness.

Here, too, we find, on the one hand, the call of Christ and his invitation to man amid the stress and stroke of the storm, and, on the other, man's positive response in a vital assertion of being, "wild and self-instressed."

Similarly, in "Hurrahing in Harvest" the poet describes a vision of Christ, only this time in ecstasy not agony. From the movement of "silk-sack clouds . . . across skies" he receives the "rapturous love's greeting" of his Saviour; and in "the azurous hung hills" (where the azure skies meet the hills on the horizon in front of him) he recognizes "his world-wielding shoulder." And so he is prompted to respond with more than usual enthusiasm, as he feels all his being caught up and united with him whom his heart loves; and once again, as in the beginning of "The Wreck of the *Deutschland*," he feels

> The heart rears wings bold and bolder
> And hurls for him, O half hurls earth for him off under his feet.

These two passages, from "The Wreck" and "Hurrahing in Harvest," together with that from "The Loss of the *Eurydice*," are again recalled—as a further development of Hopkins' Parmenidean thought—in "The Handsome Heart," as the poet reflects on the "mannerly-hearted" response of a child to his offer of a present:

> What the heart is! which, like carriers let fly—
> Doff darkness, homing nature knows the rest—
> To its own fine function, wild and self-instressed,
> Falls light as ten years long taught how to and why.

The implication here, as in the previous passages, is that man is made for God as One alone, the created "I am" of man for the uncreated "I AM" of God, according to the famous declaration of St. Augustine at the outset of his *Confessions:* "Thou hast made us for thyself, O Lord; and our heart is restless, till it finds rest in thee."

Above all, the supreme expression by Hopkins of his Parmenidean insistence on the oneness of being appears in his poetic contrast of "The Leaden Echo and the Golden Echo." On the one hand, at the heart and centre of the former, leaden echo is a feeling of despair at the disappearance of beauty, when one is merely left with "many things foredrawing away from one another." It is this voice of despair that keeps on insisting in the ears of his imagination:

> No there's none, there's none, O no there's none . . .
> . . . no, nothing can be done . . .
> O there's none; no no no there's none.

There precisely he hears the echo of non-being. But then, in stark contrast in the latter, golden echo, he hears all the more strongly the reaffirmation of being, with the response of yes:

> There ís one, yes I have one . . .
>   Somewhere elsewhere there is ah well where! one,
> Óne. . . . Yes . . . yonder.

In the former case, it is the clinging of man to merely mortal beauty that leads him to despair and the chaos of non-being; whereas his readiness to "give beauty back . . . to God" as "beauty's self and beauty's giver" brings him a renewal of hope and a reaffirmation of being.

This is the poetic philosophy that for Hopkins comes to a climax in the sharply contrasting poems that stand like the twin pillars of Hercules bestriding the "dark sonnets" of his Dublin years. On the one side stands "Spelt from Sibyl's Leaves," with its opening series of epithets:

> Earnest, earthless, equal, attuneable, | vaulty, voluminous, . . .
>   stupendous
> Evening strains to be tíme's vást, | womb-of-all, home-of-all,
>   hearse-of-all night.

—where we may recognize an echo from Hopkins' note on Parmenides of that "want of oneness" and "waste space" which is there stated to be characteristic of non-being. As for the earth, the poet continues, there is the same sense of "waste" as in the heaven

> . . . . . . For earth | her being has unbound; her dapple is at an end,
>   as-
> tray or aswarm, all throughther, in throngs; | self ín
>   self steepèd and páshed—qúite
> Disremembering, dísmémbering | áll now.

On the other side stands "That Nature is a Heraclitean Fire and of the comfort of the Resurrection," in which the former part of the poem leads, like the leaden echo, to "an unfathomable . . . an enormous dark" of "vastness," only to be offset by the sudden affirmation, as in the golden echo, of "the Resurrection, / A heart's clarion!"—when the poet finds himself "all at once" one with Christ, and his earthly "I am" as it were embraced by the heavenly "I AM" in the very word "diamond."

It is with this culminating poem of Hopkins' poetic corpus that we pass from his Parmenidean to his Heraclitean philosophy. It is perhaps appropriate that the other pre-Socratic philosopher, known in antiquity as "the weeping philosopher" and "the dark one," should only appear, in contrast to Parmenides, at the dark end of Hopkins' life and writings, at least in so explicit a manner. Yet his characteristic thought, in which he dwells on "becoming" with as much insistence as Parmenides on "being," while looking from the imagery of fire ("the Heraclitean fire") and water ("all is in flux") to the hidden idea of Reason, Law, the Way, the Word, is no less pervasive in Hopkins' poetry than the thought of Parmenides.

From the first part of "The Wreck of the *Deutschland*" we come upon the Heraclitean image of the river of time, where the poet says of the mysterious "stroke" that "it rides time like riding a river"; and he goes on to see "its swelling" in the Passion of Christ, which is "in high flood yet." Then the complementary image of fire may be seen in the doxological petition

> With an anvil-ding
> And with fire in him forge thy will.

As for the idea of the Word, which may be regarded as completing the Parmenidean idea of the One, especially as itself completed by St. John's Prologue, this may be seen first implicitly in the recognition of that mystery which is "under the world's splendour and wonder," and which "must be instressed, stressed," and last in the more explicit form of praise for the nun who

> Read the unshapeable shock night
> And knew the who and the why;
> Wording it how but by him that present and past,
> Heaven and earth are word of, worded by?

and who, like Mary before her, revealed

> ... heart-throe, birth of a brain,

Word, that heard and kept thee and uttered thee outright.

In this climax, moreover, there is a return to the Heraclitean imagery of water and fire, but with a contrastive difference. Here water appears in "the tides," "the Yore-flood," the "ocean of a motionable mind" and "the all of water," as the river of Heraclitus may be followed in its course to the open sea; while the fire is more clearly identified with Christ as the divine Word made flesh in the penultimate stanza:

> Now burn, new born to the world,
> Double-naturèd name,
> The heaven-flung, heart-fleshed, maiden-furled
> Miracle-in-Mary-of-flame,
> Mid-numberèd he in three of the thunder-throne!

When we turn, however, from the beginning to the end, from "The Wreck" to the "Heraclitean Fire," we find in the latter poem a return to the idea of fire as mere flux, as expressed in the saying of Heraclitus, not only that "All is in flux" (*"Panta rhei "*), but also that "The way up and the way down are one and the same." From various examples which are associated rather with water than with fire, the poet goes on to draw the general conclusion that "Million-fuelèd, I nature's bonfire burns on"— as it were oblivious to the fate of individuals. For them, it seems, at least as individuals, there is only a return to non-being in the "vastness" of time; and this is what fills the heart of the poet with "pity and indignation." Only what redeems the dark philosophy of Heraclitus is the light of St. John's Gospel, with its new vision of the Word not just "in the beginning" but rather in the fullness of time, and not only in the Incarnation but also more precisely in the Resurrection.

Thus, in conclusion, we may see the poetic philosophy of Hopkins as moving, in terms of these two pre-Socratic philosophers, from the One of Parmenides to the Word of Heraclitus, not so much in themselves as in the light of Christian revelation—insofar as the One of Parmenides looks to the Name of

Yahweh in the Old Testament, "I AM," and the Word of Heraclitus looks to the Word as identified with Christ by St. John in the New Testament. In this way, we may add, Hopkins has achieved a further reconciliation of Christian faith with Greek philosophy by going as it were behind its more customary and more fully elaborated forms in Plato and Aristotle to a more poetic and fragmentary, a more primitive and suggestive form, more suited to a poetic and comprehensive vision.

"The Terrible Crystal": Hopkins' Poetry after 100 Years

"... your writings [have] a rare charm — something that I cannot describe, but ... which goes to the point of the terrible; the terrible crystal."

R.W. Dixon to Hopkins
26 October 1881

Francis L. Fennell

Hopkins is a "major poet," proclaimed F. R. Leavis in 1932: "His is likely to prove, for our time and the future, the only influential poet of the Victorian age, and he seems to me the greatest."[1] How has the poet fared in the past half century? Can one make the same threefold claim now? Can one judge Hopkins to be a major poet, the best poet of his age, and the only poet of that age who exerts and will continue to exert an influence on later generations of poets? To paraphrase Matthew Arnold, is the estimate of the 1930s the real estimate?

Arnold's name reminds us of how difficult it is to answer such questions. When he wrote "The Study of Poetry" in 1880 Arnold refused to extend his analysis beyond Robert Burns, who had died in 1796, because "we enter on burning ground as we approach the poetry of times [nearer] to us ... of which the estimates are so often not only personal, but personal with a passion." We are closer in years to the first publication of Hopkins' poems than Arnold was to Burns.

Moreover the danger is not only proximity in time. We live in an era when scholars are hostile to such value questions, when they do not believe in either their validity or their usefulness. Modern critics look askance at value statements, because few who use them can define or defend their premises and because few acknowledge the ways in which valuations are the constructs of a particular culture. Leavis could bandy phrases like "major poet" or "great tradition" with cheerful insouciance. We have grown properly suspicious of that language and the kind of thinking it represents. In addition we know to remind ourselves of the cultural and political dimensions of the question, as best epitomized in Edward Said's caution that "texts are a system of forces institutionalized at some expense by the reigning culture."[2]

And yet. . . .

And yet the dangers do not deter. Somehow the need for judging, the need for making statements about relative value, survives and even overcomes our awareness of the dangers. The questions draw, even compel, attention. They do so for reasons both personal and professional.

As human beings we confront every day of our lives the challenge defined by Hopkins' own teacher, Walter Pater:

> A counted number of pulses only is given to us of a variegated and dramatic life. How may we see in them all that is to be seen in them by the finest senses? How shall we pass most swiftly from point to point, and be present always at the focus where the greatest number of vital forces unite in their purest energy?[3]

One need not fully endorse Pater's solutions—art and song— to recognize the importance of the task. How shall we make our lives count? In these short days of frost and sun, how shall we spend the time which has been given to us? And the facts that I write this essay and that you read it mean we have given at least a partial answer in favor of reading poetry. We have decided that poetry shall have some place, perhaps a very important place, in our lives. But no portion of any life, no matter how large the portion or how long the life, makes room for even a very significant part of all the good poetry produced in all ages by all cultures. In the portion of our lives given over

to poetry, whose poetry shall we read? Choose we must. Therefore spending some time thinking about whom we choose and
why we choose them becomes an appropriate and even necessary way of responding to a decision about priorities we have
to make, have in some ways already made. Taking the issue
from the general of poetry to the particular of Hopkins, we need
to ask ourselves how much of a passion shall our reading of him
be.

In addition to these private concerns, many of us have
more public and professional reasons for addressing such
questions. If we are teachers and have been sensitive to recent
discussions within the profession about canons and canon
formation, we know that we have in fact been answering those
questions all along. Every time we draw up a syllabus, every
time we type an exam, every time we compile a reading list or
establish a set of course requirements, we make decisions that
convey to others what we believe. So we cannot escape proclaiming value judgments. The only question is whether honesty, or at least candor, will compel us to be explicit rather than
implicit, to argue our case rather than pretend the answers are
obvious. Thus, in the instance of Hopkins, what do we wish to
say to our students, our colleagues, our friends about him? Do
we feel confident in urging them, in the midst of their "vari-
egated and dramatic lives," to make room for his poetry?

So, both for ourselves and for others, we judge. And in that
context centenaries are useful because they form a natural
occasion for summing up, for taking stock, for being explicit
rather than implicit. This essay, like the others in the volume,
responds to that opportunity, becomes an *essai* in the original
sense of that term.[4] The conclusions offered here reflect my
personal view of Hopkins at this time and in this place. Insofar
as they are personal, such conclusions derive their value, not
from any presumed "correctness," but rather from the occasion
they offer to those who wish to use them as a stimulus for their
own fresh response to the poet.

But the essay also has a second purpose, which is the
attempt to summarize what in another context Roman Catholics call the *consensus fidei*, the consensus of the faithful—in this
case the consensus of the faithful readers of Hopkins. I wish to

articulate what seems to me the "common ground," the agreed-upon judgments of most of those who study the poems now, one hundred years after Hopkins' death. In several important ways the judgments of an earlier time, whether Leavis' or another's, can no longer be ours. To reflect this new consensus will require an unflinching look at the poet's limitations as well as his enduring strengths.

Here at the beginning let me also sound a note of urgency for this centenary year: I would contend that Hopkins' reputation as a poet is fading.

Hard words, those. But consider the most obvious criteria by which we measure a poet's current reputation.

First, the publication of editions of Hopkins' poetry. A reader in, say, 1968 had a choice of the then-definitive fourth edition of the *Poems* edited by W. H. Gardner and Norman MacKenzie, or of four less expensive selections from the poet's work edited by Gardner or James Reeves or Graham Storey or John Pick. Now, twenty years later, we have in print only the successor to *Poems* (the Phillips edition) plus Gardner's selection.

Or take the poet's representation in textbooks and anthologies. Fr. van Beeck describes elsewhere in this volume how the new edition of the *Oxford Book of Christian Verse* cuts Hopkins' representation from nine poems to four, and four short ones at that. Fr. van Beeck gives a carefully reasoned account of what these choices reflect about the assumptions of the editors. But the process is not limited to that anthology alone. For example, X. J. Kennedy's well-known *Introduction to Poetry* shows an ever-so-gradually diminishing count, from seven poems to six to five in successive editions. The *Norton Anthology of Poetry* as another example shows a reduction also, if the first edition (1970) is compared with the third and most recent (1983). The slippage in these and other cases may not be large, certainly not as dramatic as in the *Oxford*. But we cannot disregard the trend, which at best preserves the status quo —for example, Perrine's influential textbook *Sound and Sense,* where Hopkins is always served by the same five poems—and which in other respects is downward.

Finally, and perhaps most importantly given the role which

academics now play in the determining of reputation and canonical status, observe the situation in current scholarly criticism of Hopkins. A check of the *PMLA International Bibliography*, the most accessible barometer of a poet's status within the profession, again offers hints of an ebbing tide. Compare, for example, 1987, the last year for which the bibliography is available as I write, with a decade earlier. At first glance the situation in 1987 seems to have been healthy, because Hopkins is represented by thirty entries. But a closer examination ought to provoke concern in those who love the poet. Subtract from those thirty entries the thirteen articles which appeared in *Hopkins Quarterly*, a highly specialized journal. Then subtract again the entries which cite dissertations, minor notes, and reviews of scholarship—another thirteen. We are left with exactly four entries. No books of any kind on Hopkins. No articles in major journals, with the possible exception of Norman White's piece in *English Studies*. Consider also the kinds of topics which are being addressed: "Hopkins' 'Skies of Couple-Colour': A Debt to Barnes's 'Cappled Cows'?" or "A Newly Discovered Version of a Verse Translation by Gerard Manley Hopkins."

Now go back to 1977. Here we find thirty-seven entries plus cross-references to another four. Again subtracting *Hopkins Quarterly* (fifteen) and the other category (six), we still have twenty entries. Included among them are two books as well as articles in such major journals as *PMLA, Victorian Poetry, Études Anglaises*, and *Review of English Studies*. These articles develop significant topics, such as Jacob Korg on "Hopkins' Linguistic Deviations" or Norman MacKenzie on "The Making of a Hopkins Sonnet: 'Spelt from Sibyl's Leaves.'"

Well, it may be objected, suppose these are accidental differences; after all, there are bound to be variations from year to year. Go back then still another decade, to 1967. Twenty-seven entries appear under Hopkins' name, plus one cross-reference. *Hopkins Quarterly* has not yet begun to publish. Subtracting five from the other category, we are left with twenty-three entries. Four books on Hopkins appeared that year. Journals such as *PMLA, University of Toronto Quarterly, Victorian Poetry*, and *Modern Language Quarterly* published important articles on the poet, such as Louis Rader's critique of the dark sonnets. The situation was just as healthy as it would be a decade later, and both are remarkable improvements over what would obtain in 1987, even though the profession as a whole has more scholars working and more articles being published with each passing year.

Fifteen years ago Edward Cohen could announce confidently that Hopkins' position was secure.[5] While Hopkins had always had his detractors, including influential ones such as T. S. Eliot and Yvor Winters,[6] the preponderance of opinion seemed to support the poet and his growing reputation. That assurance, I have been arguing, is no longer justified. The present challenge to Hopkins may not be as direct as was Eliot's or Winters'. Since almost all literary criticism rests now in the hands of academics, a poet can be killed gently, by neglect, even by an overspecialization which deprives him or her of a broader audience. Such challenges, while more elusive, may prove just as real as the frontal assaults of an earlier generation.

Will Hopkins receive—more importantly, does he deserve—this benign neglect? In order to answer we shall first have to look squarely at the poet's limitations. Only by doing so can those who love the poet place their enthusiasm in its proper context. Hopkins will not be well served by uncritical praise, either praise of the wrong things or praise of the right things for the wrong reasons. Furthermore, if the establishment of a poet's reputation is really in many ways a political process (a subject to which we will return), then it follows that new generations of readers can be won over to the poet only if those who engage their rhetorical skills on Hopkins' behalf recognize fully the obstacles which potential readers have to surmount.

❦

When a reader comes to a poet, especially for the first time, he or she can expect certain challenges. Some of these challenges derive not so much from the poetry itself as from the way the poetry is mediated, in other words from the nature of, or effects on, the readers themselves, and also from the weight of a critical tradition which "teaches" readers how to approach the poems. Some other challenges come from difficulties intrinsic to the poems themselves. We shall have to deal with each kind of challenge in turn.[7]

The first extrinsic limitation that can alter how we perceive Hopkins grows out of a danger against which readers have been warned by one of Hopkins' most famous contemporaries. The historical fallacy, says Arnold, may occur when we see a poet's work as important in the development of a nation's literature. If one recognizes the impact of a poet on a later generation, one is tempted to overvalue him or her. Hopkins has been given a great deal of praise of this sort, especially in the past. When Sir Herbert Read defined poetry as the productive tension between sensibility and belief and used Hopkins as his *locus classicus*,[8] or when C. Day Lewis called Hopkins' originality in diction and rhythm the poet's "gifts to posterity,"[9] or when Geoffrey Grigson praised Hopkins' influence on the ablity of later poets to "see" nature carefully and exactly,[10] they were valuing the poet for the ways he was shaping a new generation of poets. All the claims which have been made for Hopkins' influence or his precocity ("the forerunner of Modernism") need to be discounted as examples of this fallacy. Such overestimation is what Eliot found objectionable in those who praised Hopkins for his style.[11]

The truth of the matter is, first that claims for Hopkins' influence have been exaggerated, and second that whatever influence he may have exerted is now firmly in the past. Of the major twentieth-century poets only Dylan Thomas seems to have drawn heavily on the precedents set by Hopkins, and Thomas has been dead for over thirty-five years. Furthermore, Modernism, the movement with the most natural affinity for Hopkins' example, is itself a part of our past. We now live in a time of minimalist poetry inimical to Hopkins' declamatory style.

Whatever its past sins, therefore, criticism of Hopkins most probably will not carry a similar burden into the future. The historical fallacy, although it may have colored perception of the poet up till now, will not encumber our judgment much longer.

That may not be the case with a second important fallacy pointed out by Arnold. A poet, says Arnold, "may count to us on grounds personal to ourselves. Our personal affinities, likings, and circumstances, have great power to sway our estimate of this or that poet's work, and to make us attach more importance to it as poetry than in itself it really possesses, because to us it is, or has been, of high importance."[12] Here the danger is clear and present.

Let me be frank. If in our discussion of the personal fallacy we restrict ourselves for the moment just to the question of Hopkins' religion, it seems clear that over the years many readers of Hopkins appear to have been drawn to him in general because of his preoccupation with religious subjects and in particular because of his Roman Catholicism. Their own religious faith—or even deep questioning of that faith—may have led these readers to welcome a poet who felt both the consolation which such a faith can bring and also the desolation which one can feel when the only experience is of a *deus absconditus.*

To observe this predilection does not mean impugning anyone's critical integrity. Some of the people who have loved and written about Hopkins' poetry have much religious faith, some little, some none. Nor is there a correlation between one's faith (or lack thereof) and one's perspicacity: brilliant things and foolish things have been written by believers and unbelievers alike. We have no justification for drawing any conclusion about a specific critic of Hopkins simply because we know or can guess something about that person's religious beliefs.

Rather the case is this: when one examines all those who have written about Hopkins over the last sixty years, one cannot help noticing that the proportion of believers and especially the proportion of Roman Catholics (insofar as these matters can be determined or inferred) is far greater among critics of Hopkins than it is among critics as a general group. Consider the usual indices: the institution, for example, where one holds a teaching post, or where one received one's undergraduate or graduate degrees, or where one publishes a book, or even where one attends a centenary conference.[13] In all of these instances the disproportion is striking. While we can never judge an individual on these grounds, we can begin to wonder about a group. Specifically, we can suspect that what Arnold said about the personal fallacy among Scottish readers of Robert Burns may also apply to the Catholic reader of Hopkins: "Let us boldly say that much of this poetry, a poetry dealing perpetually with Scotch drink, Scotch religion, and Scotch manners, a Scotchman's estimate is apt to be personal. A Scotchman is used to this world of Scotch drink, Scotch religion, and Scotch manners; he has a tenderness for it; he meets its poet half way."[14] The Catholic reader of Hopkins may incline to meet Hopkins half way, or even a bit more than half way.

Of course a purely independent or "objective" criticism is impossible. Furthermore the personal fallacy is not a danger limited only to Hopkins, and within Hopkins' work it is not limited only to his Catholicism.[15] But the struggle to keep the personal fallacy at bay may require more energy in Hopkins' case, especially because of the forthrightness with which he put forward his religious views and the importance he himself assigned to them. "Religion, you know, enters very deep," he wrote to Alexander Baillie; "in reality it is the deepest impression I have in speaking to people, that they are or that they are not of my religion."[16] We should be just as blunt in return and pose this question: how much would Hopkins have been read in the past, how much would he be read today, if we subtracted Catholic readers and the influence of Catholic institutions and of critics or teachers informed by Catholic traditions? To answer that question suggests the possible dimensions of the personal fallacy among readers of Hopkins.

But more important than either the historical or personal fallacy is a third constraint, one which we shall have to consider in some detail. I mean the constraint which arises from the fact that almost every reader of Hopkins now comes to him with or through a large body of Hopkins criticism, even if that criticism only appears indirectly by the way it informs teaching in high schools and colleges. Taken as a whole Hopkins criticism has been remarkably effective, remarkably well done. But if one approaches it with the eyes of a fresh reader, one becomes aware that alongside the strengths of this criticism there are also some important limitations.

To understand these limitations it may be useful to go back to the fourth and fifth decades of the century. Consider first the situation in the 1930s, the great decade for the publication of primary materials on Hopkins. An improved edition of the *Poems* [17] attracted many new readers who were able to meet the poetry unencumbered by the critical prejudices with which Robert Bridges had framed the text of the first edition. The poet's letters to Bridges, Canon Dixon, Coventry Patmore, and members of his family made their initial appearance,[18] as did his *Note-books and Papers*.[19] Here was exciting new information about instress and inscape, about sprung rhythm, about Duns Scotus, about the poet's moods and his methods. Add to this the publication of the first biography[20] and the raw material for a surge of enthusiasm for the poet was ready. Hopkins proved just the poet to please the critics and poets of the 1930s, as Todd Bender and others have shown.[21] Hopkins gained, and in the next decade was to continue to gain, a wide circle of admiring readers, including influential critics such as Leavis, Thomas, William Empson, I. A. Richards, W. H. Auden, and Robert Lowell, many of whom were also practicing poets.

While enthusiasm for Hopkins suffered no abatement during the 1940s (quite the reverse), still that decade saw the beginning of trends which mark Hopkins scholarship today. Suppose we focus on four major critical books which were published during the decade. All four were excellent in their own right. The value of looking at them more closely is that they allow us to see also the dangers of Hopkins criticism, because each signals and typifies a direction which many others have taken since.

In 1942 John Pick's *Gerard Manley Hopkins: Priest and Poet* appeared in its first edition. In that book Pick related Hopkins' life, especially his religious ideas and methods as formed by the Ignatian *Spiritual Exercises*, to his achievements as a poet. There was, Pick argued, no tension between Hopkins' vocation as a Jesuit priest and his avocation as a poet. The very title of the book emphasizes the indissoluble link: priest *and* poet, not priest *versus* poet as some apparently would have it.

Pick's argument was direct, forthright, effective. Only one difficulty: the target was in many ways a straw man. Some like

Bridges had been hostile to Hopkins' Catholicism. Others had bemoaned the fact that Hopkins wrote so little because of constraints on his time or a belief that his primary duties lay elsewhere. But such musings were not different than asking what might have been the effect on, say, Keats if he had not had to nurse his brother Tom or agonize over Fanny Brawne or worry about his financial future. Moreover, critics like Bernard Kelly and Christopher Devlin had taken pains to show Hopkins as all of a piece, mind and poetry, profession and hobby, religious formation and poetic theme. In short, Pick set out to slay a hydra of his own making.

Hydras do not die. As one reads over the books on Hopkins published since 1942 one is tempted to shout with Eliot's beleagured king "Will no one deliver me from this damned poet/priest?" A matter which was never more than idle speculation has assumed mythical status, so that almost every book published on Hopkins since then must slash at the dragon again, or at the very least disavow an interest in doing so. And when the dragon is attacked, we can be sure that unity will once again triumph over disunity, harmony over disharmony.[22]

So the pervasiveness of the poet/priest theme in criticism since Pick helps us to recognize the first limitation of that criticism: its repetition of an outworn theme or subject. Certain themes and subjects—Hopkins' "Victorianness" is another common example—come up again and again, often not so much because there is a problem to be solved but because we have been habituated to thinking that comments on these themes are *de riguer*. Repetitiveness of theme and subject brings in its train repetitiveness of allusion. Breathes there a critic so free that he or she has not somewhere buttressed an argument by quoting from Hopkins' letter to Bridges of 21 August 1877 or his letter to Canon Dixon of 22 December 1880 or his retreat notes of January 1889? If the reader has ever had the experience of somehow knowing, before getting there, exactly which passage a critic is about to cite, then he or she will recognize the danger to which I am pointing.

The Pick volume was followed three years later by *Gerard Manley Hopkins*, a collection of essays put out by the Kenyon

Critics (Norfolk, CN: New Directions, 1945).   The Kenyon Critics of course did exactly what we would expect of them: they searched for tension and irony and paradox, they gave close readings, they detected a sensibility. The result was often very insightful criticism which served Hopkins' reputation quite well. But at the same time one senses the not-so-gentle pressure of the Procrustean bed. Hopkins *will* have irony, the close reading *will* reveal a conflict. The book illustrates the old principle that if you look for something long enough in a work of literature you will be pretty sure to find it.

The Kenyon Critics looked happily for their paradoxes. But they were just the type of many others who have attempted to read Hopkins according to a reigning critical fashion. If it was New Criticism in 1945, it was Chicago-school form criticism in the 1950s and Prague-school structuralism in the 1960s and linguistic analysis in the 1970s and deconstruction in the 1980s.[23] And even now some new critical fashion slouches toward New Haven or Ann Arbor or Palo Alto, urgent for birth. One need not belittle schools of criticism, for each has taught us something valuable about Hopkins. Nor can one argue that Hopkins has been singled out unfairly, because similar calipers have measured every other important poet. Rather the point is that when we survey Hopkins criticism as a whole we cannot help but notice this second type, the critic who appropriates a currently popular hermeneutics and tries to discover what it will yield when applied to Hopkins. If the result is often a trip down Pope's "high priori road," we are not surprised. In these cases too the sensation is frequently one of being able to "write" the book in the mind's eye, this time after reading its introduction.[24]

Another three years into the decade came *Gerard Manley Hopkins: A Critical Essay Towards the Understanding of His Poetry* (London: Oxford University Press, 1948) by the Dutch Jesuit W. A. M. Peters. Father Peters contended that the best *vade mecum* to Hopkins' poetry would be a copy of Duns Scotus. He very ably demonstrated the power of Scotus' influence on Hopkins' thought and practice and he established the close link between inscape and the Scotan doctrine of *haecceitas*.

Observe the method. First one examines biographical

information and the poet's letters and private papers, looking for a key to understanding the poet's practice. After finding a key one uses it to unlock the secrets of each of the important poems. That method has served many other scholars quite well. Sometimes the key resides in Hopkins' education, sometimes in his formation as a Jesuit, sometimes in his theology or philosophy. The results are often marvelously illuminating. But in the wrong hands, or in the right hands at the wrong time, the part comes to stand for the whole and we lose sight of the other dimensions of the poet's work. In other words, Peters' book, useful as it was, sometimes ran aground on shoals which have endangered many critics since then: it became reductive. And we can therefore call reductionism a third danger to which Hopkins criticism is liable.

The final year of the decade brought with it the completion of W. H. Gardner's two-volume *Gerard Manley Hopkins: A Study of Poetic Idiosyncrasy in Relation to Poetic Truth,*[25] a work which together with his edition of the poetry gave substance to the claim that he was the leading Hopkins scholar of his time.[26] This study had many virtues. Especially important was the connection which Gardner made between Hopkins' seeming eccentricities and the poetic traditions out of which they came. Gardner showed us a poet who understood his craft, who exprimented but only within the limits prescribed by traditions which he had absorbed and which he deeply respected. The very comprehensiveness of Gardner's approach—he included biography, metrics, diction, imagery, theme, source, and explication—served as an index both to its ambition and to its value.

But Gardner's work also signals a subtle but important change in assumptions about the audience. The contribution of the Kenyon Critics a few years before had been more typical of the pioneering efforts in Hopkins criticism. While several of the Kenyon Critics may have held academic positions, they were also many of them practicing poets, and they wrote as members of a broad literary community addressing other members of that community. The same assumption had informed the earlier work of critics such as Leavis, Empson, Richards, Eliot, and Read. But with Gardner the audience narrows perceptibly. His discussions of onomatopoetic theory, of Welsh *cywydd* and synapheia and the influence of Pindar, presume and draw heavily upon "scholarship" in the more limited sense of that term. After all, Gardner's work began as a Ph.D. dissertation and it retains much of that flavor. Specifically, the assumption seems to be that the reader, both of Hopkins and of Gardner, is a member of the academic community either as scholar or student. And that assumption has continued to dominate Hopkins criticism in the years since 1949. There are a few exceptions perhaps—Geoffrey Grigson and John Wain come to mind—but the trend is everywhere evident. Meanwhile the practicing poet and the general reader of poetry are no longer served as well by the published commentary on the poet as they were during the first three decades after 1918.

To sum up then: since the 1940s Hopkins criticism, that amber within which all of the poems are now preserved, has been at times repetitive, faddish, reductive, and narrowly professional. While these liabilities also mar the criticism of other poets, the pervasiveness of them does not tell against their importance.

In the future some of these constraints on our reading of Hopkins may, fortune or time favoring, dissolve, just as the historical fallacy has already begun to do. But if we turn our attention to the text, in other words to the obstacles which the poems themselves offer to those who first read them, we come to barriers which will always have to be faced so long as Hopkins has readers who are new to his work.

The most obvious difficulty for a new reader of Hopkins is the one which has been experienced (and often complained about) for such a long time: his unusual poetic style. Bridges registered the first objection to it, both to the poet and later to the world at large, when he faulted Hopkins for "oddity" and "obscurity." Bridges' description hardly bears improving upon: frequent ellipsis, destructions of ordinary syntax, odd rhymes, word coinages, obscure diction, extraordinary condensations of language. These "faults" were for Bridges eccentricities which the reader would have to learn to forgive. To his list we can add some others, such as disruption of the usual grammatical functions of words or the frequency of assonance, alliteration, and internal rhyme. To read Hopkins for the first time is indeed to enter a world counter, original, and strange.

Yet the unusualness of Hopkins' style created more of a barrier for Bridges and his contemporaries than it does for us. The reaction to Hopkins by his early readers much resembles the typical response to a strikingly original composer, such as Beethoven in the nineteenth century or Schoenberg in the twentieth. At first horror, then grudging acceptance, then perhaps approval and even admiration: that has been Hopkins' fate as well as theirs. Like concertgoers, we poetry readers have managed to learn and to adjust. I daresay the new reader of Hopkins in 1989 meets obstacles no more severe than those faced by, say, the new reader of Donne or of Eliot, where the archaic diction and contrived metaphors of the former or the dry, allusive, detached voice of the latter prove just as strange and just as formidable to the novice as anything Hopkins wrote. The history of English literature does offer examples of writers who have so violated stylistic conventions that they no longer gain a hearing. (The Joyce of *Finnegan's Wake* or the Pound of some of the *Cantos* may well fall into this category.) But Hopkins cannot be numbered among them. Hopkins will never be an "easy" poet, but his stylistic features, however much they may need to be explained to each new generation, will never prove to be more than a temporary barrier to a fuller appreciation of his poems.

Of the impermanence of the next limitation, however, one which grows out of his stylistic features, I am not so sure. Hopkins designed his poems so that they would offer an experience which was preeminently aural. The poet himself never tired of emphasizing the importance of this feature. "My verse is less to be read than heard, as I have told you before," he reminds Bridges in one letter. Despite the reminder he has to repeat the lesson a few months later: ". . . you must not slovenly read [*Eurydice*] with the eyes but with your ears, as if the paper were declaiming it at you."[27] Such exhortations appear frequently in Hopkins' letters to Bridges and to others. We know too that Hopkins composed aloud, weighing the sounds and their relationship to each other, and that he gave fully expressive renderings of the poems to those with whom he shared them in person.[28] His most consistent defense even of his stylistic oddities was they they would disappear when the poems were declaimed oratorically.

Yet, like Bridges, we forget. We read rather than listen. We teach others to read rather than hear. Despite the occasional nod to Hopkins' principles, we introduce new readers to him in our schools and colleges by explaining the text rather than recreating the sound. Only in a few rare moments, when we try reading him aloud perhaps, or when we listen to one of the old Caedmon records or attend one of the Hopkins one-man plays,[29] do we feel a stirring of the kind of response Hopkins wanted to call forth from his hearers.

Whether or not this "silence" is an irreversible condition of our existence, we at least need to acknowledge the way in which we truncate our experience of so aural a poet as Hopkins by limiting ourselves to reading him. When we read or teach Hopkins as a disembodied text, even more when we write an article or a book on him, our relationship to our subject is like that of a musicologist studying Mozart. Musicology has a real and an important place, and the labors of its better practitioners provide an incalculable benefit. But we would never dream of substituting a musical score or a text about Mozart for the experience of hearing his music played. Only in performance does the music retain its vitality, only in performance does it win a new generation of admirers.

So far I have discussed this limitation as if the responsibility for it lay solely with us. But after all it was Hopkins who deliberately created a poetry that depended so heavily upon the ear, it was Hopkins who employed such an array of polyphonic devices that only a complete "listening" could do them justice. For most poets the adjuration to hear them rather than read them becomes a truism—if we and they suffer from our inevitable failure to do so, the suffering can be borne. With Hopkins the case is otherwise. The poet himself is the one who determined that his works would occupy that rare space where text ends and performance begins, and he did so at a time and in places and circumstances where his wish for a declamatory reading stood very little chance of ever being fulfilled by others. Dylan Thomas affords an instructive comparison. Thomas too wanted to be heard as well as read. But he had both the means and the will to create the effect he wanted, and through his many public readings, his radio performances, and his recordings he educated our ears to hear him properly. The measure of his success lies in the fact that many of us cannot now read a poem like "And Death Shall Have No Dominion" without in our "mind's ear" hearing that rich and melodious voice through which we first encountered the work.

There is still another limitation to Hopkins: the slenderness of the material we have to use.

Of the poetry itself one can point to perhaps a couple of dozen poems which are significant works in reasonably finished form. For the rest we must make do mostly with fragments: letters, snatches of recollections, a few sermons, journal entries that cover only certain years.[30]

Such a slender collection has implications for the range of a poet, an issue to which we will come shortly. But the most immediate danger is the temptation it offers to misrepresent, to mistake the part we now read for the whole of what Hopkins said and wrote. Think first of what we know Hopkins wrote but which is missing: some of his poems; the majority of his family letters; portions of his correspondence with Bridges, Dixon, and Patmore, along with the reciprocal side of the correspondence (except in Dixon's case) which would give the rhetorical context for Hopkins' responses; letters to other friends, some of whom we know about, others of whom we probably do not; the majority of his sermons; most of the notes from lectures he heard; many of the notes and texts for lectures he gave, both at Roehampton and in Dublin; the drafts of his unpublished books and articles on subjects ranging from science to Greek metrics and Egyptology; many of his retreat notes; portions of his spiritual journal, a counterpart to his quotidian journal and the one where he recorded the deepest and most sensitive events of his inner journey. Then think of what we know Hopkins himself destroyed: drafts of his early poems (the so-called "slaughter of innocents"); miscellaneous notes and papers; countless drafts of letters (the extant letters frequently note how earlier drafts were thrown away because the writer felt he had been too blunt or impolitic—exactly the reason we would like to have them). Subtract also from the material we do have the long dutiful commentaries on poems by others, the social chit-chat, the discussions of music, the political rant.

What remains, when compared to the possible whole, is small. Put simply, these texts must carry a disproportionate weight, a weight which in good critical conscience they ought not have to bear. If modern criticism has taught us about the silences within a text, how much more do we have to recognize the silences of many other kinds in this poet's *oeuvre*. The recognition is humbling. Contemporary students of classical Greek literature, for example, know that the texts handed down to us constitute only a very small and perhaps unrepresentative fraction of the literature produced in those long-ago centuries. They are somewhat chary, therefore (certainly more so than earlier scholars had been), of offering important-sounding generalizations about matters like "the meaning of Greek tragedy." Faced on the one hand with only a fraction of Hopkins and on the other hand with a consuming desire to understand and then generalize about those wonderfully haunting poems, we are not always as judicious as we might be, do not always acknowledge the frailty of our evidence.

This slenderness of materials also suggests the final limitation of Hopkins' texts, their small range. Here we need to examine two kinds of range. The first is range of form. In his mature poetry Hopkins restricted himself almost exclusively to the sonnet, either the Petrarchan or his "curtal" adaptation. We have besides the sonnets an ode and a few other poems of mixed or indeterminate form. The rest are fragments, translations, and poems in Welsh or Latin. Put that body of poetry over against any of Hopkins' contemporaries: Tennyson, for example, who wrote elegies, odes, sonnets, verse narratives, idylls, ballads, verse dramas, lyrics, dramatic monologues, and even a "monodrama" and a "medley"; or Browning, who like Hopkins had a favorite form but in addition to his dramatic monologues wrote verse dramas, narratives, sonnets, poetic addresses, lyrics, and "parleyings." Even Rossetti, who was similar to Hopkins in his preference for the sonnet, his small output, and his treatment of the muse as a part-time dalliance, managed to employ such diverse forms as the literary ballad, the dramatic monologue, the lyric, and the ballade. If control of the poetic medium includes mastery of some or many of the diverse forms which it offers, then Hopkins' achievement must be found in some degree wanting.

Range of subject is almost equally limited. It would not be unfair to say that with a few exceptions Hopkins' mature poetry confines itself to two subjects, nature and religion. And since many of the nature poems have a religious dimension, and many of the religious poems draw upon images from nature, the restriction becomes even more pronounced. Perhaps we can dramatize the matter by realizing how many areas of life Hopkins' poetry ignores. Almost nothing, for example, about family life. Nothing about that most constant of all subjects, the relationship between the sexes. Almost nothing about social life or political life, this last despite the fact that Hopkins was a man of at times passionate political convictions. Very little travel poetry ("Inversnaid" might be the exception), although Hopkins was a frequent vacationer. Very little about other people. Nothing about matters historical or philosophical, very little about subjects musical or scientific or artistic or literary, despite the fact that Hopkins was *au courant* in all of these areas. When one thinks of Tennyson, whose poetry ranged over these subjects and more, who was both responsive to the movements of his time and anxious to interpret them for others, the difference is striking.

If we think about these textual limitations taken as a group, we cannot help but speculate on the causes of them. Certainly one cause was the poet's isolation. This isolation stemmed partly from his chosen vocation, which brought him fourteen different assignments in the twenty-one years of his membership in the Society of Jesus. Such frequent shifts of location disrupted friendships and made it impossible for this very lonely man to have any sense of rootedness. (Remembering his choice in 1868 between the Jesuits and the Benedictines, one wonders what would have been the poet's lot had he joined the latter order with its vow of stability of place.) We can add to these disruptions the distance which his religion and his vows—especially of celibacy and obedience—placed between him and many of his earlier ties.

But the isolation was more than just a matter of circumstance. Hopkins courted isolation too: not just by his choice of vocation or even of personality (to the extent that personality reflects conscious and unconscious decisions), but also by the deliberate limitation of his "audience." As a poet Hopkins chose to have the attention only of Robert Bridges, and later of Canon Dixon and Coventry Patmore. These readers had much in common with him: school and university associations (Dixon, Bridges), clerical profession (Dixon), mutual friends (Bridges), religion (Patmore), even humility before Christ as "the only just literary critic" (Dixon, Patmore). Frank and helpful as these men often were, they could not offer the broad spectrum of response that would have come from publication or from a more diversified circle of readers.

Hopkins' letters show that he wanted very much to win the approval of these readers. But he also distinguished carefully between his chosen few and the broad public. "I do not write for the public," he tells Bridges. "You are my public and I hope to convert you."[31] That sounds independent and courageous until one realizes that Hopkins harbored a suspicion of the public which bordered on disdain. Time and again the poet's letters reject suggestions from Bridges and others about how he could modify certain passages in the interests of greater intelligibility and a wider readership. It is a rare Hopkins poem that was meant to be read by anyone outside of his circle (somewhat of an affront to us, if you think about it). Whenever he does aim more broadly, he dismisses the product and implies contempt both for the audience and the effort: "The sonnet (I say it snortingly) aims at being intelligible."

Isolation was compounded by stubbornness. To read the letters is to acknowledge that Sir Robert Stewart had it right:

> Indeed my dear Padre . . . I saw, ere we had conversed ten minutes on our first meeting, that you are one of those special pleaders who never believe yourself wrong in any respect. You always excuse yourself for anything I object to in your writing or music so I think it is a pity to disturb you in your happy dreams of perfect ability. . . . [You] are impatient of correction, when you have previously made up your mind on any point. [32]

The letters also suggest that to the stubbornness must be added a set of strong prejudices. Keats was too sensual, Tennyson too Parnassian, Swinburne too archaic. Byron was a barbarian, Whitman a scoundrel. Like many sensitive and intelligent people, Hopkins expressed convictions about his own abilities partly through attacks on the achievements of others.

We should recognize an additional influence: the fact, too often ignored, that Hopkins was not after all a professional poet. I noted earlier how the "poet versus priest" controversy involves a misunderstanding. The misunderstanding grows partly out of a natural confusion between the importance *we* place on Hopkins' poetry and the importance *he* placed on it. There could be no poet vs. priest simply because the contest would have been unequal—poetry for Hopkins was never a vocation, never a profession, never a commitment in any way equivalent to his dedication to his ministry.

Because we value his poetry so much, we tend to overlook Hopkins' own attitude toward it. He loved reading poetry (only someone with that love could have spent countless hours writing out elaborate criticisms of such a minor poet as Canon Dixon). He loved writing poetry (only a few of the late sonnets elicit from him any indication that creating poems—as distinct from copying them—was ever anything but a pleasure). And he developed interesting and defensible theories about poetry. But consider the usual criteria which would mark someone as a professional in any activity. Devotion of time? Even at the height of his productivity Hopkins never averaged more than a half dozen or so completed poems a year. Despite a busy schedule he had time to compose, as he himself admitted. Consistency of interest? Hopkins alternated periods of poetic activity with long stretches of comparative inactivity. Besides the seven years of elected silence (1868-1875), he experienced many long periods when he chose not to write (during his tertianship at Roehampton) or when he had distractions either from other duties (during the early months in Liverpool) or from depression of spirits (e.g., the late Dublin years). Yet nowhere do we hear any expressions of great regret. He never seems to have found it difficult to give up writing and never seems to have missed it very much when he returns to it.

Singlemindedness of interest? As an undergraduate at Oxford Hopkins gave more attention to his future as an artist than to his poetry, as a professor in Dublin he gave more to his music. We would force the evidence if we said that among all of his avocations poetry was any more than *primus inter pares*. Absorption in his craft? Hopkins admitted that his poetry reading was more deep than wide, and he made little effort to keep up with contemporary developments.

The simple truth is that, in Hopkins' time and in our own, others have valued his poetry more than he did. If Jerome Buckley is right to include among the essential attributes of a major poet "dedication to the poet's calling,"[33] then Hopkins falls short. Poetry, he tells Bridges quite frankly, is a luxury. The necessity was his commitment to being a Jesuit priest. If the priesthood was his profession and if writing verses did not belong to that profession per se, then he could cultivate poetry only as an avocation—if you will, as a hobby. Those who ascribe Hopkins' misery during his years in Dublin to a faltering of his creative instinct have it backwards. The source of his self-torment was his belief that he had failed as a priest; the resulting depression made it impossible to write poetry, on the principle so well enunciated by Coleridge in his "Dejection" ode.

Of course Hopkins was a man of many virtues: tenderness, patience, humor, good will, and an abundance of sympathy. But when one takes into account his isolation, his stubbornness, and his comparative indifference to the fate of his poetry (again the comparison with Tennyson proves instructive), the picture emerges of a man and an artist so trapped within his own "wall of personality" that communication with others becomes extraordinarily difficult. Perhaps all of the constraints on our reading of Hopkins, whether from outside the texts or from the texts themselves, can be subsumed under this one core problem of relationship with audience. If even his closest friends such as Bridges —a man from the same social milieu who went to school with Hopkins and visited and corresponded with him often—could so frequently misunderstand the poet, then we can suspect some basic failure in rhetorical adjustment. As *rhetor* Hopkins could have learned much from his master,

Newman. The reader of Hopkins' poetry often has the curiously paradoxical experience, on the one hand of feeling the "bidding" power of the work and the desire of the poet to reach out to the reader (Elisabeth Schneider is surely right in saying that Hopkins did want to be understood[34]), and on the other hand of grasping at something or someone that moves further away the closer we come.

By way of summary: we have in Hopkins a poet who is preeminently aural, but instead we read; we have a poet who more than most provokes our curiosity, but who has left us only a small amount of material on which we are tempted to over-rely. We also have a poet whose narrowness of range both in form and subject limit his achievement. Add to these limitations the fact that we approach Hopkins through a body of criticism which has provided much but which has often fallen victim to the historical or personal fallacy and the major achievements of which, given its repetitive, faddish, reductive, and narrowly professional tendencies, may lie mostly in the past.

If that were all, Hopkins might well deserve the neglect into which he seems to be falling. But limitations must be weighed against a poet's enduring strengths—a subject which we now can address.

❧

Although many would wish to extend the list, those who love Hopkins can I think agree on four qualities as the virtues most characteristic of his poetry: originality, command of language, immediacy, and craftsmanship. We shall consider each in turn.

Of these four virtues, perhaps the chief glory of Hopkins' poetry is its striking originality. Our first awareness upon reading him is of originality of voice. Simply, no other voice in English poetry sounds like this:

> I caught this morning morning's minion, king-
> dom of daylight's dauphin, dapple-dawn-drawn Falcon

or like this:

> Nor mouth had, no nor mind, expressed
> What héart héard of, ghost guéssed: . . .

or this:

> But ah, but O thou terrible, why wouldst thou rude on me
> Thy wring-earth right foot rock? lay a lionlimb against me?

In his best work the poet has a voice which is singular, fresh, inimitable.

Just how distinctive that voice is we can discover by putting Hopkins next to some of his contemporaries. There is nothing in him of the laureate:

> The splendour falls on castle walls
> And snowy summits old in story;
> The long light shakes across the lakes,
> And the wild cataract leaps in glory.

While he is often sad to the point of despair, Hopkins' melancholy has none of the studied languor of Arnold's:

> How sweet to feel, on the boon air,
> All our unquiet pulses cease!
> To feel that nothing can impair
> The gentleness, the thirst for peace—

Browning speaks in many voices lest one good one should corrupt the world; but, despite the variety of masks, we have little difficulty finding the right key for reading him, either as he speaks *in propria persona:*

> This world's no blot for us,
> Nor blank; it means intensely, and means good.

or as he speaks through a Hyde-like alter ego:

She thanked man, —good! but thanked
Somehow—I know not how—as if she ranked
My gift of a nine-hundred-years-old name
With anybody's gift. Who'd stoop to blame
This sort of trifling?

No mature poem by Hopkins could ever be mistaken for a work by these or other Victorian poets. Nor is his voice distinct only from his contemporaries. If one looks backward, to the Romantics and then beyond, or forward, to the Modernists and then nearer, the singularity remains. Hopkins is *sui generis*.

Furthermore this voice of Hopkins has what I call the power of *endearment*. For a poet to have staying power with us he or she must have a voice which touches us in the same way the voices of friends and family touch us. In fact, psychologists tell us that the first thing a newborn baby learns to recognize is voice. We become deeply yet unconsciously attached to the voices of those we love, and nothing becomes more closely identified with them than the sound of their words. More than just a function of pitch or timber or accent, voices function metonymically—*become* them (in both senses of that word)— and endear them. Anyone who has lost a family member through death and then encountered his or her voice on a tape recording knows how deeply affecting that experience can be, more affecting than even picture or object would occasion. Poetry works the same way. If poets can through their voices mark off their *selves* in the poetry—establish their *haecceitas,* if you like the Scotan terms—then they can become lodged in our minds and hearts the way people become lodged. Singularity makes endearment possible. If a poet's voice does not strike our ear as distinctive and "real," it stands little chance of rooting itself in our affections.

This singularity of Hopkins' voice and its consequent power of endearment have been felt by generations of readers. Any attempt to explain the voice is doomed to at least partial failure. Of course we can list adjectives, but they fall short, are not *it*. By the same token we can name the devices by which he creates the voice, such as alliteration and assonance and colloquial diction; yet *how* never substitutes adequately for *what*. These relative failures should not distract us from acknowledging that few who have felt the power of that voice would doubt its uniqueness, its ability to make us aware of itself and to move us.

Moreover Hopkins prized this distinctiveness of voice and deliberately cultivated it. Partly the effort grew out of an awareness of his own individuality:

> ... I consider my selfbeing, my consciousness and feeling of myself, of *I* and *me* above and in all things, which is more distinctive than the taste of ale or alum, more distinctive than the smell of walnut leaf or camphor. . . . Nothing else in nature comes near this unspeakable stress of pitch, distinctiveness, and selving, this selfbeing of my own. Nothing explains it or resembles it, except so far as this, that other men to themselves have the same feeling.[35]

Partly too it grew out of his desire to avoid what he called Parnassian, the language of poets who have submitted to the style and especially to the diction of poets who have preceded them. For Hopkins this echoing of other poets amounts to a plague: "The echoes are a disease of education, literature is full of them; but they remain a disease, an evil."[36] This aversion may account for the fact that Hopkins has proven surprisingly resistent to certain strains of modern criticism. The task of finding out how his poems amplify other texts, how they cannot be understood except as commentary on those other texts, becomes exceedingly difficult in his case. Few poets have done more to make precarious the venture of establishing "intertextuality" or proclaiming an authorless text.

Nor is Hopkins' originality a matter only of voice—it also characterizes his vision. We often find in his choice of subject and his development of theme a fresh approach, a new and singular way of looking at things. As an example, consider the early poem "Spring and Death," written about the time he entered Oxford. Much of it shows the work of an apprentice (the iambic quadrameters, the triplets, the Pre-Raphaelite mannerisms). But for a poem by a newly matriculated eighteen-year-old student we find some unusual turns. The juxtaposition of

spring and death in the very title alerts us to expect a disruption
of our usual associations. For the speaker spring does have its
customary lush, damp, and fragrant qualities. But in a dream
he encounters Death personified, who marks the flowers which
he will destroy in the fall. If the first surprise is the presence of
death in a time of joyous rebirth, a second awaits:

> But the Spring-tide pass'd the same;
> Summer was as full of flame;
> Autumn-time no earlier came.
> And the flowers that he had tied,
> As I mark'd, not always died
> Sooner than their mates. . . .[37]

and then a third, as the speaker thinks of the predestined
flowers:

> . . . and yet
> Their fall was fuller of regret:
> It seem'd so hard and dismal thing,
> Death, to mark them in the Spring. [17]

Nevertheless the tone of that final address blends regret and
acceptance, not anger and protest. At each point in the poem
our usual expectation of a poem on spring has been thwarted.
The young Hopkins avoids the obvious, redefines the theme,
hints finally at a mystery.

If Hopkins could give a fresh turn to so common a subject
as a schoolboy poem on spring, we can anticipate an even more
inventive poet in his mature works. Donald Walhout in the
fourth essay of this volume demonstrates the way Hopkins
kept in such careful balance the often opposing powers of
freedom and necessity. Only a mind which penetrates the
empty cliché and is unsparing in the conduct of its own self-
examination could place the poet, as Walhout shows that
Hopkins is placed, "among the small number of writers who
[experience] the tension and yet the reality of both of these
poles."

Another of Hopkins' enduring strengths, one which has its

origin in his search for a distinctive voice, is his remarkable command of language. If, as Denis Donoghue has recently argued, the very function of a poem is to prolong our contemplation of its words, then each of Hopkins' mature works stands as a powerful objet d'art. He taxes the language to its last farthing:

> wherever an elm arches,
> Shivelights and shadowtackle in long I lashes lace,
>   lance, and pair.
> Delightfully the bright wind boisterous I ropes,
>   wrestles, beats earth bare
> Of yestertempest's creases; in pool and rutpeel parches
> Squandering ooze to squeezed I dough, crust, dust;
>   stanches, starches
> Squandroned masks and manmarks I treadmire toil there
> Footfretted in it. Million-fuelèd, I nature's bonfire
>   burns on. [181]

These lines from "That Nature is a Heraclitean Fire" encapsulate Hopkins' techniques for stretching the limits of the English language. He makes the reader accept the word coinages as spontaneous, inevitable. James Milroy has demonstrated convincingly that Hopkins best exemplifies the everyday language "purified"—more so than even Wordsworth does.[38]

This heightening of ordinary speech is of course one of those features of Hopkins' verse that makes him seem so much our contemporary. Perhaps his modernity in poetic language develops out of his obsession with language itself —an obsession which our own time has pushed to its limits. Todd Bender shows in an essay earlier in this volume how Hopkins thought long and deeply about language, and pursued his inquiries to a point where he felt comfortable "correcting" the most distinguished etymologist of his day. Whether or not Hopkins was right about "scope" and "scape" is beside the point; the important fact was that he recognized language as a pliable instrument, and he valued words not just for their denotative or connotative powers but also for their "properties," their ability to suggest by sound or by analogy other words and other meanings. One need only read Hopkins' letters and journals to appreciate his sensitivity to the effects his words could have.

Nor should we forget the aural dimension of Hopkins' language, discussed earlier. For someone with such a command of sound, Hopkins still surprises us with his restraint, his avoidance of the cheap effect. He does not let alliteration and assonance trivialize the poetry by turning it into an incantation. In lines like these the magnificent sound never tempts us to neglect the sense:

> Wiry and white-fiery and whírlwind-swivellèd snow
> Spins to the widow-making unchilding unfathering deeps. [113]

> Áll félled, félled, are áll félled;
> Of a fresh and following folded rank
> Not spared, not one
> That dandled a sandalled
> Shadow that swam or sank
> On meadow and river and wind-wandering weed-winding bank. [142]

> My cries heave, herds-long; huddle in a main, a chief-
> Woe, wórld-sorrow; on an áge-old ánvil wínce and síng—
> Then lull, then leave off. [167]

Hopkins plays with all the stops pulled out. To change the metaphor, he is an aerialist of the word performing without a net. There is an occasional crash landing, as in the concluding lines of "Harry Ploughman":

> Churlsgrace too, chíld of Amansstrength, how it hángs or hurls
> Them—broad in bluff hide his frowning feet lashed! raced
> With, along them, cragiron under and cold furls—
> With-a-fountain's shining-shot furls. [177]

But for the most part the poet emerges unscathed, creator of a poetic language that—once properly *heard*—cannot be forgotten. As Agnes Donohue illustrates in her contribution to this book, sounds in Hopkins' poetic language function in remarkably complex ways, even helping to define character, such as the barbaric but self-conscious and tormented villain Caradoc of "St. Winefred's Well." The memorability of Hopkins' words comes not from their sound taken in isolation but from the way sound helps to establish meaning.

An additional feature of Hopkins' language, one that grows naturally out of the respect he gave to words, is its sacramentality. Margaret Ellsberg in her recent book has shown how Hopkins always wanted to bring into play this sacramental dimension of words by allowing them to "transubstantiate."[39] It may be more than accidental that those qualities of Hopkins' language that Ellsberg calls "baroque"—his exuberance, his vigor, his explosiveness, his desire for spectacle—coexist in Hopkins with a theological sensibility that has its origin in the seventeenth-century Council of Trent.

A third enduring strength of Hopkins is what I call his *immediacy*, his absorption in the *now*. Other writers more characteristically live in the then (of the past) or the when (of the future). Among Hopkins' contemporaries we think of Carlyle, for example, who cannot recognize the present except in the light of the (better) past or the (dire) future; or of Ruskin, who cannot even observe the weather without putting it on trial for what it portends; or of Tennyson, who bemoans humanity's descent from a purer past into the "hot swamp of voluptuousness" yet paradoxically looks forward to "the vision of the world, and all the wonder that would be." In his poetry Hopkins is almost never nostalgic. We find in him no sentimentality about past eras like Rossetti's medieval world or Swinburne's pre-Christian Hellenistic age. Nor does he offer any equally sentimental idealization à la Macaulay of what "progress" will accomplish. While Hopkins may sometimes use apocalyptic imagery and borrow apocalyptic themes[40] he is quite different in the way he uses them. Destruction and creation are for Hopkins continuous, the world is always ending and always being reborn. If a ship founders, the occasion brings with it both physical death and spiritual new life, both terror and hope.

Therefore in a Hopkins poem we experience what Patricia Ball calls "his ability to keep us in the presence of the thing itself."[41] At harvest time the stooks "barbarous in beauty" and the "silk-sack clouds" are real stooks and real clouds, vividly present to us. Felix Randal is not an idealized type of the brave and honest workingman; like the real human being he is, he curses, he sobs, he pines, and eventually he breaks. Even the "black hours" and "cliffs of fall" which the poet encounters within himself have an almost shocking immediacy. And curiously enough this quality in Hopkins is precisely what takes his poems out of the Heraclitean flux, precisely what makes them live in a "time out of time" because, as Carol Christ has pointed out, only by this intense immediacy can one leap to the transcendental.[42] In the opening essay of this book David Downes dramatizes this virtue very effectively by showing how Hopkins appeals to modern readers who share this consciousness. The very immediacy of a Hopkins poem, his concentration on this moment, this place, this scene, frees it of its historical accidents. In tasting every moment, says Downes, Hopkins through his poetry textualizes himself—and thus, in ways that would have surprised him very much, triumphs over the circumstances of his often dismal and banal everyday life.

A corollary of this quest for the immediate in Hopkins is the sensuousness of his verse. The natural world he seizes directly, physically, whether it is

> . . . a juicy and jostling shock
> Of bluebells sheaved in May [141]

or the time

> When drop-of-blood-and-foam-dapple
> Bloom lights the orchard-apple
>   And thicket and thorp are merry
>   With silver-surfèd cherry. [140]

His most insistent appeal is for us to *see:*

> Look, look: a May-mess, like on orchard boughs!
> Look! March-bloom, like on mealed-with-yellow
>   sallows! [129]

But we also hear "the air of angels" in Henry Purcell's music,

smell the "Comforting smell breathed at the very entering" of
the cottage remembered "In the Valley of the Elwy," taste the
bitterness of "God's most deep decree," feel the

> Wild air, world-mothering air,
> Nestling me everywhere,
> That each eyelash or hair
> Girdles. . . . [158]

Nor does Hopkins exclude the human body from this natural
world, whether it is the "downdolfinry and bellbright bodies"
of the young boys at the swimming hole in "Epithalamion" or
Harry Ploughman's

> Hard as hurdle arms, with a broth of goldish flue
> Breathed wound; the rack of ribs; the scooped flank; lank
> Rope-over thigh; knee-nave; and barrelled shank— [177]

The term "photoeroticism" which John D. Rosenberg bestowed
on Ruskin applies with equal force to Hopkins, because the
eye—not just the physical eye but also the mind's eye, the eye
with which we his readers can also see—proves to be a source
of the most exquisite pleasure, a pleasure made more intense
for both writers by asceticism or self-deprivation in other parts
of their lives. (The parallel with Ruskin also reminds us of the
similarities between Hopkins and Ruskin's idol Turner. Both
artists had a way of distorting "reality" in the interest of deeper
truths about that reality and their own experience of it.)

Another corollary is one to which we—following Hopkins—
can give the very Victorian term *earnestness*. The reader finds
in Hopkins a determination to be candid if not almost confron-
tive which is rare in the poetry of his age or any age. Most of the
time we overhear a poet as he or she "ruminates aloud," as it
were; Hopkins speaks to us directly, feelingly, beseechingly. In
fact he sought this quality precisely because of the importance
he assigned to it: "[A] touchstone of the highest or most living
art is seriousness; not gravity but the being in earnest with your
subject—reality."[43] He echoes Arnold in that sentence but turns

him upside down. Seriousness for Hopkins is not the "high seriousness" which Arnold demanded—Hopkins dismisses that as mere gravity of tone. He requires instead seriousness about oneself and one's own experience, exactly the kind of "dialogue of the mind with itself" that Oxford's Professor of Poetry had observed and then condemned in his own earlier efforts. Arnold damns the Romantic enterprise, at least in his poetics; Hopkins accepts the revolution as a *fait accompli*. In fact the failure to take oneself seriously, the "want of earnest," was for Hopkins "the deepest fault a work of art can have."[44]

Yet the essay by Alison Sulloway earlier in the volume points to a quality that softens this image of the earnest, almost aggressive Hopkins. For her a distinctive feature of the poetry is its rendering of an "archetypally feminine self," a self that manifests itself in many poems through a variety of voices and devices. This feature may prove one of the strongest guarantors of Hopkins' perdurability as a poet. On the one hand it connects Hopkins through archetypes to a poetic tradition which cannot be effaced because of its foundation in an indestructible core of the human psyche. On the other hand it points forward, toward the increasing emphasis which our own century now places on the integration of masculine and feminine selves. A poet like Hopkins who understands intuitively the need for this integration and transcendence seems likely to fare better in an age deeply influenced by Carl Jung. Regarding the permanence of the Romantic revolution, Hopkins was right and Arnold was wrong; if this newer revolution proves equally permanent, as I believe it will, then Hopkins will be read with enthusiasm in a way he never would have foreseen. (This would also be one of the few ways in which he wrote better than he knew.)

As a final enduring strength of Hopkins' work I would point to its *perfection*. Partly this perfection is a function of both his small output and the brevity of his finished works. Hopkins has rigorous standards: "... if we criticize in the rigour of justice no human work except short pieces of music and small examples of the arts of design could stand."[45] The larger the work, the greater the chance for imperfection. One might for the right reason undertake the risks inherent in a larger work; but—

especially if an artist has a temperament which does not permit living with imperfections in his or her work—preference must be given to shorter pieces where this drive for perfection has a better chance of fulfillment. Driven in just this way, Hopkins concentrated on giving shorter poems an extraordinary degree of finish. Anyone who has seen drafts of his poems knows the laborious revision to which he subjected them, and we have besides his own testimony about the process.[46]

Hopkins' objections to the Parnassian language of poets may have been another motivating factor. To avoid the language of the poetic tribe and employ instead a "purified" everyday speech becomes an increasingly more difficult task the further one is removed by tradition or circumstance from one's language roots. Hopkins' opposition to the Parnassian was not that it was too refined and elevated—rather that it was too easy, too "natural" for poets to adopt.[47] Purifying everyday language in the same way one would purify a chemical, by distillation, would be much harder, and therefore more rewarding if done well. The difficulty of sustained composition in this mode exerted at least some pressure on the poet to keep his works short. If a poet writes something of the length of *The Idylls of the King* or *The Ring and the Book* or "Sohrab and Rustum," the temptation to at least occasionally borrow from the Parnassian must be overwhelming, even if (as was not always the case) one saw it as a danger one should avoid. By accepting the confines of the sonnet and other shorter structures, Hopkins freed himself to labor on the perfection of form and language which meant so much to him and which mirrored so well the perfectionism he exhibited in the conduct of his life. If this trait is the obverse of that narrowness of range we noted earlier, "for such loss . . . / Abundant recompense."

Whatever the reason, Hopkins gave to his poems the kind of care few have emulated. Each finished poem is the product of a man who thought long and deeply about English prosody, who weighted the effects that each consonant and each vowel can create, who researched and experimented with words from a wide variety of sources, and who mastered the most intricate relationships of form and structure. The strongest testimonial to the successful union of these aspects of his craftsmanship comes from the way his poems have provoked critical comment and exegesis. Few poems since Keats's odes have received the attention given to, say, "The Windhover." Hopkins is not only witty in himself, but the cause that wit is in others.

And in this case too Hopkins seems to have backed the right [r]evolutionary cause. From his century to ours the emphasis is more and more on the shorter work, the smaller but more polished performance. Who now would have the courage or audacity to undertake an epic like the 10,565 lines of *Paradise Lost*? Arnold, aware of the trend and its concomitant burdens, shrank from it:

> People do not understand what a temptation there is, if you cannot bear anything not *very good*, to transfer your operations to a region where form is everything. Perfection of a certain kind may there be attained, or at least approached, without knocking yourself to pieces, but to attain or approach perfection in the region of thought and feeling, and to unite this with perfection of form, demands not merely an effort and a labour, but an actual tearing of oneself to pieces, which one does not readily consent to. . . .[48]

To the honor of Hopkins be it said that he not only accepted the challenge, he often conquered it.

To return then to the question with which we began: Is it still possible to endorse the judgment of the 1930s, that Hopkins is a major poet, perhaps the greatest poet of his age? To put the issue another way: how likely is it that Hopkins will be celebrated as vigorously in 2089 as he is today?

That Hopkins has important limitations as a poet is a conclusion I have taken some pains to establish. The language of praise accorded to him in the thirties was an excessive language.

True, Hopkins' poetry may be shedding some of its encumbrances, especially those which have their origin not so much in the poems themselves as in how the poems are mediated. For instance, the historical fallacy has been fairly well exposed, now that Modernism is no longer modern. The influence of the personal fallacy, especially as it applies to Roman Catholics, may also prove ephemeral. The intellectual Catholic of Hopkins' day bears a much closer resemblance to the Catholic of the 1940s and 1950s than either does to the serious Catholic of the 1980s or 1990s. The latter finds himself or herself like Arnold's anguished visitor to the Grande Chartreuse, "Wandering between two worlds, one dead, / The other powerless to be born." The intellectually secure because hermetically sealed world that Hopkins knew, the world of Aquinas and infallibility and miracles and encyclicals and doctrines, has in the space of two short decades passed away forever. Many of the Catholic beliefs which Hopkins dramatized or celebrated in his poetry no longer carry the force of conviction that until quite recently they did. If Dante no longer attracts a disproportionate number of Catholic scholars because all aspiring readers of the poet have to immerse themselves in the unfamiliar environment of a fourteenth-century world view, so too by the next generation everyone, Catholic and non-Catholic alike, will have to be instructed in the equally foreign premises of post-Tridentine Catholicism.[49]

But other limitations remain. If we put Hopkins up against some important definitions of "major poet," he falls short. Eliot's requirement of *maturity*, for example, obligated a poet to maturity of mind, manners, and language as well as a comprehensiveness of vision.[50] Maturity of mind, manners, and language Hopkins may indeed have possessed. But we have had occasion to see that comprehensiveness of vision is not the distinguishing feature of a poet whose range of form and subject is as narrow as Hopkins'.

Yet Eliot like Arnold before him was in pursuit of what he called "universal authors," those whom every educated person should read. If Hopkins fails on these terms, it means simply that he is not "major" in the same way that Chaucer, Shakespeare, Milton, and Wordsworth can be said to be major. Are there other, perhaps more useful ways to approach the question?

If we consider Hopkins' strengths as we have defined them—originality, command of language, immediacy, craftsmanship—his superiority to most of his contemporaries becomes immediately evident. Tennyson and Browning may have greater claim to our esteem because of more extensive range and the other fruits of a lifetime's dedication to their calling. But aside from these two, which Victorian poets can rank with Hopkins? Possibly Arnold, because of his sensitivity to and accurate reflection of the intellectual and social nuances of his time; but readers often wonder if they receive thereby an adequate compensation for the almost unvaried melancholy of Arnold's tone and the more than occasional flatness of his diction. Not Rossetti, whose poetry for all of its gifts is betrayed by solipsism, Parnassian language, and a narrowness of subject that exceeds even Hopkins' own. Not Swinburne, for whom the term "maturity of mind" is merely amusing. Certainly not the Decadents, whose laborious search for perfection of form led far too often to triteness and insipidity of content. If Leavis' proclamation of Hopkins as the greatest poet of his age overstates the case, the exaggeration is at least not unconscionable.

Therefore, if we accept a more modest definition of "major poet"—for example, as a poet whose virtues establish him or her as one of the perhaps half-dozen poets who epitomize what an important age of an important national literature can at its best produce—Hopkins will have a secure place. In the future he will be read, I think, in much the same way Keats will be read. Both can be seen as poets who for different reasons did not have the opportunity and perhaps the experiential resources for rivalling the poets who bestrode their age—Wordsworth, for example. But they will be honored as poets who extended the possibilities of the language, poets who created a new and exciting idiom for capturing both the sensory delights of an external world they embraced as formative yet mystifying, and the anguish of an internal world they endured as terrifying yet revelatory. Both poets have shown the power to claim for themselves new generations of readers who not only respect their craftsmanship but also love them for their tonally rich yet seductively familiar voices. As poets with fresh things to say, they both evoke and provoke. And Hopkins like Keats haunts us with the forever unanswerable "what if. . . ."

Will Hopkins be read in 2089? Will the current gentle slide in his popularity be arrested or reversed? No one can offer any guarantees. But if we accept Said's claim about texts being institutionalized by a culture, the fact remains that any "culture" is at bottom simply people. Hopkins will be "institutionalized" so long as there are people who love his poetry and want to share that enthusiasm with—even "enforce" it upon—others. The fate of Hopkins' poetry rests with the dedication and the rhetorical power of those who testify, not just to other enthusiasts but to new or as-yet-unpersuaded readers, about their own engagement with the poet's words.

For those who love Hopkins, therefore, now is the acceptable—the only acceptable—time.

APPENDIX

Round-Table Discussion:
Hopkins after One Hundred Years

At the conclusion of the Hopkins Centenary Conference the participants engaged in a round-table discussion on the general theme of the conference, "Hopkins after One Hundred Years." Identified in this transcript are six of the contributors to this volume and the editor, who served as moderator; several members of the audience also took part in the quite spirited conversation.

FENNELL: Let me start by supposing that Hopkins could have foreknown that he would be published and would indeed be successful one hundred years later. What would surprise him, do you think, about how we read him today? Not the *fact* that we read him, but *how* we read him.

SULLOWAY: This is something that I'm sure has troubled all of us at one time or another—I tried to cope with it in one essay or another, and messed it all up, I can assure you. It seems to me that he would have been deeply gratified that we care in a human sense—or he would say in a "manly" sense—about what he did, his vocation. I think that some of my colleagues on the panel would join me in saying he would have been shocked at some of us. He would have been shocked at the likes of me, saying some of the things I have said and will say. That troubles me but I go right on doing it.

WALHOUT: I have a feeling the papers he would have liked most might have been Professor Donohue's and Professor Bender's because they dig right into the linguistic and literary aspects of the poetry, and that's exactly what he did. So I think he would look on those very favorably, and about some of the others of us I'm not so sure. But I'd like to think also that Hopkins, being a very wide ranging person with many interests and talents, would understand that once literary works are put into the public domain they're no longer just a private possession of Hopkins or anybody else. Maybe there are dimensions of those works now in the public domain that other people can probe and fathom that he perhaps didn't think about, so maybe—or at least we'd like to persuade ourselves to think—he would look on this work as showing nuances, angles and perspectives that he didn't necessarily think of explicitly at the beginning but he might be very fond of.

DOWNES: I'd like to suggest that he may very well be embarrassed today. A lot of books on the bookshelf deal so much with his life; that his problems, which were real and honestly faced, would take such prominence I think he would be very embarrassed by. This would be true for many reasons including social and familial as well as religious. There's been, as we all know, a great deal of attention about the so-called "priest and poet" conflict and a lot of attention to his neurasthenic problems. I often think when I go to a conference like this and hear my own paper, in a way I keep forgetting that if you read Hopkins' letters and at least a few accounts of those who knew him, he was a cut-up, he was in his class a kind of Jesuit jokester, he was a lot of fun. He was a far more balanced human being than sometimes we remember and I think he'd be a bit embarrassed by our serious interest in his occasional malfunctions.

AUDIENCE MEMBER: You asked the question, how is he read today. I would ask that in a very literal way. Someone once said to me, "I have no difficulty reading him, except when I pay attention to his markings." Does everyone pay attention to the markings? Does *anyone* pay attention to the markings?

DONOHUE: If I try to follow his markings, I can't do it. But in a letter to Bridges, Hopkins finally acknowledges this difficulty; he talks about "I have marks here," "this is a six stress line," "this is an eight stress line," "I wonder where I should put the marks," and then he begins remembering that Bridges' voice doesn't put the same accents as his own voice does, and he finally admits that everyone is going to read it according to the way he takes in a line, the way he sees and hears it. Even as to sprung rhythm, I certainly am not qualified to talk about it, and again I'm not trying to make light of Hopkins' seriousness, but I do think that the distinction of "sprung" rhythm is often more imaginary than real.

SULLOWAY: Thank you. I've always harbored that secret too. I've tried to describe it to students and they'll throw up their hands, and I'll throw up my hands, and I'll say, "Just *read* it!"

FENNELL: One thing to remember is that when he submitted the manuscript of "The Wreck of the *Deutschland*" he had all the markings there, and the editor said, "we'll take it but you've got to get rid of those markings," and very reluctantly Hopkins agreed. Now unfortunately the rest of the poems were never published either, but if he'd met with a similarly forthright editor for those, he might have bowed, and we might not even see the markings today. When I teach Hopkins, I must confess that I read it as I feel I ought to and let the marks guide me only where I am in some doubt. Do any of the panelists feel differently about the marks?

VAN BEECK: I'm absolutely orthodox. I follow them very carefully, but I read Hopkins not in a colloquial tone at all. I read him loudly and very slowly, the way Dylan Thomas read his own poetry. Hopkins sounds best to me when I play him like Brahms, when I play him with a broad beat.

DOWNES: I might remark that professional readers have very different versions of reading Hopkins too. If you listen to John Gielgud or Cyril Cusack read him, they're very different. I suppose each bespeaks his own approach to poetry in general, which suggests to me that while I think there's real metrical acuity to what Hopkins was talking about —he did know a lot about metrics and the history of metrics and that's what interested Robert Bridges (remember that later Bridges wrote a work on Milton's metrics) —art overcomes technique in a way, and so we all find a way to react and respond. I tend to be on the side that is more concerned about those stresses. But I notice that when students read back to me in class and they appreciate Hopkins, they do a lot of subjective response to the text, which suggests they work differently too.

AUDIENCE MEMBER: I think Hopkins deliberately put those marks in because he was trying to work against a traditional iambic beat and it's pretty hard to do.

VAN BEECK: The best example of that is his last poem, which is entirely iambic, with one exception. The sonnet to Bridges is entirely iambic except one line "I want the one rapture of an inspiration," there's an anapest there.

SULLOWAY: He wasn't a musician for nothing either. Though his music is not the quality of the poetry, he knows the value of a line that isn't perfectly iambic. What do you do when you read, "The world is charged with the grandeur of God"? It's not iambic, and then he starts off "it will flame out like shining from shook foil," which *is* an iambic line, and then "generations have trod"; so he moves back and forth from iambs to anapests and dactyls. What are you to do as you read to a class? "Gen-uh-ra-tions"? You can't do that. And yet he had such an extremely scrupulous ear about every syllable.

VAN BEECK: His interest in Latin verse forms—all these regularly irregular lines were part of that.

BENDER: It seems that this question is more complicated than we have yet admitted. To be sure, we have some metrical markings. And the question is, should we follow the metrical markings in order to recreate historically the authorial intention for the phonology of the line? But if that is indeed our goal, then the vowel qualities should be reconstructed to the way Oxfordshire dialect would have sounded in, say, 1875. And we could make a stab at that— we have the Daniel Jones pronouncing gazeteer and some other things that would allow us at least to recognize that the sounds of those poems in Hopkins' performance would have been very different from the sound of those poems read by an American undergraduate from South Carolina as opposed to Maine or a person from Africa. All of these latter have charming effects, but are so different from Hopkins' expectations of how English should sound that we are very near to a phonetic translation of some kind. The sign system has been altered and drifts further and further from Hopkins' intention. This is perhaps to be regretted, but lacking a way to stop it we need to recognize that this is the nature of systems of code: to drift under the pressure of the interpretive mechanism that is brought to bear on them. The issue seems to have built into it a primacy of authorial intention with reference to the sound. I would raise two questions: if we agree with that, what can we do about it? And I think not very much. And the second possibility is that if we don't agree with that, how are we to avoid falling into total chaos, where the signification, sound— every feature of Hopkins' language—has drifted into a world which he would not recognize? I have no answer to either of those questions—I've managed perhaps to confuse the issue rather than answer it.

DONOHUE: We talk about the rhythms of ordinary speech that he used in his speech one hundred years ago; whatever we're doing, we're just making stabs at it.

DOWNES: I noticed someone recording this; future generations may look at this and say "what in the world were those people doing, talking about this poet?" It may seem very archaic that we're reading him and responding to him this way, and it may not be recognizable to the readers of a later time. Is that a fair implication?

BENDER: Might I say that in what you just said you had an

implied distinction between what is said and the fact of a response. What will be constant, so long as there's human intelligence, is that minds will reach out and respond to these cunning systems of signification, although what the poems say or how the poems sound or the medium which carries this code may vary in ways that we cannot even imagine. As our minds reach back and try to construct Sanskrit, for instance, over all that time and space what is constant is the *activity*. It is the activity of this conference that will be replicated in one hundred years, not the content of it.

WALHOUT: I wonder if there's a comparison between what Professor Bender is saying and the return to doing music with original instruments. There's a British conductor who's redoing all the Beethoven symphonies with original instruments on the ground that the way Beethoven "heard" it was quite different from the way it is now. The orchestras now are fuller, the instruments sound different. He's done an awful lot of research to reconstruct what earlier instruments were like in order to record those versions again. Now you could argue, which is the better? Should we go back to Beethoven's intentions, at least to the way he thought of it, or should we go for the fuller orchestra? I suppose we could say the authorial intention is a fallacy there, so by the same token we should look on these poems as objective works that continue on with their significance apart from the author, without trying to get back to the authorial intention, which is a fallacy. But it seems like you could also say there are multiple ways of viewing them and one is not necessarily a fallacy so that one way of hearing the music is the way Beethoven heard it, one way of hearing Hopkins' poems is the way he intended it, but there are many other ways of doing it too as time goes forward, as new consciousness and new experiences bring more to it. You wouldn't have to look on one as a fallacy; there are a variety of rich ways of doing the whole thing.

VAN BEECK: As for the original question I'd like to say something about being a Jesuit one hundred years later. Hopkins of course was an intensely private man, and to the extent I understand the Jesuits one hundred years ago, I'm amazed at how much he did without spiritual direction, without the sharing of prayer experience, which has only become a thing among Jesuits within the past twenty-five years. What astounds me is the application to Hopkins of things I've come to understand as a Jesuit within the past twenty-five years, especially when it comes to the combination of sensuousness and contemplation. The enormous freedom Hopkins obviously has in associating prayer with tenseness around the midriff; the association in "The Wreck of the *Deutschland*" of prayer and the experience of diarrhea as a picture of surrender to Christ. The sonnets on "Patience" and "To Bridges" have dreadfully relaxed last lines. All these are experiences which we now know, having developed much more of a community of contemplative prayer, are part of the experience of bringing one's whole self into prayer and into the presence of God. The more I begin to understand what prayer is over the last twenty-five years, I realize how little we knew about it as a community up to around 1965. And I marvel at the fact that Hopkins apparently discovered much of this for himself.

AUDIENCE MEMBER: Going back to the topic of language, rhythms, and the different ages and developments of that, I wonder if we don't have a case for the theory that language was originally a poetic, sung language. In many cultures meanings were given by intonation, and we speak in Western culture about "musical" languages like Italian. I don't know of anybody saying that about English. I'm wondering if we haven't lost that sense of music in language. The English professors can argue that point if they want. But we're talking about ordinary language as though it were ordinary: there may be a second language based on music and rhythm, and if that's so, I guess I'd want to ask a question about whether there isn't a limit to structures of language and sounds of language. Consequently, even though there are diversities, there's a connection. There are limits to human phonological possibilities, to speaking, hearing, listening. Someone like Hopkins is touching at the core and central usage of Western language, if you want to limit it to Western language as such. We all operate within that limitation.

SULLOWAY: There's something that struck me. The world is opening up for people of all races to travel all around the globe and settle, and in addition some people are forced to move all around the globe for various reasons of tragedy, and therefore we have this melding, as Todd Bender said, of accents. I can imagine classrooms one hundred years from now at Loyola, and I can imagine a Ghanian sitting here as a Jesuit, along with people of every race, both sexes, from all over the globe. They will be reading Hopkins, and our memory of how *we* read him, to say nothing of how *he* read himself, is going to disappear in a sense. What then is left? I happen to think a great deal would be left, although I'm bound to mourn that we don't yet know or we've lost the knowledge of what the exact musical sounds were of Hopkins' sense of language and how it shifted when he moved from Hampshire to Oxford, Oxford to Wales, Wales to wherever. He was sensitive to every little timbre of dialect.

AUDIENCE MEMBER: Following on from what you said regarding what will be left. Not being a lexicographer or a linguist, I still think that the iambic rhythm is long in English, and the value of alliteration is something that goes way back in the language and assonance as well. When I find myself puzzled about the meaning of any poem of Hopkins' I go away in my closet and read it aloud and it straightens out for me. I don't think I'll inflict it upon you now but I could go to any poem I've never read before, I think, and read it aloud, and its meaning would become evident to me, and my mistakes would make me back up immediately, and discover, just from the reading aloud, what the truer meaning is. I think Mr. Gardner's note on the opening of "The Wreck of the *Deutschland*" is mistaken. And the alliteration tells you. The alliteration—when it moves with the iambic rhythm there's no trouble. The alliteration tells you when you ought to set the iambic rhythm aside, because the alliteration overrides the iamb.

SULLOWAY: "Giver of breath and bread"—that's triplicate rhythm. That's sometimes the way I have to do it, too. I just kind of go with the alliteration. Two things: go with the alliteration—this is iambic and clearly what he meant, he wasn't a sonneteer for nothing. Then also go with the diacritics and other marks whenever I can. I don't know what else we can do.

FENNELL: Could I pose another question. We've been talking about the last one hundred years, and even forecasting the next one hundred. But just in the space of your own lifetime, how has your reading of Hopkins changed from when you first encountered him to the way you read him now?

DONOHUE: Well, I for one found that when I focused on his "introduction"—I was missing the interpretation. I was missing the poem. I know it's important to him. However, there's so much in the poetry beyond putting an accent here and an accent there, that once I got old enough to not pay much attention to all his concern with sprung rhythm and accents, I felt much happier. I always felt happy reading him, but I don't feel that I'm flouting an order from the poet.

SULLOWAY: I think I appreciate him more. I'm much more critical of him as woman to man; at the same time I care more about him. There's one thing that has never changed for me personally, Hopkins rescued me from a life at Dunkin' Donuts. He rescued me in the sense that I was able to do some work on him that got some recognition. I used to ask him in the middle of the night, just open my mouth and say, "What do you want of me?" And I would get some sort of response. I still find that going on, even though I change, join the feminist movement, have children and grandchildren, quarrel with faculty, make peace with the world, and so forth. There's something about Hopkins that doesn't change. If you have any love, respect, and affection for him at all it simply never leaves you, no matter how you lchange. What he would have thought of me, or if he would have liked me at all, that's of no account. The fact that we have these conferences, the fact that we have so many ways of looking at him, that he had this kaleidoscopic personality, that he handled it with such grace in the flippant and theological sense of the word—I don't think that leaves me. And I suspect my colleagues on this panel feel the same way no matter how much they've changed about him, or grown with him, or departed perhaps from him.

WALHOUT: Maybe I can comment and cheat a little bit and go back and say something first about musicality. Whether the original languages were more musical or not would be something that others would have to answer. But whatever the answer is, does that mean we should try to recover the musicality of another age today and go back in some way? I think what you could say is there are different kinds of musicality. Just as music itself is developing, so there can be different kinds of musicality in poetry at different times. Perhaps different kinds of poetry capture their own kinds of musicality. I'm not sure that just because original languages were more musical, if they were, that that would give us a good reason to reduplicate them rather than finding other dimensions for poetry. The relation to this question is that I've found that Hopkins can mean a lot of different things to different people. I think Professor Bender had it right at the beginning, there are many different reasons that people have because of the richness of the poetry. Musicality would be one, and other linguistic elements would be another. But there are other reasons people have for appreciating the poetry, and the same would be true one hundred years from now.

Endnotes to Essays

Religious Consciousness in Hopkins
(David A. Downes)
(pp. 1 – 32)

[1]See, for example, Jeffrey Mehlman, *A Structural Study of Autobiography: Proust, Sartre, Levi-Strauss* (Ithaca, N.Y.: Cornell University Press, 1974).

[2]Paul Jay, *Being in the Text: Self-Representation from Wordsworth to Roland Barthes* (Ithaca, N.Y.: Cornell University Press, 1984).

[3]*The Journals and Papers of Gerard Manley Hopkins,* Rev. 2d. ed., Humphry House and Graham Storey, eds. (London: Oxford University Press, 1959), 129. (Hereafter *Journals*)

[4]Jacques Lacan, *The Language of Self: The Function of Language in Psychoanalysis,* tr. Anthony Wilden (Baltimore: The Johns Hopkins Press, 1968), 60.

[5]*Journals*, 289.

[6]Paul Ricouer, *The Conflict of Interpretations: Essays in Hermeneutics,* ed. Don Ihde (Evanston, Ill.: Northwestern University Press, 1974), 466-67.

[7]Thomas Browne, "Religio Medici," in *Seventeenth-Century Prose and Poetry,* ed. R. Coffin and A. Witherspoon (New York: Harcourt Brace, 1946), 364.

[8]*Journals,* 289.

[9]*Journals,* 290.

[10]*Oxford Authors: Gerard Manley Hopkins,* ed. Catherine Phillips (London: Oxford University Press, 1986), 177. Numbers after poems in the text refer to pages in this edition.

[11]*The Sermons and Devotional Writings of Gerard Manley Hopkins,* ed.

Christopher Devlin (London: Oxford University Press, 1959), 123. (Hereafter *Sermons*)

[12]Alfred Borello, *A Concordance to the Poetry in English of Gerard Manley Hopkins* (Metuchen, N.J.: Scarecrow Press, 1969), 235-36.

[13]*Journals*, 230.

[14]*Sermons*, 199.

[15]Ibid., 140.

[16]*Journals*, 230.

[17]*Sermons*, 140.

[18]Ibid., 197.

[19]Ibid., 154.

[20]Donald Walhout, "Modes of Religious Response in Hopkins' Poetry," *Hopkins Quarterly* 12 (1985-86): 93-94.

[21]Matt 16:24-26 in *The New English Bible with Apocrypha*, ed. Donald Ebor *et al* (Oxford and Cambridge: Oxford and Cambridge University Presses, 1970).

[22]Northrop Frye, *The Great Code: The Bible and Literature* (New York: Harcourt Brace Jovanovich, 1982), 166.

[23]*Great Code*, 166.

[24]*Sermons*, 34-38.

[25]James Finn Cotter, "Apocalyptic Imagery in Hopkins' 'That Nature is a Heraclitean Fire and of the Comfort of the Resurrection,'" *Victorian Poetry* 24 (1986): 261-75.

Hopkins, Male and Female, and the "Tender Mothering Earth" (Alison Sulloway)
(pp. 33 – 54)

[1]In recent terminology, the noun "gender" and the gerund "gendered" allude to those traits assigned to either sex according to the assumptions about what is sexually appropriate on certain continents, countries or sections of these countries at any specific millennia, century, or decade. The adjective "sexual" now tends to be reserved mostly for the discrete anatomical and reproductive differences in the two sexes.

[2]"God's Grandeur," poem 31 *The Poems of Gerard Manley Hopkins*, 4th Ed., ed. W. H. Gardner and Norman H. Mackenzie (London: Oxford University Press, 1967). All references to Hopkins' poems are based on this edition.

[3]"The Wreck of the *Deutschland*," poem 28, stanza 34.

[4]*The Sermons and Devotional Writings of Gerard Manley Hopkins*, ed.

Christopher Devlin, (London: Oxford Univ. Press, 1959), 48-49.

[5]*Sermons*, 114, 108.

[6]*Further Letters of Gerard Manley Hopkins including his Correspondence with Coventry Patmore*, 2d Ed., ed. C. C. Abbott (London: Oxford University Press, 1956), 310; *Sermons*, 63-68.

[7]For the controversy over whether Hopkins did or did not suffer from the machismo common in Victorian England, see Sandra Gilbert and Susan Gubar, *The Madwoman in the Attic: The Woman Writer and the Nineteenth-Century Literary Imagination* (New Haven: Yale University Press, 1979), 3-4; Donna Moder, "Aspects of Androgyny, Oedipal Struggle, and Religious Defence in the Poetry of Gerard Manley Hopkins," *Literature and Society* 1 (1986) 2-4; Jeffrey Loomis, "Birth Pangs in Darkness: Hopkins' Archetypal Christian Biography," *Texas Studies in Literature and Language*, 28(1986):81-106; Alison G. Sulloway, "Gerard Manley Hopkins and 'Women and Men' as 'Partners in the Mystery of Redemption,'" in *Texas Studies in Literature and Language*, 31 (Spring 1989). For Hopkins' letter comparing women's art to unfertilized hen's eggs, see *The Correspondence of Gerard Manley Hopkins and Richard Watson Dixon*, ed. C. C. Abbott (London: Oxford University Press), 133.

[8]*Sermons*, 122-23.

[9]"As kingfishers catch fire," poem 57.

[10]"Binsey Poplars," poem 43; "God's Grandeur," poem 31; "The May Magnificat," poem 42.

[11]*The Letters of Gerard Manley Hopkins to Robert Bridges*, 2d impression, ed. C. C. Abbott (London: Oxford University Press, 1955), 319-20.

[12]"Duns Scotus at Oxford," poem 44.

[13]*Journals and Papers of Gerard Manley Hopkins*, ed. Humphry House and Graham Storey (London: Oxford University Press, 1959), 84-114.

[14]*Sermons*, 283; Norman H. Mackenzie, *A Reader's Guide to Gerard Manley Hopkins* (London: Thames & Hudson, 1981), 231-35.

[15]*Further Letters*, 308-9. But see Hopkins' eager comments on Marie Lataste in *Sermons*.

[16]Ruth Salvaggio, *Enlightened Absence: Neoclassical Configurations of the Feminine* (Urbana: University of Illinois Press, 1988), x; Catherine Keller, *From a Broken Web: Separation, Sexism and Self* (Boston: Beacon Press, 1986), 10-15. See also *The Spiritual Exercises of St. Ignatius*, trans. Anthony Mottola; introduction by Robert W. Gleason, S.J. (Garden City, N.Y.: Doubleday & Co. Inc., 1964), 39-40.

[17]"The May Magnificat," poem 42.

[18] "Spring," poem 33.

[19]"The Starlight Night," poem 32; emphasis mine.

[20]"In the Valley of the Elwy," poem 34.

[21]Rosa Mystica," poem 27.

[22]The May Magnificat," poem 42; "The Blessed Virgin compared to the Air we Breathe," poem 60.

[23]"The Windhover," poem 36.

[24]"Pied Beauty," poem 37.

[25]"God's Grandeur," poem 31.

[26]For instance, see Daniel Harris, *Inspirations Unbidden: The "Terrible Sonnets" of Gerard Manley Hopkins* (Berkeley: University of California Press, 1982). For a fine, balanced pair of Jesuit responses, see Father Christopher Devlin's introductions to Hopkins' sermons and his spiritual writings in *Sermons*, 3-12 and 107-21; and Robert Boyle, S.J., "'Man Jack the Man Is': *The Wreck* from the Perspective of 'The Shepherd's Brow,'" *Readings of "The Wreck,"* ed. Peter Milward, S.J. and Raymond Schoder, S.J. (Chicago: Loyola University Press, 1976), 101-9. Richard Giles has written a brilliant essay, "'The Shepherd's Brow': Hopkins 'Disparadised,'" *Victorian Poetry* 23 (1985): 169-87. The essays of Boyle and Giles can also be found in *Critical Essays on Gerard Manley Hopkins*, ed. Alison G. Sulloway (Boston: G. K. Hall, 1989).

[27]Keller, *From a Broken Web*, 10-11; 35-36.

[28]Poem 69.

The Choices of Two Anthologists:
(Frans Jozef van Beeck, S.J.)
(pp. 55 – 72)

[1]*The Oxford Book of Christian Verse* (Oxford: Clarendon Press, 1940), ed. Lord David Cecil, 492-503. Henceforth *OBCV*.

[2]*The New Oxford Book of Christian Verse* (Oxford and New York: Oxford University Press, 1981), ed. Donald Davie, 249-51. Henceforth *NOBCV*.

[3]By comparison, in *The Faber Book of Religious Verse*, edited by Dame Helen Gardner (London: Faber and Faber, 1972), Hopkins occupies the largest space, 15 full pages, immediately followed by T. S. Eliot with 14 1/2, George Herbert and Henry Vaughan with 13, and John Donne with 12. This is a collection of "religious" verse, although "the majority of the poems in this book are Christian poems." In stating the critical principles that guided her in

determining what makes poetry religious, the editor very briefly explains that religion involves commitment or obligation, that it involves some form of revelation and the response to it, and that the latter may include the expression of doubt.

[4]F. R. Leavis, *New Bearings in English Poetry* (London: Chatto and Windus, 1932), 159-93. See. also Leavis' *The Common Pursuit* (London: Chatto and Windus, 1952), 44-72, and his *retractatio* entitled *Gerard Manley Hopkins: Reflections After Fifty Years* (London: The Hopkins Society, 1971).

[5]For a comprehensive account, see W. H. Gardner, *Gerard Manley Hopkins (1844-1889): A Study of Poetic Idiosyncrasy in Relation to Poetic Tradition*, 2 vols. (London: Secker and Warburg, 1948, 1949).

[6]William Peters, S. J., *Gerard Manley Hopkins: A Critical Essay towards the Understanding of His Poetry* (Oxford: Oxford Univerity Press, 1948). In his old age, Father Peters summed up the reflections that had come to him during a lifetime of familiarity with Hopkins, which, he writes, had developed into "an affinity . . . , a certain kinship, and, in the end, without being either sentimental or arrogant, a friendship": *Gerard Manley Hopkins: A Tribute* (Chicago: Loyola University Press, 1984).

[7]For the range of meaning of the word "catholic," see Avery Dulles, *The Catholicity of the Church* (Oxford: Clarendon Press, 1985), 185.

[8]This description of the poet's relationship to idioms and the cultural communities behind them is analogous (as well as complementary) to T. S. Eliot's analysis of the poet's relationship to the literary tradition developed in "Tradition and the Individual Talent." My reason for applying Eliot's theory to idioms and their corresponding communities is that the literary tradition in which poets and writers live (some, like Virginia Woolf and James Joyce, more exclusively than others, like D. H. Lawrence and Saul Bellow) remains connected with other worlds of reference.

[9]See Lord David Cecil's remarks in his introduction (*OBCV*, xixii), and Donald Davie's in his (*NOBCV*, xviii).

[10]*OBCV*, v; xxxxi. *NOBCV*, xxxxii.

[11]*NOBCV*, xviii.

[12]*NOBCV*, xvii.

[13]*NOBCV*, xviiiixix.

[14]*NOBCV*, xixxx.

[15]*NOBCV*, xxxxi .

[16]*NOBCV*, xxi .

[17]*NOBCV*, xxi.

[18]See John Henry Newman's characterization of liberal Evangelicalism in n. 25: it tends to identify the "dispensation" (of salvation) with its "revelation" or "manifestation."

[19]Philipp Melanchthon states, "But as for one who is ignorant of the other fundamentals, namely, 'The Power of Sin,' 'The Law,' and 'Grace,' I do not see how I can call him a Christian. For from these things Christ is known, since to know Christ means to know his benefits . . . In his letter to the Romans . . . what does [Paul] discuss? He takes up *the law, sin, grace, fundamentals on which the knowledge of Christ exclusively rests*" [*Loci Communes Theologici*, in *Melanchthon and Bucer*, ed. Wilhelm Buck (Philadelphia: Westminster, 1969), 21-22; italics added].

[20]Philipp Melanchthon's *Loci Communes Theologici* of 1521, "the first systematic theology of the evangelical Church" [Hans Engeland in *Melanchthon on Christian doctrine: Loci Communes* , 1555, ed. Clyde Manschrek (New York: Oxford University Press, 1965), xxxii], follows, after a characteristically anthropological introduction on the human faculties and on free will, the following theological sequence: Sin— Law— Gospel— Grace—Justification—Faith. That this sequence is thematic and intentional is demonstrated by Melanchthon's foreword to the 1555 edition of the *Loci:* "God has given us the most fitting order [. . .]. He puts his doctrine in the form of a story" (xlvi).

[21]For a much fuller treatment of this entire background, see Frans J. van Beeck, S.J., *God Encountered*, vol. 1, *Understanding the Christian Faith* (San Francisco: Harper and Row, 1989), § 20.

[22]There is a world of painful discord in the background of George Herbert's harmonious lines: "Come, my Way, my Truth, my Life:/. . ./Such a Truth, *as ends all strife*" (italics added). Note John Toland's preface to his *Christianity not Mysterious* of 1696, addressed to "the well-meaning Christian . . . with all the Sincerity and Simplicity imaginable." Equipped with these two long-lost virtues, Toland inveighs against the "foreseen Wranglings of certain Men, who study more to protract and perplex than to terminate a Controversy." What Toland wants is simply the Gospel: it is ". . . not the Articles of the East or West, Orthodox or Arian, Protestant or Papist, consider'd as such, that I trouble my self about, but those of Jesus Christ and his Apostles." This basic Christianity above all sectarian division has Reason as its natural associate, for the contestants in the theological battles invariably end up having "Resource to Railing when Reason fails them." Just like Reason, Religion "is always the same, like God its Author, *with*

whom there is no Variableness, nor Shadow of changing." See *Christianity not Mysterious*, ed. Günther Gawlick (Stuttgart Bad Canstatt: F. Fromann Verlag, 1964), x, xiv, xvii, xiii. The scriptural reference is to Jas 1:17.

[23]Consider Melanchthon's expression: "In his letter to the Romans *when he was writing a compendium of Christian doctrine,* did Paul philosophize about the mysteries of the Trinity . . . ?" (*Loci Communes Theologici* [1521], 212; italics added).

[24]For a fuller treatment of this development, see Frans Jozef van Beeck, S.J., *God Encountered,* vol. 1, *Understanding the Christian Faith,* §28.

[25]John Henry Newman, who received Hopkins into the Catholic church, had come to distrust the tradition of liberal Evangelicalism in which he had been raised. His description, which first appeared in 1835, in one of the early *Tracts for the Times,* is accurate enough to be still worth quoting. Newman wrote: "That theology is as follows: that the Atonement is the chief doctrine of the Gospel; again, that it is chiefly to be regarded, not as a wonder from heaven, and in its relation to the attributes of God and to the unseen world, but in its experienced effects on our minds, in the change it effects when it is believed. To this, as if to the point of sight in a picture, all the portions of the Gospel system are directed and made to converge; as if this doctrine were so fully understood, that it might fearlessly be used to regulate, adjust, correct, complete, everything else. Thus, the doctrine of the Incarnation is viewed as necessary and important to the Gospel, *because* it gives virtue to the Atonement; of the Trinity, *because* it includes the revelation, not only of the Redeemer, but also of the Sanctifier, by whose aid and influence the Gospel message is to be blessed to us. It follows that faith is nearly the whole of religious service, for through it the message or Manifestation is received . . . . . Thus the dispensation, in its length, depth, and height, is practically identified with its Revelation, or rather its necessarily superficial Manifestation. Not that the reality of the Atonement, in itself, is formally denied, but it is cast in the background, except so far as it can be discovered to be influential, viz., to show God's hatred of sin, the love of Christ, and the like . . . And the Dispensation thus being hewn and chiselled into an intelligible human system, is represented, when thus mutilated, as affording a remarkable evidence of the truth of the Bible, an evidence level to the reason, and superseding the testimony of the Apostles. That is, . . . Rationalism, or want of faith, which has in the first place invented a spurious gospel,

next looks complacently on its own offspring . . ." [*Essays Critical and Historical*, Vol. I, 4th edition (London: Basil Montagu Pickering, 1877), 47–48].

[26]This may also help explain why Davie prefers George Herbert to John Donne: the latter's world—his mother was a sister of the Jesuit Jasper Heywood—is much more Catholic in scope. (I suspect, though, that Davie's reading of George Herbert may be determined by liberal Evangelical hindsight, which would make Herbert look quite a bit more like an Evangelical, and certainly more plainspoken, than he actually is.)

[27]*NOBCV*, xxv. Davie cites both Donne and Hopkins for poetic honesty the quality that gives the impression that they "speak of their Maker only of and for themselves, not for themselves in communion with others." He then rightly suggests that this is a misinterpretation of Donne.

[28]*OBCV*, xxxxxxi.

[29]*OBCV*, xixii.

[30]Note the literary and theological prejudices implied in this expression. It suggests that the Hebrew Scriptures are more original, and hence, inherently more poetic. At the same time, however, it continues, in a secular vein, the widespread (ultimately Marcionist) misconception that the God of the Hebrew Bible is a debased version of the New Testament God of love. Cecil explains that "the Hebrew psalmists . . . spill themselves without shame in their invocations to God; show themselves rancorous or self-pitying or boastful just as the mood dictates. Their mode of expressing themselves is equally uninhibited. 'The Lord awaked out of sleep like a giant refreshed with wine'; no devotional writer of later days would permit himself to use such an image about the All Holy, All Wise object of his adoration" (*OBCV*, xii). This all sounds very nice and knowing, but it is written only to suit the romantic preconception. The authors of the psalms were not original religious and poetic geniuses any more than the authors of the ballads were halfclad, half-crazed bards plucking harps and improvising from windswept promontories, as John Martin's well-known painting would have us believe. The Hebrew psalms are, of course, both original and conventional, and they reflect the faith and the community worship of Israel. And the God the Hebrew Scriptures know of is as All-Holy and All-Wise as the God professed in the New Testament. The latter's "sentiments" of "love, reverence, humility" are not blandly "unexceptionable"; and its aspirations— as all who read the New Testament text can see for themselves—are

for a great deal else besides the individual benefits of "a purer soul and stronger faith" (cf. *OBCV*, xii-xiii).

[31]*OBCV*, xii-xiii.

[32]See Friedrich Schleiermacher, *On Religion: Speeches to its Cultured Despisers* (New York: Harper and Row, 1958).

[33]*Ibid.*, 23-45.

[34]For a longer explanation of the affinity between Schleiermacher and Wordsworth, see van Beeck, *Christ Proclaimed: Christology as Rhetoric* (New York: Paulist Press, 1979), 548-66.

[35]*OBCV*, xii .

[36]"It is doubtful whether [Blake] should appear in a book of Christian verse at all. If he was a Christian, he was certainly a heretic" (*OBCV*, xxvi). Cecil is not the first to associate original talent with heresy as a vocation. Schleiermacher himself attributed to the individual theologian an oracular ability to keep the tradition "mobile" by means of necessary "heterodoxy" See John E. Thiel, "Theological Responsibility: Beyond the Classical Paradigm," *Theological Studies* 47 (1986): 573-98.

[37]Not surprisingly, the Romantic movement in Continental Europe, in keeping with its strong antirationalist bias, had early affinities with Roman Catholicism. The names of Joseph de Maistre and Friedrich Schlegel come to mind, as well as, of course, the latter's friend and protégé, the German poet Novalis, whom Schleiermacher memorialized in the third edition of his *Speeches* (*On Religion*, 41, 104, 184). Novalis' leanings towards Catholicism remained in suspense when he died in 1801, at the age of twenty-nine. Later on, in the thirties, in Paris, the typically romantic patriotism of the Polish freedom fighter and refugee Bogdan Jański, the founder of the later Congregation of the Resurrection, had profoundly Roman Catholic roots.

[38]Margaret R. Ellsberg, *Created to Praise: The Language of Gerard Manley Hopkins* (New York and Oxford: Oxford University Press, 1987), 20-45.

[39]*Odyssey*, A, 45.

[40]Evelyn Underhill, *The Essentials of Mysticism and Other Essays* (London and New York: J. M. Dent and E. P. Dutton, 1920), 71-72.

[41]What T. S. Eliot writes about appreciating Dante also applies, *mutatis mutandis*, to appreciating Hopkins: "My point is that you cannot afford to *ignore* Dante's philosophical and theological beliefs . . . You are not called upon to believe what Dante believed, for your belief will not give you a groat's worth more of understanding and appreciation; but you are called upon more and more

to understand it. If you can read poetry as poetry, you will 'believe' in Dante's theology exactly as you believe in the physical
reality of his journey; that is, you suspend both belief and disbelief.
I will not deny that it may be in practice easier for a Catholic to
grasp the meaning, in many places, than for the ordinary agnostic;
but that is not because the Catholic believes, but because he has
been instructed. It is a matter of knowledge and ignorance, not of
belief or scepticism. The vital matter is that Dante's poem is a
whole; that you must in the end come to understand every part in
order to understand any part. . . . it is necessary to read the philosophical passages of Dante with the humility of a person visiting a
new world, who admits that every part is essential to the whole.
What is necessary to appreciate the poetry of the *Purgatorio* is not
belief, but suspension of belief" ["Dante," in *Selected Essays 1917-
1932* (New York: Harcourt Brace, 1932), 218-20].

[42]Melanchthon's statement: "All the benefits of the Gospel are
included in the idea of the forgiveness of sins" is quoted by Hans
Engelland in *Melanchthon on Christian Doctrine: Loci Communes
1555*, xl.

[43]Schleiermacher, *On Religion*, 39.

[44]Ibid., 36, 103.

[45]van Beeck, *Christ Proclaimed*, 548-66.

[46]Schleiermacher, *On Religion*, 247.

[47]David Jenkins, *Guide to the Debate About God* ,(London: Lutter-
worth Press, 1966), 30.

[48] Robert Preyer,"Tennyson as an Oracular Poet," *Modern Philology*
55 (1958): 239-251.

[49]For the concept of "responsive identity," see van Beeck, *Christ
Proclaimed*, esp. 270–72, 327–28.

[50]Ibid., n. 41.

[51]Chapters 4 and 5 in Father William Peters' *Hopkins: A Tribute* are
a good instance of this, written by a spiritual director of no mean
experience.

Freedom and Necessity in the Poetry of Hopkins (Donald Walhout)
(pp. 73 – 93)

[1]Gabriel Marcel, *Being and Having* (New York: Harper & Row,
1965), 117-18.

[2]J. B. Korolec, "Free Will and Free Choice," in *The Cambridge History
of Later Medieval Philosophy*, ed. Norman Kretzman, Anthony

Kenny, and Jan Pinborg (Cambridge: Cambridge University Press, 1982), 638.

[3]Donald Walhout, *Send My Roots Rain: A Study of Religious Experience in the Poetry of Gerard Manley Hopkins* (Athens: Ohio University Press, 1981), Chapter 2.

[4]See Alvin Plantinga, "On Ockham's Way Out," *Faith and Philosophy* 3 (1986): 245, The entire article (235-69) is an excellent discussion of the subject.

[5]The actual phrase is "we Aristotelian Catholics." See *The Letters of Gerard Manley Hopkins to Robert Bridges,* 2d ed., ed. C. C. Abbott (London: Oxford University Press, 1955), 95.

[6]Numbers in parenthese refer to the numbering of the poems in *The Poems of Gerard Manley Hopkins,* 4th ed., ed. W. H. Gardner and N. H. MacKenzie (London: Oxford University Press, 1967).

[7]*The New Catholic Encyclopedia* (New York: McGraw-Hill, 1967), 6: 93.

[8]Albert Hakim, *Historical Introduction to Philosophy* (New York: Macmillan 1987), 205.

Giving Beauty Back: Hopkins' Echoes (Agnes M. Donohue)
(pp. 95 – 114)

[1]From the 4th edition of *The Poems of Gerard Manley Hopkins,* ed. W. H. Gardner and N. H. MacKenzie (London: Oxford University Press, 1967), 315. All references and quotations are from this edition.

[2]*Poems,* 310-11.

[3]"Take breath and read it with the ears, as I always wish to be read, and my verse becomes all right." *Letters of Gerard Manley Hopkins to Robert Bridges,* ed. C. C. Abbott (London: Oxford University Press, 1935), 79.

[4]Bridges' "Preface" to Hopkins' poetry, quoted in *Poems,* 240.

"Scope," "Scape," and Word Formation in the Lexicon of Hopkins
(Todd Bender)
(pp. 115 – 125)

[1]"Spring," No. 33 in *The Poems of Gerard Manley Hopkins,* 4th Ed., ed. W. H. Gardner and N. H. MacKenzie (London: Oxford University Press, 1967, 1984). References in the text will be to number,

[stanza], and line in this edition.
[2]*Further Letters of Gerard Manley Hopkins*, 2d Ed., ed. C. C. Abbott
(London: Oxford University Press, 1956), 284.
[3]*Further Letters*, 437.
[4]*The Letters of Gerard Manley Hopkins to Robert Bridges*, 2d Ed., ed. C.
C. Abbott (London: Oxford University Press, 1955), 66.

Hopkins on "Man" and "Being" (Peter Milward, S.J.)
(pp. 127 – 144)

[1]The topics were first addressed in separate lectures which I gave
at Loyola College in Baltimore, Maryland, during the fall of 1988.
[2]*The Note-Books and Papers of Gerard Manley Hopkins*, ed. Humphry
House (London: Oxford University Press, 1937), 98.
[3]*Note-books and Papers*, 98.
[4]*Note-books and Papers*, 98.
[5]*The Sermons and Devotional Writings of Gerard Manley Hopkins*, ed.
Christopher Devlin (London: Oxford University Press, 1959), 151.
[6]*Note-books and Papers*, 100.

"The Terrible Crystal" (Francis L. Fennell)
(pp. 145 – 182)

[1]*New Bearings in English Poetry* (London: Chatto and Windus,
1932), 159. Leavis' claim is the best known, perhaps because it was
delivered with his customary magisterial tone, but it was not the
only one: William Empson, I. A. Richards, Malcolm Cowley,
Herbert Read, and C. Day Lewis were part of the chorus intoning
Hopkins' virtues and the potency of his influence.
[2]"The Text, the World, and the Critic" in *Textual Strategies*, ed. J.
Herari (Ithaca: Cornell University Press, 1979), 188.
[3]*The Renaissance*, ed. Kenneth Clark (London: Collins, 1961), 222.
[4]Even this is an oversimplification, of course. I cannot escape the
limitations of the form itself. For example, who is the "I" who
speaks? What kind of pretense is involved when this very sentence, which seems to exist before the "essai" begins, which implies
that the trial is now to be undertaken with the outcome not yet
known, is in fact being written after the completion of the essay's
first draft?
[5]"The Present State of Hopkins Scholarship," *Hopkins Quarterly* 1

(1974): 7.

[6]Winters' objections in *The Function of Criticism* (London: Routledge and Kegan Paul, 1957) are the ones most frequently cited. Yet he was only criticizing specific poems from a specific perspective, a rhetorical fact often overlooked by those who refer to him. Winters granted that Hopkins was among the twelve or fourteen best poets of the century, no mean praise. Still one can apply to him what might be called the Salmon Rushdie principle of critical response: it's not what you say that counts, it's what many people *think* you say.

With Eliot the case is still more complex. While he did criticize those who extolled Hopkins for his style ("What Is a Classic?"), he also in "Religion and Literature" suggested indirectly that Hopkins might be a great poet. *Selected Prose of T. S. Eliot,* ed. Frank Kermode (London: Faber and Faber, 1975), 99.

Perhaps more telling than Eliot's or Winters' comments was the judgment implied by William Marshall's anthology *The Major Victorian Poets* (New York: Washington Square Press, 1967), which included selections from Tennyson, Browning, Arnold, Rossetti, and Swinburne—but not Hopkins.

[7]This is not the place to enter upon the sensitive question of how many other limitations there may be —of whether in fact, as some would have it, we cannot properly "read" at all. I have restricted myself to those kinds of limitations which most critics would agree can exist.

[8]"Gerard Manley Hopkins," *English Critical Essays, Twentieth Century,* ed. P. Jones (London: Oxford University Press, 1933), 360-68.

[9] C. D. Lewis, *Hope for Poetry* (Oxford: Blackwell, 1934).

[10]Geoffrey Grigson, *Gerard Manley Hopkins* (London: British Council, 1955).

[11]Eliot, *Selected Prose,* 129.

[12]Matthew Arnold, *Selected Prose,* ed. P. J. Keating (London: Penguin, 1970), 342.

[13]For example, information collected by Joseph Feeney, S.J., of St. Joseph's University indicates that of the twenty-seven Jesuit colleges and universities in the United States, about a dozen expected to hold some sort of commemoration of Hopkins during or near the centenary year. Of course non-Catholic institutions like the University of Texas are having programs too. But would almost half of these institutions have such plans? The question answers itself.

[14] Arnold, *Selected Prose*, 360.

[15] For example, I have always wondered if part of the fascination that Hopkins has exerted could be attributed to his introspective nature and to his lonely and unrecognized life. Academics too are often introspective people who work in relative obscurity but nurse deep convictions about their as-yet-unappreciated talents, as anyone who has spent some time around a department water cooler will know.

[16] *Further Letters of Gerard Manley Hopkins*, 2d Ed., ed. C. C. Abbott (London: Oxford University Press, 1956), 245.

[17] *Poems*, edited by Charles Williams (London: Oxford University Press, 1930).

[18] *The Letters of Gerard Manley Hopkins to Robert Bridges, The Correspondence of G. M. Hopkins and R. W. Dixon*, and *Further Letters*, all edited by C. C. Abbott and published by the Oxford University Press (1935, 1935, and 1938, respectively).

[19] *Note-books and Papers of Gerard Manley Hopkins*, edited by Humphry House (London: Oxford University Press, 1937).

[20] G. F. Lahey, *Gerard Manley Hopkins* (London: Oxford University Press, 1930).

[21] Todd Bender, *Gerard Manley Hopkins: The Classical Background and Critical Reception of His Work* (Baltimore: Johns Hopkins University Press, 1966).

[22] The most recent example is Margaret Ellsberg's *Created to Praise: The Language of Gerard Manley Hopkins* (London: Oxford University Press, 1987), 4; there are many others. As an example of one who raises the question but then says he will not answer it, see Donald McChesney, *A Hopkins Commentary* (London: University of London Press, 1968), 6-7.

[23] As examples of each, one could cite Alan Heuser's *The Shaping Vision of Gerard Manley Hopkins* (London: Oxford University Press, 1958), J. Hillis Miller's *The Disappearance of God: Five Nineteenth Writers* (Cambridge: Harvard University Press, 1963), James Milroy's *The Language of Gerard Manley Hopkins* (London: Andre Deutsch, 1977), and Michael Sprinker's *"A Counterpoint of Dissidence": The Aesthetics and Poetry of Gerard Manley Hopkins* (Baltimore: John Hopkins University Press, 1980), respectively.

[24] Take Sprinker's book: when the very first sentence quotes Kristéva and the second Derrida, and when the next paragraph quotes Harold Bloom and proposes reading Hopkins "in the most extreme terms possible" in order to "liberate those texts from the weight of a critical tradition that has rendered them innocuous"

(3)—well, we know where we are.

[25]W. H. Gardner, *Gerard Manley Hopkins*, 2 vols. (London: Secker and Warburg, 1949). Although the two volumes came out together in 1949, the first volume had first appeared in 1944.

[26]The title was awarded by John Pick in *The Victorian Poets: A Guide to Research*, 2d Ed., ed. F. Faverty (Cambridge: Harvard University Press, 1968), 342.

[27]*Letters to Bridges*, 46, 51-52.

[28]See, for example, the bewildered author of a reminiscence of Hopkins in *The Month* (August 1919), probably Br. Clement Barraud, who while he was at St. Bueno's had to listen to the "Wreck of the *Deutschland*" being read aloud during the early stages of its composition.

[29]The English actor Peter Gale has given frequent performances of his *Hopkins!* in Great Britain and Ireland, with occasional tours of the States. In this country *Immortal Diamond*, written by William Van Etten Casey, S.J., is acted by Henry Wright.

[30]Some confessional notes and other unpublished materials such as portions of the spiritual journals remain under the control of the Jesuit order. But even if some or all of them are published soon (as has been promised), much of their contents seems to have been revealed already by Paddy Kitchen and others—See *Gerard Manley Hopkins* (London: Hamish Hamilton, 1978).

[31]*Letters to Bridges*, 46.

[32]*Letters to Bridges*, 319.

[33]Jerome Buckley, *Tennyson: The Growth of a Poet* (Cambridge: Harvard University Press, 1960), 254.

[34]Elisabeth Schneider, *The Dragon in the Gate: Studies in the Poetry of G. M. Hopkins* (Berkeley: University of California Press, 1968), 106.

[35]*Note-books and Papers*, 309-10.

[36]*Letters to Bridges*, 206.

[37]*The Oxford Authors: Gerard Manley Hopkins*, ed. Catherine Phillips (London: Oxford University Press, 1986), 17. All subsequent quotations are followed by the page number from this edition.

[38]James Milroy, "Hopkins the Purist: Some Comments on the Sources and Applications of Hopkins' Principles of Poetic Diction," in *Vital Candle: Victorian and Modern Bearings in Gerard Manley Hopkins*, ed. J. North and M. Moore (Waterloo, Ontario: University of Waterloo Press, 1984).

[39]Margaret Ellsberg, *Created to Praise: The Language of Gerard Manley Hopkins* (Oxford University Press, 1987), 50f.

[40]See, for example, the final chapter of Alison Sulloway's *Hopkins*

and the Victorian Temper (New York: Columbia University Press, 1972).

[41]Patricia Ball, *The Science of Aspects: The Changing Role of Fact in the Work of Coleridge, Ruskin, and Hopkins* (London: Athlone Press, 1971), 123.

[42]Carol Christ, *The Finer Optic: The Aesthetics of Particularity in Victorian Poetry* (New Haven: Yale University Press, 1975), 146-47.

[43]*Letters to Bridges*, 225.

[44]*Further Letters*, 360.

[45]Ibid. 326.

[46]Ibid. 379.

[47]One wonders too if another reason might have been Hopkins' notion of poetry as an unsuitable profession for an aspiring saint. After all, in a *lifetime* given to poetry, as distinct from creative outbursts, there would have to be much that is uninspired. To object to Parnassian may be the equivalent of saying "look what I save myself from."

[48]*Poetry and Criticism of Matthew Arnold*, ed. Dwight Culler (Boston: Houghton Mifflin, 1961), 526.

[49]I skirt an even larger question. Suppose Annie Dillard is right that critics only interpret art objects (objects shaped by an artist), and that observers of the object called "nature" can therefore interpret it only when they assume an "artist" behind the work (God)—see *Living by Fiction* (New York: Harper and Row, 1982), 144. Then what might be the fate of a nature poet like Hopkins in an age which sees nature as an authorless text?

[50]Enunciated in "What Is a Classic?" (*Selected Prose*).

Contributors

TODD BENDER is Professor of English at the University of Wisconsin-Madison. Besides numerous articles on Hopkins and other writers he is the author of two standard works on the poet: *Gerard Manley Hopkins: The Classical Background and Critical Reception of His Work,* and (with Robert Dilligan) *A Concordance to the Poetry of Gerard Manley Hopkins.*

AGNES MCNEILL DONOHUE is Professor Emeritus of English at Loyola University of Chicago. Her most recent book is *Hawthorne: Calvin's Ironic Stepchild.* She also has published another book on Hawthorne and one on John Steinbeck as well as many articles on such modern writers as Flannery O'Connor, Doris Lessing, and Iris Murdoch. She has taught several graduate seminars on Hopkins.

DAVID A. DOWNES has written eight books, four on Hopkins: *Hopkins' Sanctifying Imagination, The Great Sacrifice: Studies in Hopkins, Victorian Portraits: Hopkins and Pater,* and *Gerard Manley Hopkins: A Study of His Ignatian Spirit.* He has also written numerous articles on the poet and serves on the Editorial Board of the *Hopkins Quarterly.* Formerly Dean of the College of Humanities and Fine Arts, he is currently Professor of English at California State University, Chico.

FRANCIS L. FENNELL is Professor of English at Loyola University of Chicago. His most recent book is *Dante Gabriel Rossetti: An Annotated Bibliography*. He has also published two other books and several articles on Victorian literature and related topics.

PETER MILWARD, S. J., currently teaches at Sophia University in Tokyo, Japan. He is the author of four books on Renaissance literature, including two on Shakespeare. In addition he has written two books on Hopkins (including *A Commentary on the Sonnets of G. M. Hopkins*) and has co-authored two more with Raymond Schoder, S. J.: *Readings of "The Wreck"* and *Landscape and Inscape: Vision and Inspiration in Hopkins' Poetry*.

ALISON SULLOWAY is Professor Emeritus of English at Virginia Polytechnic and State University. She has written *Gerard Manley Hopkins and the Victorian Temper* as well as several articles on the poet; she is also the editor of *Critical Essays on Gerard Manley Hopkins*, forthcoming later this year. She serves on the editorial board of the *Hopkins Quarterly*.

FRANS JOZEF VAN BEECK, S.J. holds the Cody Chair of Theology at Loyola University of Chicago. His books on theological topics include *God Encountered: Understanding the Christian Faith* and *Christ Proclaimed: Christology as Rhetoric*. Since his graduate training was in English literature, he has also published articles on literary figures, including Hopkins.

DONALD WALHOUT is Professor of Philosophy and Religion at Rockford College. He is the author of *Send My Roots Rain: A Study of Religious Experience in the Poetry of Gerard Manley Hopkins* and also of several articles on the poet, as well as of books and articles on philosophical topics.

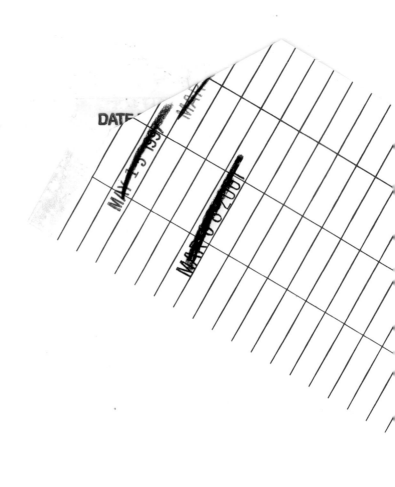